LETTERS FROM TWO WORLD WARS

A SOCIAL HISTORY OF ENGLISH ATTITUDES TO WAR 1914–45

Ernest Sanger

With a Foreword by
Field Marshal Lord Carver

ALAN SUTTON

First published in the United Kingdom in 1993 by
Alan Sutton Publishing Limited
Phoenix Mill · Far Thrupp · Stroud · Gloucestershire

First published in the United States of America in 1993 by
Alan Sutton Publishing Inc · 83 Washington Street · Dover · NH 03820

British Library Cataloguing in Publication Data

Letters from Two World Wars: A Social
History of English Attitudes to War, 1914–45
  I. Sanger, Ernest
  940.3

  ISBN 0–7509–0294–9

Library of Congress Cataloging in Publication Data
Sanger, Ernest.
  Letters From Two World Wars / E. Sanger.
    p.   cm.
  Includes bibliographical references and index.
  ISBN 0-7509-0294-9 : $30.00
  1. World War, 1914–1918—Personal narratives, British. 2. World
War, 1939–1945—Personal narratives, British. 3. English letters.
I. Title.
D640.A2S26 1993
940.4′8141—dc20
[B]   92–42384
                                                              CIP

Typeset in 10/12 Palatino.
Typesetting and origination by
Alan Sutton Publishing Limited.
Printed in Great Britain by
The Bath Press, Avon.

Contents

List of Illustrations

Foreword

Letters provide a truer picture of life in wartime than any other medium. Accounts written some time after the event, with access to historical records, may produce a more accurate version of what actually occurred. Poems and pictures may reflect the emotions of participants, but tend to be written or painted for effect. Personal letters to family or friends come straight from the heart and tell us, with few or no reservations, what the writer thought and felt in his or her experience of war, in battle or out of it.

These letters from soldiers, sailors, airmen, nurses, civil defence workers and civilians in both wars remind us that war has both positive and negative aspects. The negative ones are obvious: death, wounds, fear, anxiety, extremes of discomfort, physical and psychological stress, and the suffering inflicted on all involved – comrades, family and friends, the enemy and the inhabitants of the battlefield. The positive ones are often not generally recognized: the challenge which draws physical and moral strength out of those who face it to a degree of which they themselves, and others, are surprised to find them capable, deepening the intensity of life lived in the present, with little thought for past or future; the strong bonds of affection and mutual respect which bind bodies of fighting men together, as they face the same dangers and challenges, their lives dependent on each other's skill, support and sympathy; the simplification of life in many ways, particularly for the lower ranks; a keen appreciation of the beauties of nature, coming partly from living in the open air, partly from the realization of how much one would miss them, if killed or deprived of sight; for some, a strengthening of religious or patriotic faith.

All these positive and negative aspects of life in wartime are reflected in this skilfully chosen and varied collection of letters from both world wars, many of which are intensely moving.

Field Marshal Lord Carver

Acknowledgements

I wish to record my gratitude to the late Miss Ursula Somervell who first started collecting war letters with me, to my old colleagues Charles Keeley and William Lough, and to Dr David Chandler, Head of War Studies at the Royal Military Academy, Sandhurst, who read my manuscript and recommended many valuable amendments. Dr Peter Thwaites and Mr Roderick Suddaby, Keepers of the Department of Documents at the Imperial War Museum, have been most helpful in providing facilities for study in the Reading Room.

I am greatly indebted to the authors of letters, or their estates, and to editors, publishers and agents, for their kind permission to reproduce letters contained in books, newspapers and periodicals, or kept in archives. My thanks are also due to the many writers of sometimes anonymous letters put at my disposal. I am afraid it has often proved impossible to trace copyright holders or to elicit replies from them: if, not for lack of trying, I omitted to obtain any necessary authorization, I hope I shall be forgiven.

The author wishes to thank the following for giving their permission to use copyright material:

B.T. Batsford for extracts from R. Rhodes James, *Gallipoli*, 1965, G. Bennett, *The Battle of Jutland*, 1964 and *Naval Battles in the First World War*, 1968; Cambridge University Press for extracts from *Letters of Charles Sorley*, 1919, Baroness Wester Wemyss, *Life and Letters of Lord Wester Wemyss*, Eyre & Spottiswoode, 1935, and *Private Papers of Douglas Haig*, ed. R.N.W. Black, Eyre & Spottiswoode, 1952; Curtis Brown & John Farquharson on behalf of the Estate of Sir Winston Churchill for extracts from W.S. Churchill, *The Second World War*, vols I–V, Cassell, 1948–54, Randolph Churchill, *Churchill*, Heinemann, 1969, and Martin Gilbert, *Churchill*, Heinemann, 1986; Miss Artemis Cooper for extracts from *A Durable Fire. The Letters of Duff and Diana Cooper*, Hamish Hamilton, 1983; Leo Cooper for extracts from *Rifleman Alex Bowlby*, 1969; David & Charles Publications, Newton Abbot, Devon, for an extract from S.W.C. Pack, *Operation 'Husky'*, 1977; J.M. Dent for an extract from J. Laffin, *Letters from the Front 1914–16*, 1973; Faber & Faber for extracts from W.S. Robson, *Letters from a Soldier*, 1960, *Letters of Rupert Brooke*, ed. G. Keynes, 1968, and S. Sassoon, *Memoirs of an Infantry Officer*, 1931; Victor

Gollancz for extracts from L. Housman, *War Letters of Fallen Englishmen*, 1930; A.P. Watt on behalf of the Trustees of the Robert Graves Copyright Trust and Paul O'Prey for extracts from R. Graves, *Goodbye to All That*, Cassell, 1929, and *Selected Letters of Robert Graves*, ed. P. O'Prey, Hutchinson, 1982; Harper Collins Publishers and authors or their estates for extracts from F.H. Keeling, *Letters and Recollections*, Allen & Unwin, 1918, Alun Lewis, *In the Green Tree*, Allen & Unwin, 1948, C. Sykes, *Wingate*, Collins, 1959, *Keyes Papers III*, ed. P.G. Halpern, Allen & Unwin, 1972–81, Raymond Asquith, *Life and Letters*, 1982, ed. J. Joliffe, Collins, 1980, and D. Fraser, *Alanbrooke*, Collins; William Heinemann for extracts from A.J.L. Scott, *History of the 60 Squadron RAF*, 1920; Sir Michael Howard for an extract from *Horizon* VII, no. 42, 1943; the Trustees and the Director General of the Imperial War Museum and Mr E. Carracher, Mrs Cross, Mr J. Durant, Mr N.A. Fenwick, Mr P.G. Hardman, Mrs Hatfield, Miss E. Hughes, Mrs Lodden, Mrs Montford, Miss P.J. Murphy, Miss A. Parry, Miss P. Rowbery, Mrs Toomey, the estate of Captain A.V.S. Yates; Longman Group for extracts from X.F. Walker, *Young Gentlemen*, 1938, and O. Creighton, *With the 29th Division in Gallipoli*, 1916; Macmillan Publishing Company New York for extracts from F.B. Maurice, *Life of General Lord Rawlinson*, Cassell, 1928, J. Charteris, *At G.H.Q.*, Cassell, 1931, J. Connell, *Auchinleck*, Cassell, 1959; The Society of Authors as the literary representative of the Estate of John Masefield for an extract from his *Letters from the Front*, ed. P. Vansittart, Constable, 1984; Viscount Montgomery of Alamein for extracts from his father's letters to Alanbrooke, held in the Liddell Hart Centre for Military Archives, King's College London, and published in N. Hamilton, *Monty*, Hamish Hamilton, 1981–6, and in *Monty and the Eighth Army*, ed. S. Brooks, Bodley Head for the Army Record Society, 1991; The Paul Nash Trust for extracts from *Paul Nash*, ed. M. Eates, Lund Humphries, 1948; the estate of the late Sonia Brownell Orwell and Martin Secker & Warburg for an extract from *Orwell's Collected Essays, Journalism and Letters*, 1968; Oxford University Press for extracts from Thomas Jones, *Diary with Letters*, 1954, and *Collected Letters of Wilfred Owen*, ed. H. Owen and J. Bell, 1967; Random House UK and authors or their estates for extracts from F. Owen, *Tempestuous Journey*, Hutchinson, 1954, *Correspondence of Admiral Lord Fisher*, ed. A.J. Marder, Cape, 1959, J. Cornford, *A Memoir*, ed. P. Sloan, J. Cape, 1938, and R.E. Harris, *Billie. The Nevill Letters*, MacRae, 1991; Benedict Read and the Herbert Read Trust for extracts from H. Read, *The Contrary Experience*, Faber & Faber, 1963; Routledge for extracts from S. Keyes, *Minos of Crete*, ed. M. Meyer, 1948, and Bertrand Russell, *Autobiography*, Allen & Unwin, 1968; Mr George Sassoon for reproduction of his father's poem 'The General'; Sir Stephen Spender for an extract from *Citizen at War*, Harrap, 1945; The Controller of Her Majesty's Stationery Office for extracts from W.S. Churchill, *The Second World War*, Cassell, 1959, and S.W. Kirby, *The War against Japan*, 1957; Mr George Stephenson for extracts from *Ivor Gurney's War Letters*, Carcanet Press, 1982; *The Times* for a letter from FO V.A.W. Roseware, published 18 June 1940; Virgin Publishing for an extract from M. Moynihan, *Greater Love, Letters Home 1914–18*, W.H. Allen, 1980.

Introduction

The letters are shockingly real,
Like the personal belongings
Of someone recently dead. . . .

Like a poignant glove
Surviving a well-known hand,
They can outlast our bodies. . . .
ROY FULLER, 'WAR LETTERS'

In recent years, catering for a massive revival of interest in war, on the part of the young generation which has never experienced it and of the old which likes to relive its memories, a number of anthologies of English letters and poetry of the First and Second World Wars have been published; but, as far as I am aware, this is the first attempt to concentrate on an analysis of the attitudes the conflicts evoked. It is therefore not so much the story of the two world wars as these attitudes that form our subject and which often throw a revealing light on society's perceptions in general.

The reader interested in English attitudes to war from 1450 to 1900 may refer to the companion volume, *Englishmen at War: A Social History in Letters.* The threefold purpose of both studies is to provide: a) a continuous selective narrative for the general reader of successive English wars (in this case the two world wars), accompanied by brief summaries of the causes, principal actions and social features of the wars, as witnessed by our letter writers; b) a sourcebook for the student of history, with short details of the circumstances in which the letters were written and of the personalities involved; c) a socio-psychological study of English attitudes to war which are highlighted by significant quotations from the letters in the captions and comments, and by contemporary poetry (or prose) at the beginning of each chapter.

Letters written in wartime provide the truest and most moving testimony of attitudes to war. A systematic list of the themes and attitudes which characterize these letters from the two world wars can be found in the Conclusion. This list is only partly identical to that found in the previous book – some themes disappear, others emerge: for example jingoism, looting, or mutiny are mainly characteristic of the earlier period, while admission of fear, consciousness of the obscenity and insanity of war, cynical humour, or acceptance of self-sacrifice are largely features of twentieth-century conflicts.

The English serviceman tends to become a resolute, steeled fighter only gradually; anger and vengefulness inevitably grow in the heat of battle at the sight of comrades being butchered or blown to pieces, but the conscience of a deeply humane race cannot be silenced entirely:

> This bloody steel
> Has killed a man.
> I heard him squeal
> As on I ran.
>
> He watched me come
> With wagging head.
> I pressed it home,
> And he was dead.
>
> Though clean and clear
> I've wiped the steel,
> I still can hear
> That dying squeal.
> Wilfred Gibson (1878–1962), 'The Bayonet'[1]

Revulsion against violence was rare before the First World War when this poem was written; in the Second World War, killing became increasingly distant, unconscious and efficient. But, in any case, the basest beastliness, often forced out by fear and self-defence, coexists in war with the most elevated idealism which, for most people, excuses and justifies the former. Mythicizing self-delusion reaches truly heroic proportions:

No nation has ever produced a military history of such verbal nobility as the British. Retreat or advance, win or lose, blunder or bravery, murderous folly or unyielding resolution, all emerge alike clothed in dignity and touched with glory. Everyone is splendid whatever the fiasco; disasters are recorded with pride. Other nations attempt but never quite achieve the same self-esteem.[2]

This superiority complex, arising from the historic inviolability of the island's sea defences and the long experience of ultimate victory, led to defeats and bloody sacrifices in the early stages of war being turned into

1 J. Laffin, *Tommy Atkins*, Cassell, 1966, p. xix.
2 M.P. Hussey, *Poetry in the First World War*, Longman, 1967, p. 66 f.

legends of glory – for example the evacuation from Dunkirk in 1940. Unlike most British generals, Allenby believed intelligence to be more important than courage, and criticized his colleagues for having 'no more brain or backbone than a bran doll'; he called the First World War 'a lengthy period of general insanity' and thought that 'all our disasters have been caused by our contempt of the enemy'.[3] Montgomery held similar views about incompetence in the Second World War.

The horrible casualties and the greater involvement of the civilian population in the First World War resulted in a revulsion against war and a reluctance to face up to the unavoidable necessity of resisting the Nazi threat two decades later. There was a deep fear of bombing, gas, and other yet unknown means of mass extinction, and in place of the excited enthusiasm at the beginning of the First World War which everyone, including the politicians and military leaders, was convinced would be over soon, in 1939 there was a feeling of frustration in face of the apparent futility of war; only gradually a hesitant people realized that it had to take up arms again to preserve the hard-earned heritage of the English way of life. But the more reluctantly it had entered the war, the more grimly it hung on against reason during the dark days of 1940–1. German bombing consolidated morale at home and the closer social solidarity, created by common suffering, stiffened resistance.

Having the most up-to-date weapons had always had a decisive influence on the outcome of battles, but the invention and skilful handling of the largest number of war engines of the best design and quality gradually superseded individual and collective initiative based on personal courage. Sea-fights with sailing ships, in which after bold and clever manoeuvring the enemy was out-gunned and sunk or boarded, and land battles with cavalry charges and hand-to-hand fighting became a thing of the past. In the twentieth century opposing warships could hardly be discerned in the distance and yet gunnery took an increasingly accurate toll of these armoured dreadnoughts; in the same way, the vast armies of soldiers were helpless against cannon, machine-guns, and, later, tanks and planes, and were mercilessly massacred. The fight between men was replaced by the fight between machines and it became the main purpose to destroy the machines rather than the men who directed them; this was particularly true of air warfare, the last vestige of individual combat.

In 1914 a soldier could write home that he 'longed for the rough and tumble of war as for a football match', and, at home, 'a sedentary, urbanized people find the spectacle of war even more attractive than a spectacle of football', with the Press treating war as a sort of glorified match;[4] this attitude quickly altered when the men at the front were pitted against all-powerful

3 B. Gardner, *Allenby*, Cassell, 1965, pp. 51, 66.
4 Hussey, op. cit., p. 4.

engines of war. 'Fun' would change into 'Hell', the patriotic rhetoric into agonized protest or resigned acceptance:

> War – A dirty, loathsome, servile murder-job:–
> Men, lousy, sleepless, ulcerous, afraid . . .
> Men driving men to death and worse than death:
> Men maimed and blinded: men against machines –
> Flesh versus iron, concrete, flame and wire:
> Men choking out their souls in poison gas:
> Men squelched into the slime by trampling feet:
> Men, disembowelled by guns five miles away . . .[5]
>
> Gilbert Frankau

For the first time war had become too monstrous to be enjoyed after the initial exuberance:

> The truth about war is that it is an evil, not only because men suffer and die in it but because it destroys the meaning of life. . . . War is not an adventure, but a disaster; it has no glamour or romance or nobility.[6]

The Second World War, although much more murderous overall, was never felt to be so terrible, because the new technicians of war were much better equipped and looked after, and more motivated; but, foremost, they were without illusions about the character of war and free of war hysteria and lofty notions: 'This life dulls one's awareness of tragedy,' wrote an airman, shot down in 1944, 'we just don't get tied up in knots by our imagination, because it would then be impossible to fulfil our duties not only efficiently, but cheerfully. . . .'[7]

Distance, the concern with effective handling of the machinery of war, and dispassionate dealing with casualties, tended to hide the reality of war, although the mental strain claimed many many more victims despite the fact – and perhaps a little because of it – that battle became a cold, impersonal matter of logistics and numbers. However, unrelenting attacks of doubtful value had survived the First World War, in actions like Monte Cassino in 1944 or the bombing offensive against German cities.

It all changed in 1945 – with the event of the atomic bomb. The poet Robert Southey had foreseen almost two centuries previously that the mechanist and chemist were to take over: 'The novel powers which, beyond any doubt, will be directed to the purposes of destruction, are so tremendous. . . .'[8] The

5 N. Angell, *The Great Illusion*, Heinemann, 1910.
6 J. Ellis, *Eyedeep in Hell*, Croom Helm, 1976, p. 174.
7 C.B. Purdom, *Everyman at War*, J.M. Dent, 1930, p. vii.
8 J. Farrar, *Unreturning Spring*, Chatto & Windus, 1968, p. 189 f.

long history of conventional warfare has since come to an end, at least on a world scale, apart from relatively minor convulsions constantly flaring up here and there. It is therefore a suitable time to take stock and describe the attitudes of Englishmen at war and, in their light, speculate on the chances that the contradiction between the horrendous scientific techniques of the third millenium and the latent heritage of age-old mental impulses may be reconciled.

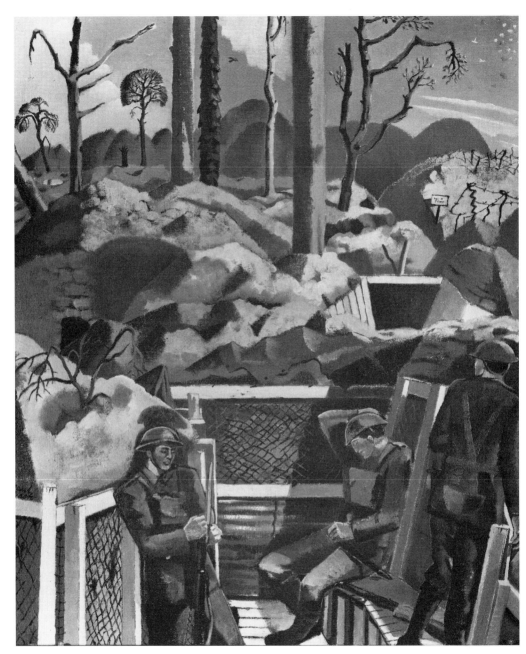

Spring in the Trenches, Ridge Wood, 1917, by Paul Nash (*see* pp. 76–7). *(Imperial War Museum, London)*

PART ONE

THE FIRST WORLD WAR

'. . . it is all the best fun'

Once in a generation a mysterious wish
for war passes through the people . . .
only by intense suffering can the nations grow
GENERAL SIR IAN HAMILTON

Why did Britain break out of a century of 'splendid isolation', shielded by her Navy, and get embroiled in a continental war on an unprecedented scale, sending almost a million men to death? Was the war avoidable? Looking back, the self-destruction of Europe seems sheer madness but, at the time, irresistible forces drove the nations into tragedy: the automatic operation of alliances on both sides (Britain entered the Entente Cordiale with France in 1904, and the Triple Entente with Russia and France in 1907); the German bid to equal Britain in naval rearmament, refusing any agreed limitation, accompanied by a military build-up to five million men under arms with superb training and equipment, and a rapid increase in population and industrial potential – in short, German rivalry threatening British naval superiority and markets, as well as the 'balance of power' on the continent.

These Great Power considerations alone would not have carried along public opinion in Britain; what united the country was the German invasion of Belgium, contrary to the 1839 guarantee of Belgian neutrality in the Treaty of London. This was a ruthless attack on a small country in the Channel area, always vital to Britain, abandoning morality for strategic necessity (openly spelt out in the Reichstag by the Chancellor, Bethmann-Hollweg: 'Gentlemen, this is a breach of international law'). The subsequent spread of 'Hun' atrocity stories (like cutting off the breasts of violated nuns and the hands of children) did the rest to rouse a fundamentally peaceful people to war fever.

When put into action the alliance system released plans for mobilization, and rigid strategic preparations, immediately evident in the plan by the dead hand of Field Marshal Schlieffen to overwhelm France in six weeks. The insistence of Sir Henry Wilson, Director of Military Operations, on dispatching the British Expeditionary Force to Mabeuge in Picardy (instead of landing it directly in Belgium), was based similarly on plans worked out three years previously.

The gigantic arsenal of war materials, and the huge armies ready to use them, exerted, in the prevalent state of mass hysteria, fatal pressure of their own for attack as the best means of defence. It was pride, mutual fear and elaborate preparations which plunged Europe into the First World War: 'The lamps are going out all over Europe,' said sadly Sir Edward Grey, the Foreign Secretary. The first total war, fought with rapidly developing technological means of mass destruction, had started between gigantic forces of balanced strength, and was to be pursued with unparalleled determination to the point of complete exhaustion.

O N E

From Offensive to Deadlock (1914–15)

O all of us, both horse and foot
And the proud artillery,
We're going to the merry wars . . .
And we shall moulder in the plains of France
Before these leaves have ceased from their last dance
EDWARD SHANKS (1892–1953)

Fascination, Faith and Fury

War broke: and now the winter of the world
With perishing great darkness closes in . . .
RUPERT BROOKE, 1914

Thou through the flood
Shall win to Salvation,
To Beauty through blood
ROBERT BRIDGES, THE TIMES, 8 AUGUST 1914

Churchill castigates the madness of war and the trance-like drift towards catastrophe a week before the British declaration; but he confesses, with horror, his own happy elation.[1]

---

1 A.G. Gardiner wrote in 1912 about Churchill: 'Remember he is a soldier first, last and always. He will write his name big on our future. Let us take care that he does not write it in blood.'

1

'A hideous fascination'

Winston Churchill (1874–1965), First Lord of the Admiralty, to his wife.

28 July 1914

. . . Everything tends towards catastrophe and collapse. I am interested, geared up and happy. Is it not horrible to be built like this? The preparations have a hideous fascination for me. I pray to God to forgive me for such fearful moods of levity. Yet I would do my best for peace, and nothing would induce me wrongfully to strike a blow. I can't feel that we in this island are to any serious degree responsible for the wave of madness which has swept the mind of Christendom. No one can measure the consequences. I wondered whether those stupid Kings and Emperors could not assemble together and revivify kingship by saving the nations from hell but we all drift on in a kind of dull cataleptic trance. . . .

The proverbial British belief in the salutary effect of reverses and the certainty of always winning the last battle which alone matters, inspire the young naval officer with deep confidence.

2

'We'll get them in the end'

Sub-Lieutenant (later Commander Lord) Stephen King-Hall (1893–1966), a popular broadcaster during the Second World War, welcomes initial reverses.

[HMS *Southampton*] 27 August 1914

Dearest Parents,

At the moment of writing the Germans are doing nicely in Belgium, to be expected of course, I, even, am preparing myself to see them in Paris. But nothing, nothing, not even the annexation of France ought to make us give in. Everyone who is serving ought to feel that he has dedicated himself to win or die.

I feel and know that the feeling will grow as the War goes on. I almost welcome the idea of initial reverses, and the idea of being knocked out has quite begun to lose any unpleasantness which it may naturally have had in the sudden transition from peace to War.

Whenever I feel a bit fed up on Watch, and there is a good deal of Watchkeeping, I just comfort myself with thinking that however long we have to wait, it may be months or even years, we'll get them in the end, the Empire will never give in until there isn't an Empire, and then it hardly matters, does it? . . .

We are all in good spirits, and growing more efficient every day, though I fear we have a long while to wait before we attain the super-human hardiness and war-worthiness of our forefathers off Brest . . ..

Love and kisses to all. We sail at day-break.

Yours,
Stevie

But 'Jacky' Fisher, the creator of the dreadnought fleet ('Hit first, hit hard, and keep hitting'), soon to be brought back from retirement at the age of seventy-four to succeed Prince Louis of Battenberg as First Sea Lord, storms against fools, sycophants and snobs in high places, and what he called, in a letter to Jellicoe, the 'regular menagerie of "Charity Admirals"'.

3

SHOOT THE ADMIRALS

Admiral Lord Fisher (1841–1920) writes to George Lambert, Civil Lord of the Admiralty, about the 'criminal folly' of sending 'play-soldiers' to France.

August 28th, 1914

Private and Secret

I went to London for a *tête-à-tête* with Winston, and that gave me a 'set-back', but I am once more quite right and go for a good long walk every day in Richmond Park, and think over some of the poor d–d fools that Winston has now surrounded himself with! *I'm not sure he don't like it!* (What a clear-out I would have!!) And certainly two British Admirals ought to be shot, *and Winston knows it*!! I wrote to him and said I supposed they would be promoted instead, as they are both Court sycophants. However, this is the price we ought to pay for a disguised republic, and the d–d strain of snobbishness that pervades the feudal relics of the British race – no court-martial, but shoot them! Also, of course (as possibly you know), I am dead against having sent our soldiers on the Continent. *Simply criminal folly!* And if I am not mistaken, the masses of our countrymen agree with me. Neither Press or Parliament represents the real thought of the people. Our Navy and *our Navy alone* is our one and abiding *sure* defence. *DOUBLE IT IF YOU DON'T FEEL SAFE!* But to pile on 'play-soldiers' as we are now doing, and for which we could have 60 Dreadnoughts and 600 submarines, is really silly! Only it's so tragic! However, what's the good of my letting fly at you! So no more.

Naval Battles, Refugees and Invasion Scare

> *. . . as swimmers into cleanness leaping,*
> *Glad from a world grown old and cold and weary*
> *. . . we have found release.*
> RUPERT BROOKE

5

The North Sea fleet at Scapa Flow and Rosyth kept a long-distance watch on the German Navy, ready to pounce as soon as it left the safety of its port defences, as Nelson had done outside Brest and Toulon. The first confused encounter occurred in Heligoland Bight when Vice-Admiral Sir David Beatty tried to cut off a German destroyer patrol which, in turn, lured the light British ships into the Bight within range of their heavy cruisers there. Three German cruisers were sunk and one was crippled for no loss on the British side. The German admiral perished with his whole crew in the *Cöln*.

4

'Jolly exciting although I was in a beastly funk'

E.T. Hodgson, a fifteen-year-old midshipman, sends his parents a breathless account of the Battle of Heligoland Bight, and describes how the flagship *Cöln* was 'biffed to blazes'.

HMS *Invincible*, Sept. 6th, 1914

Dear Mum and Dad

Thanks *awfully* for all the ripping things you sent me this week. I got the chocolates and they are awfully good, the magazine, the *Riddle of the Sands* which I am reading now, the soap and all your letters, also the shortbread; if you were thinking of sending any more I think I should prefer gingerbread.

I can give you an account of the battle so here goes. On 28th of August I went on deck at five and saw us join up with the first Battlecruiser squadron and a flotilla of destroyers. We all put on clean shirts in order that it would be all right if we were wounded. After breakfast signals began to come in by W.T. that our destroyers were engaged, soon after this they sounded off 'Action' and I went off to my station. We were cruising about in rather an erratic way and going pretty fast. Suddenly there was the shout from submarine look-outs that some had been sighted and almost immediately we began firing with the Q.F.s;[2] they saw about three periscopes but I don't think we hit them, the destroyers also tried to ram them, anyhow we managed to drive them off.

We now heard we were chasing some cruisers and they again sounded off action, I sprinted off to my station expecting to get a shot in my gizzard every minute. The three ships in front[3] now began blazing away with their 13.5s big guns, it made a tremendous row and enormous flash as they fired the whole broadside, going as fast as we were we soon came up on one cruiser,[4] she had got one funnel left standing, her mainmast knocked over, and her fore top mast her bridge was still intact, she was frightfully down by the head and there were piles of wreckage on the deck, we passed pretty close and I almost thought I could see the men stretched out on the

2 Quick-firers.
3 *Lion, Princess Royal* and *Queen Mary*.
4 *Mainz*, torpedoed by *Laertes*.

deck, she had had a terrific hammering, the destroyers all closed round to rescue the survivors as she soon sank, the leading ships were still firing and I believe soon sank another cruiser,[5] there was a tremendous lot of smoke and mist ahead and I could not see much of what was going on, there seemed to be a big cloud of smoke on our port bow with great flashes coming from it and shells began to burst, after a bit it cleared and we saw another cruiser[6] about a mile off rather smashed up with two funnels bent in a curious way and minus the fore top mast, directly we saw her we fairly loosed off as quick as we could go from all the port side turrets, 8–12" going like smoke there were huge flashes all over her as our shells burst, we found the range after the third shot and biffed her to blazes, they fired at us a bit but the poor chaps were soon wiped out, one shell burst somewhere over our heads a bit cut a fragment out of the quarter-deck, it made a good row and I felt all queer inside and was glad there were not many more, we knocked one funnel over and she was soon on fire all over and smoking like anything, they were awfully plucky however and although the flag came down once I distinctly saw them haul up a new one, they could not have possibly been braver poor chaps, they fired a torpedo at us which slid by about five yards away, a deuced near thing, the people in the ship astern thought it had got us, we were having to dodge floating mines nearly all the time. Altogether it was jolly exciting although I was in a beastly funk at times. . . .

Love from TIDDLES

On 22 September three armoured cruisers were sunk by a single German U-boat, a mine blew up the super-battleship *Audacious* (news kept secret throughout the war), and on 16 December Scarborough, Hartlepool and Whitby were bombarded by nine German cruisers which had slipped out undetected and escaped pursuit in the mist. However, after the sinking of the battle-cruiser *Blücher* at Dogger Bank on 24 January 1915, the German fleet did not venture out again from the protection of their minefields and coastal guns for the next two years.

In South American waters, off the Chilean coast, Graf Spee's squadron destroyed a weaker force under Rear-Admiral Sir Christopher Cradock at the Coronel Islands. In revenge, they were intercepted off the Falkland Islands on 8 December by Vice-Admiral Sir Doveton Sturdee with the battle-cruisers *Invincible* and *Inflexible*, and the armoured cruisers *Carnarvon*, *Cornwall* and *Kent*; the armoured cruiser *Scharnhorst* was sunk with the admiral and all hands, and the *Gneisenau* went down too; of the light cruisers, the *Leipzig* blew up, the *Nürnberg* sank, and only the *Dresden* escaped, but not for long. This spelt the end of German cruiser warfare on the oceans.

The public school boy, having overcome his 'moldy funk', thinks it is 'jolly exciting', except when the enemy ships stop firing and are still sunk.

---

5 *Ariadne.*
6 *Cöln*; both were sunk.

5

BEASTLY TO SEND THE ENEMY TO THE BOTTOM

Midshipman E.T. Hodgson describes what he felt during the Battle of the Falkland Islands. He was killed at Jutland, aged seventeen.

HMS *Invincible*, Port Stanley, Dec. 1914

. . . I was frightfully excited and very keen to be at them not at all like the moldy funk I was in at Heligoland, when I thought about it I was quite surprised, I suppose it was knowing exactly what we were going to take on . . . .

With their second salvo they hit us and the rest of the shells either fell short or went off with the most awfully sort of moaning noise. The one I heard at Heligoland was mere skittles to it, the shells came just before the sound and you would hear the awful Whoooo and then bang. The first whistles fairly made me duck as it always makes you think it is coming through the eye slits.[7] We all ducked like rabbits for the first few shots but soon got used to it and did not mind it at all. . . . I got simply to loathe their painfully accurate salvos.

A lot were drowned before our eyes but I had got used to seeing those two poor ships gradually smashed up that it did not impress me much, although it made me absolutely fed up with actions, and I felt I did not want another again for at least a month. . . . My general impression was that as long as the enemy are firing back at you it is jolly exciting but when they have stopped firing but it is still your duty to send the poor chaps to the bottom it is then it is so beastly. . . .

I should think you must have felt rather bucked about me as it is quite the largest and best action of the war so far. You can be sure I was jolly thankful to get out of it safe. . . .

Another midshipman gives a more detailed account of the battle.

6

'Glad to save such plucky foemen'

A.C. Jelf describes the sinking of the *Scharnhorst* and the *Gneisenau* in the Battle of the Falkland Islands.

HMS *Carnarvon*, Dec. 9, 1914

. . . The whole fleet slipped their cables and got under way. Full speed was the order, and we formed battle-line in single line ahead. In a short time the speed was 20 knots, soon increased to 22. The *Invincible* and *Inflexible* then left the line, and flashed past us all. The enemy were seen in single quarter line making away to the southward.

---

7 He was stationed in the conning-tower.

Survivors from the German cruiser *Gneisenau* being picked up by HMS *Inflexible* after the Battle of the Falkland Islands, December 1914.
(Royal Naval Museum, Portsmouth)

Men of the Royal Gloucestershire Hussars in the firing line at Gallipoli, 1915. *(Reproduced by permission of the Trustees of the Royal Gloucestershire Hussars)*

Meanwhile we cleared for action; woodwork of all sorts went overboard from all ships; guard rails went down and decks flooded with inches of water . . . .

At about one o'clock the battle-cruisers opened fire on the enemy with their twelve-inch. The range was about 18,000 to 20,000 yards. The battle-cruisers were hitting the flagship *Scharnhorst* well. We closed in on her and reduced the range to 10,000 yards. Her third funnel was shot away about four o'clock. She soon had a heavy list to port, and the *Gneisenau* took her place. B. turret put the finishing touch to her, hitting her aft. At 4.16 the *Scharnhorst* sank. She had fought magnificently to the last against great odds.

We continued firing at the *Gneisenau*, and it was splendid to see the way they fought three big ships. Several shells passed near and over us, but we were not hit at all. (A sea has just come into the gun-room splashing all over the letter. Please excuse this.) At about 5.45 one of her funnels went, and she got a heavy list to starboard. One by one her guns were knocked out, but she continued firing to the last and went down at 6.2, blazing. A pall of smoke hung over the spot where she sank.

We lowered what boats we had (two small cutters and one whaler) as fast as we could. I went away in the third cutter. It was slightly rough and very cold. It was an hour before the ship had got to the scene of the sinking and had lowered her boats. We saved about 150. It was horrible, so I will say no more. I got one officer and about 16 men into my boat. There were none left struggling in the water when we returned . . . .

It was extraordinary to see the lack of animosity against us. We were very cheery saving them. It was a case of 'Buck up, old chap, you're all right', &c. They said they did not want to fight us. We were glad to save such plucky foemen.

To begin a birthday in the Falklands with the greatest naval action of the war, then to round Cape Horn, and finish up with a glass of champagne, is an extraordinary experience. . . .

When the Germans besieged and bombarded Antwerp, three naval brigades were landed as an advance guard to support Belgian resistance; but General Rawlinson's two divisions came too late to prevent the fall of the city on 10 October. The poet Rupert Brooke was there, who hailed war as a regenerator of life forces linked to death. He wrote to John Drinkwater: 'Come and die. It'll be great fun. And there's great health in the preparation. . . .'

7

'A Dantesque Hell'
RUINS AND REFUGEES

Sub-Lieutenant Rupert Brooke (1887–1915) tells Leonard Bacon what he saw during the Antwerp expedition.

Anson Batt. RND, 11 Nov 14

. . . It hurts me, this war but I'm glad to be under it for Belgium. That's what breaks the heart to see and hear of. I marched through Antwerp, deserted, shelled, and burning, one night, and saw mined houses, dead men and horses: and railway trains with their lines taken up and twisten flung down as if a child had been playing with a toy. And the whole heaven and earth was lit up by the glare from the great lakes and rivers of burning petrol, hills and spires of flame. That was like Hell, a Dantesque Hell, terrible. About there – and later – I saw what was a truer Hell. Hundreds of thousands of refugees, their goods on barrows and hand-carts and perambulators and waggons, moving with infinite slowness out into the night, two unending lines of men, the old men mostly weeping, the women with hard white drawn faces, the children playing or crying or sleeping. That's what Belgium is now: the country where three civilians have been killed to every one soldier. That damnable policy of 'frightfulness' succeeded for a time. It's queer to think one has to be a witness of one of the greatest crimes of history . . . .

Well, we are doing our best. Give us what prayers or cheers you can. It's a great life, fighting, while it lasts. The eye grows clearer and the heart. But it's a bloody thing, half the youth of Europe blown through pain to nothingness, in the incessant mechanical slaughter of these modern battles. I can only marvel at human endurance . . . .

Six months later Brooke died ingloriously of blood poisoning on the way to Gallipoli, but acclaimed as a new Sir Philip Sidney, he became a national legend.

Meanwhile, there were all sorts of rumours going round: one million Russians landing in Aberdeen on their way to the Western Front, their boots still covered with snow, Angels fighting alongside the BEF at Mons – so why not a German invasion? All four regular divisions had gone to France, and Britain, with the Navy away at Scapa Flow, was only protected by the Territorial Army.

8

SCARE OF A CHRISTMAS INVASION

Admiral Fisher, First Sea Lord, relates the rumours to Vice-Admiral Sir David Beatty.

Admiralty, 7.11.1914

My dear Beatty,

. . . Just off to see the King who wants me urgently, he says. Probably Prince Albert has got a stomach-ache! . . .

The latest German scare from our Minister at The Hague is that 150,000 Germans will land, half at Dundee, the other at Oban, and the feint of 20,000 men at Norwich four days sooner! This is to be on Christmas Day when we are all supposed to be drunk . . . .

Neither you or Jellicoe can be in on the job – you can't get there in the time, nor indeed to cut them off with your rear well strewed with mines and covered by sub-marines, as it will be a flying escapade, I expect, on the part of the Germans.

Yours till death,
Fisher

9

250,000 GERMANS TO STRIKE A BLOW AT LONDON

F.S. Oliver (1864–1934) relates reports to his brother in Canada about German artillery hidden in England.

November 20th 1914

. . . We have had by far the worst scare of invasion this week that there has been yet. Apparently the tides on the 17th, 18th and 19th are the most favourable for a long time to come for disembarkation of an invading force in Essex and Suffolk, and the authorities came to the conclusion that an invasion was going to be tried seriously. I suppose they had information from their spies at Emden of activity among the transports, movement of troops, etc.

The idea was that the Germans were going to make a desperate effort; their vessels were to draw out our southern main battle fleet and keep it engaged while they ran 250,000 first line troops right across the North Sea at full speed to the English East Coast and struck, if possible, a blow at London. They were not going to bring any cavalry, but only motor cars and motor bicycles in great numbers. They were not going to bring any heavy artillery – some reports said that was because they had already got it hidden away here – but only field guns. They were to be put on flat-bottomed barges and hauled ashore at high tide. Anyway, whether this was wholly true, or wholly false, there was a tremendous stir. The Southern command was denuded of troops, which were hurried up to the neighbourhood of Harwich, Colchester and Huntingdon.

'I adore war' – 'all a great game'

And when the burning moment breaks,
And only joy of battle takes
Him by the throat, and makes him blind . . .
And in the air death moans and sings
JULIAN GRENFELL, 'INTO BATTLE'

The voice of a schoolboy rallies the ranks:
Play up! Play up! And play the game!
SIR HENRY NEWBOLT (1862–1939)

God! How I hate you, you young cheerful men
ARTHUR WEST (1891–1917)

Haldane's army reforms of 1906–12 had created a highly trained professional Army, supported by a General Staff, an Officers' Training Corps, and a Territorial Army. When Lord Kitchener, alone expecting a long war of attrition when everybody believed in quick victory, appealed for one hundred thousand volunteers on the famous poster 'Your King and Country need Y O U', two and a half million came forward. ('If Kitchener was not a great man,' said Mrs Asquith, 'he was, at least, a great poster.')

The BEF of 160,000 under the command of Sir John French, a hot-tempered cavalry officer of by-gone days, reached Mons on the other side of the Belgian frontier on 22 August and clashed with the First Army under von Kluck. The 'Old Contemptibles' (a label coined by War Office propaganda, mistranslating the Kaiser's description of the BEF as 'insignificant' – fourteen divisions as against ninety-five German and sixty French – by 'a contemptible little Army'[8]) held off German forces two to three times superior to them, before they saved themselves by retreating 160 miles, in conformity with the French left wing, to a line extending from Ypres to La Bassée.

10

'We were preparing to die'

Lieutenant (later Field Marshal Earl) Harold Alexander (1891–1969), under fire for the first time, describes to his mother the retreat from Mons.

28 August 1914

. . . We were surrounded on all sides by thousands of the enemy, and there was only one Brigade, ourselves. . . . It was a death-trap, there being absolutely no cover at all. We had just to lie down on the open road. There we lay, 20 or 30 yards from the Germans face to face, only it was so dark that you could hardly see in front. The ground was covered in cartridges, rifles and dead men whilst we could hear the wounded Germans moaning or talking just in front. We were preparing to die on top of the mound when the orders came for us to retire gradually and noiselessly. This we did, and we were out of the town before light dawned. We had about 150 killed and wounded.

At the First Battle of Ypres, from 12 October to 11 November, the BEF resisted the German onslaught at the cost of 50 per cent casualties. The danger of being cut off from the Channel ports was averted and the whole front froze into a maze of trenches for the next three years. The defensive superiority of the machine-gun behind barbed wire, backed by heavy artillery, had brought the war of movement to a standstill; reinforcements, travelling by rail, could close gaps faster than infantry could advance. Kitchener confessed: 'I don't know what is to be done, this isn't war!' After the failure of their Marne offensive, the Germans dug in for the rest of the war, having taken Belgium and North-east France, with all France's iron and four fifths of its coal.

---

8 *'Verächtlich kleines Heer'* changed into *'verächtliches kleines Heer'*.

Initially, the war was like a scouts' picnic adventure for young officers typical of the generation of eager, well-conditioned public school boys with a rural background. They found manhood in the exhilarating excitement of fighting and the affection they felt for their fellow soldiers grew out of the common pursuit of killing the enemy whom they despised; yet they could feel ashamed when actually faced with a prisoner.

For most of the subalterns there was no time to get worn down by trench warfare: they fell in a ratio of 6:1 to the soldiers. Julian Grenfell (Eton–Balliol–Regular Army) who was a zestful poet ('Into Battle' is perhaps one of the best war poems) confessed: 'I *adore* war. . . . Nobody grumbles at one for being dirty.' But although he enjoyed killing he is not insensitive to the misery caused by war:

> The wretched inhabitants here have got practically no food left. It is miserable to see them leaving their homes, and tracking away, with great bundles and children in their hands and the dogs and cats left in the deserted villages are piteous.[9]

11

'It is all the best fun'

Captain Julian Grenfell (1888–1915), 1st Royal Dragoons, sends to his parents his first impressions of Flanders.

November 3rd, 1914

. . . I have not washed for a week, or had my boots off for a fortnight. . . It is all *the* best fun. I have never felt so well, or so happy, or enjoyed anything so much. It just suits my stolid health, and stolid nerves, and barbaric disposition. The fighting-excitement vitalizes everything, every sight and word and action. One loves one's fellow man so much more when one is bent on killing him. And picnicking in the open day and night (we never see a roof now) is the real method of existence.

There are loads of straw to bed-down on, and one sleeps like a log, and wakes up with the dew on one's face. . . . The Germans shell the trenches with shrapnel all day and all night; and the Reserves and ground in the rear with Jack Johnsons, which at last one gets to love as old friends. You hear them coming for miles, and everyone imitates the noise; then they burst with a plump, and make a great hole in the ground, doing no damage unless they happen to fall into your trench or on to your hat. They burst pretty nearly straight upwards. One landed within ten yards of me the other day, and only knocked me over and my horse. We both got up and looked at each other and laughed. . . .

---

9 L. Housman, *War Letters of Fallen Englishmen*, V. Gollancz, 1930, p. 117.

Julian Grenfell was hit in the head by a splinter of a heavy Jack Johnson on the Menin Road at Ypres that he had called 'the little hill of death'. He cheerfully said 'I think I shall die', and, the next day, wrote the following letter in pencil on bloodstained paper.

12

'Julian of the 'Ard 'Ead'

[14 May 1915]

Darling Mother, Isn't it wonderful and glorious that at last after long waiting the Cavalry have put it across the Boches on their flat feet and have pulled the frying pan out of the fire for the second time. . . . We are practically wiped out but we charged and took the Hun trenches yesterday. I stopped a Jack Johnson with my head and my skull is slightly cracked. But I'm getting on splendidly. I did awfully well. To-day I go down to Wimereux, to hospital, shall you be there? All all love. Julian of the 'Ard 'Ead. Longing to see you and *talk*! Bless you!

The fracture of his skull, lacerating his brain, turned septic after the operation, and he died on 26 May.

Julian's younger brother, Billy, a lieutenant in Flanders, wrote to his mother two months before he was himself killed:

The more I think of darling Julian, the more I seem to realise the nothingness of death. He has just passed on, outsoared the shadow of our night, 'here where men sit and hear each other groan', and how could one pass on better than in the full tide of strength and glory and fearlessness. So that there is no interruption even in the work which God has for him. Our grief for him can only be grief for ourselves.

How beautiful his poem is. It perfectly expresses the unity and continuity of all created things in their Maker. I pray that one tenth of his gay spirit may descend on me.[10]

To Lieutenant Kenneth Garnett, war was like a game of 'bears'. He wrote to his mother:

This is all a great game – so very childish – but I am such a child as to love it. And you poor people at home pay for us to play 'bears' as we used to do when I was four – only now the game is very greatly glorified. Do you remember the Fort at Sea View? We have our peepholes just the same, and fire at anything we like – only this is much more fun. . . .[11]

10 Ibid., p. 115.
11 Ibid.

Another public school boy who survived four years as an infantry officer confessed twenty years later that he looked back on them 'as among the happiest I have ever spent', although 'they contained moments of boredom and depression, sorrow for the loss of friends and of alarm for personal safety'.[12]

13

'A most ripping day'

Captain Graham Greenwell describes to his mother his arrival at the front.

Romorin, Ploegstert Wood, May 24, 1915

I am enjoying myself tremendously. I cannot believe I am within two miles of this ridiculous war; it sounds just like an Aldershot Field Day. . . . I am supremely happy and have had the most interesting day of my life. I can't believe it is true. . . . I mounted in the most divine sunshine to *ride* up to the trenches! . . . I have had a most ripping day: I can't remember ever having had so much pleasure and excitement, seeing so many old friends and experiencing such new sensations. I can see that one must be resigned to keeping one's clothes on all day and night for weeks at a time and to getting sleep always in the open and only for an hour or two on end; but it is all so delightfully fresh after England that the unpleasant side of it does not strike me, though all my friends have been trying to instil into me the gospel of 'frightfulness'.

A week later the initial excitement was beginning to wear off: 'It is a curious life, depressing at times, on the whole rather boring but occasionally exhilarating.'

On 10 March 1915 the First Army under General Sir Douglas Haig launched its first attack on Neuve Chapelle. It was an attempt to break out towards Lille, in face of withering German machine-gun fire from wire-protected emplacements left completely intact by the preliminary shelling. The casualties were frightful: after a week, of 700 men of the Scottish Rifles only 145 survived, under the command of a second lieutenant. It was the last time officers led their men into action sword in hand, among them Major Ferrers.

The following extract is an unexcited, stoic account of what it was like to leave the trench to advance through the barbed wire, come under fire and lie there wounded alone.

12   G.H. Greenwell, *Infant in Arms*, Allen Lane, 1972.

14

OVER THE PARAPET

Major E.B. Ferrers writes to Lieutenant M.D. Kennedy a week after being wounded in the attack.

No. 7 Field Hospital, 18 March 1915

. . . I got through the wire and over the parapet. . . . When I got there the cupboard was bare, and someone shot me, as I thought in the right ankle, as I started for the next trench. This was really rather a relief as no one else was up and I was feeling exceedingly lonely. I couldn't walk so I lent up against the parapet and waved my sword. . . . I could see the lads all hung up in wire and I fancy some were firing . . . but before I could appreciate the situation I took it again in the right thigh. As it came out very low down right in the middle of the stomach I accepted that as final and being fallen on my back partly on sandbags and partly in a puddle I concluded to stay as long as I was and take stock of my worldly affairs. I doubted that I'd live very long but as I'd had all I'd ever wished for I didn't worry much over that. I calculated the lads would have finished with the wire and be coming over the parapet soon and I thought if I saw them started for the next trench that would do me very well. I made out that I had a bit of a chance if I could only keep absolutely still. Never did I feel the least doubt, but it was very lonely on my side of the parapet. I could see down towards the hedge for a few yards and by screwing round my head I could see toward the Bosches' 2nd trench but that was about all.

Presently someone tumbled through the fence, looked very lost for a moment but bucked up no end when he saw me. He started to Holla the rest on like a good 'un and when that produced no immediate result said to me, 'It's no good Sir they won't come'. I said 'Don't you worry about the lads they'll come all right'. There was some sort of frightful battle going on behind my head. . . . I think they'd got some Bosches round a corner and were killing them; but I couldn't twist my head round to make sure. . . .

[The letter goes no further because Ferrers fainted at that point.]

Attitudes Towards Germans and Brutalization

The average German was just a decent poor devil like everyone else
C.E. MONTAGUE (1867–1928), 'DISENCHANTMENT'

I have blindly killed,
And nameless hearts with nameless sorrow filled
PAUL BEWSHER (1894–1966), 'NOX MORTIS'

When you see millions of mouthless dead
Across your dreams in pale battalions go,
Say not soft things as other men have said . . .
CHARLES SORLEY, UNTITLED POEM

Initial contempt and detestation of the enemy, and the wish to wreak vengeance upon them tended to melt away under the shock of personal human contact. Julian Grenfell recounts in the letter quoted above:

We took a German Officer and some men prisoners in a wood the other day. One felt hatred for them as one thought of our dead; and as the Officer came by me, I scowled at him, and the men were cursing him. The Officer looked me in the face and saluted me as he passed; and I have never seen a man look so proud and resolute and smart and confident, in his hour of bitterness. It made me feel terribly ashamed of myself. . . .

Fraternizing on Christmas Day became a feature of trench warfare, despite horrified displeasure higher up the ranks: in 1915, for example, Sir John French ordered an artillery barrage to prevent a recurrence. In a number of attacks footballs were dribbled or kicked into the enemy lines, in a literal identification of war as a game, but on Christmas Day 1914 regular matches were played in a friendly spirit in no man's land. In one of them, the Lancashire Fusiliers beat the Saxons 3:2; then both sides crept back to their lines in obedience to their patriotic duty of killing each other: 'There was not an atom of hate on either side that day; and yet, on our side, not for a moment was the will to war and the will to beat them relaxed. It was just like the interval between the rounds in a friendly boxing match.'[13]

15

CHRISTMAS PARTY WITH THE ENEMY

Captain Sir E.H.W. Hulse Bart, describes to his mother how they were singing, drinking and hare hunting with the Germans on Christmas Day half-way between the trenches. He was killed three months later, aged twenty-five.

[Flanders] December 28th, 1914

My dearest Mother,

Just returned to billets again after the most extraordinary Christmas in the trenches you could possibly imagine. Words fail me completely in trying to describe it, but here goes!

During the 24th the usual firing took place, and sniping was pretty brisk. We stood to arms as usual at 6.30 a.m. on the 25th, and I noticed that there was not much shooting; this gradually died down, and by 8 a.m. there was no shooting at all. At 8.30 a.m. I was looking out, and saw four Germans leave their trenches and come towards us; I told two of my men to go and meet them, *unarmed* (as the Germans were unarmed), and to see that they did not pass the halfway line. We were 350–400 yards apart at

---

13 B. Bairnsfather in J. Terraine, 'Christmas 1914', *History Today*, December 1979, p. 781 ff.

this point. My fellows were not very keen, not knowing what was up, so I went out alone, and met Barry, one of our ensigns, also coming from another part of the line. By the time we got to them, they were three quarters of the way over, and much too near our barbed wire, so I moved them back. They were three private soldiers and a stretcher-bearer, and their spokesman started off by saying that he thought it only right to come over and wish us a happy Christmas, and trusted us implicitly to keep the truce. He came from Suffolk, where he had left his best girl and a 3½ h.p. motor-bike! He told me that he could not get a letter to the girl, and wanted to send one through me. I made him write out a postcard in front of me, in English, and I sent it off that night. I told him that she probably would not be a bit keen to see him again.

I was dressed in an old stocking-cap and a man's overcoat, and they took me for a corporal, a thing which I did not discourage, as I had an eye to going as near their lines as possible. . . . I asked them what orders they had from their officers as to coming over to us, and they said *none*; they had just come over out of goodwill. They protested that they had no feeling of enmity towards us at all, but that being soldiers they had to obey. They said that unless directly ordered, they were not going to shoot again until we did.

We talked about the ghastly wounds made by rifle bullets, and we both agreed that neither of us used dum-dum bullets, and that the wounds are solely inflicted by the high-velocity bullet with the sharp nose, at short range. They think that our Press is to blame in working up feeling against them by publishing false 'atrocity reports'. I told them of various sweet little cases I have seen for myself, and they told me of English prisoners whom they have seen with soft-nosed bullets; we had a heated, and at the same time, good-natured argument.

I kept it up for half an hour, and then escorted them back as far as their barbed wire, having a jolly good look round all the time, and picking up various little bits of information which I had not had an opportunity of doing under fire! I left instructions with them that if any of them came out later they must not come over the half-way line, and appointed a ditch as the meeting place. We parted after an exchange of Albany cigarettes and German cigars, and I went straight to Headquarters to report.

On my return at 10 a.m. I was surprised to hear a hell of a din going on, and not a single man left in my trenches; they were completely denuded (against my orders)! I heard strains of 'Tipperary' floating down the breeze, swiftly followed by a tremendous burst of 'Deutschland über Alles', and as I got to my own Coy. Headquarters dug-out, I saw, to my amazement, not only a crowd of about 150 British and Germans at the half-way house which I had appointed opposite my lines, but six or seven such crowds, all the way down our lines. I bustled out and asked if there were any German officers in my crowd, and the noise died down (as this time I was myself in my own cap and badges of rank).

I found two, but had to talk to them through an interpreter, as they could neither talk English nor French. I explained to them that strict orders must be maintained as to meeting half-way, and everyone unarmed; and we both agreed not to fire until the other did, thereby creating a complete deadlock and armistice. . . .

Meanwhile Scots and Huns were fraternizing in the most genuine possible manner. Every sort of souvenir was exchanged, addresses given and received, photos of families shown, etc. A German N.C.O. with the Iron Cross, – gained, he told me, for conspicuous skill in sniping, – started his fellows off on some marching tune. When they had done I set the note for 'The Boys of Bonnie Scotland, where the heather and the bluebells grow', and so we went on, singing everything from 'Good King Wenceslaus' down to the ordinary Tommies' song, and ended up with 'Auld Lang Syne', which we all, English, Scots, Irish, Prussian, Wurtembergers, etc., joined in. It was absolutely astounding, and if I had seen it on a cinematograph film I should have sworn that it was faked! . . .

From foul rain and wet, the weather had cleared up the night before to a sharp frost, and it was a perfect day, everything white, and the silence seemed extraordinary, after the usual din. From all sides birds seemed to arrive, and we hardly ever see a bird generally. Later in the day I fed about 50 sparrows outside my dug-out, which shows how complete the silence and quiet was. It is the first time, day or night, that we have heard no guns, or rifle-firing.

Just after we had finished 'Auld Lang Syne' an old hare started up, and seeing so many of us about in an unwonted spot, did not know which way to go. I gave one loud 'View Holloa', and one and all, British and Germans, rushed about giving chase, slipping up on the frozen plough, falling about, and after a hot two minutes we killed in the open, a German and one of our fellows falling together heavily upon the completely baffled hare. Shortly afterwards we saw four more hares, and killed one again; both were good heavy weight and had evidently been out between the two rows of trenches for the last two months, well-fed on the cabbage patches, many of which are untouched on the 'no-man's land'. The enemy kept one and we kept the other.

It was now 11.30 a.m., and at this moment George Paynter arrived on the scene, with a hearty 'Well, my lads, a Merry Christmas to you! This is d—d comic, isn't it?' and he then said, 'Well, my boys, I've brought you over something to celebrate this funny show with', and he produced from his pocket a large bottle of rum (not ration rum but the proper stuff). One large shout went up, and the nasty little spokesman uncorked it, and in a heavy ceremonious manner, drank our healths, in the name of his 'camaraden'; the bottle was then passed on and polished off before you could say knife. . . .

One of the enemy told me that he was longing to get back to London: I assured him that 'So was I'. He said that he was sick of the war, and I told him that when the truce was ended, any of his friends would be welcome in our trenches, and would be well-received, fed, and given a free passage to the Isle of Man! At 4.30 p.m. we agreed to keep in our respective trenches and told them that the truce was ended. They persisted, however, in saying they were not going to fire, and as George had told us not to, unless they did, we prepared for a quite night, but warned all sentries to be doubly on the alert. But not a shot was fired . . .

Christmas fraternization was possible because hatred of the enemy in the opposite trench was rare, in contrast to the Hun-baiting hysteria at home, whipped up by the Press. 'Strange to say', observes Major-General Charteris, 'our men fraternize far more readily with the German prisoners than with their French allies'.[14] Richard Aldington remembers:

They had no feeling of hatred for their enemies on the other side of No Man's Land. In fact they were almost sympathetic to them. The fighting

14 *At G.H.Q.*, Cassell, 1931, p. 221.

was so impersonal as a rule that it seemed rather a conflict with dreadful hostile forces of Nature than with other men. You did not see the men who fired.[15]

It was widely felt that the German front-line soldiers shared the same predicament, caused by fumbling diplomats and top brass, and hatred was reserved for 'fat patriots' at home, as in the lines of Edward Thomas (1878–1917), 'This is no Case of Petty Right or Wrong':

> I hate not Germans, nor grow hot
> With love of Englishmen, to please newspapers.
> Beside my hate for one fat patriot
> My hatred of the Kaiser is love true . . .

Sergeant-Major Keeling, in his letters, also opposed the hatred of the Germans stirred up by journalists and the plans to humiliate Germany: 'I have no sympathy with people who want to execrate the whole German nation. . . . It does not help to win the War. Women seem to be particularly bad.' At the front, he asserts, few hate their enemies: 'I feel as sorry for the Germans as for our own men in the bombardments, and am none the worse soldier for that.' The front soldier's hatred was directed towards profiteers and high wage earners at home.[16]

16

VILE TO KILL GERMANS

Brigadier-General Philip Howel voices this growing revulsion in a letter to his wife. He was killed the following year, aged thirty-eight.

15.9.15

. . . It is VILE that all my time should be devoted to killing Germans whom I don't in the least want to kill. If all Germany could be united in one man and he and I could be shut up together just to talk things out, we could settle the war, I feel, in less than an hour. The ideal war would include long and frequent armistices during which both sides could walk across the trenches and discuss their respective points of view. We are really only fighting just because we are all so ignorant and stupid. And if diplomats were really clever such a thing as war could never be. . . .

---

15 *Death of a Hero*, Chatto & Windus, 1929, p. 255.
16 F.H. Keeling, *Letters and Recollections*, Allen & Unwin, 1918, p. 259 ff.

17

THE GERMAN SOLDIER IS NO BARBARIAN

Second Lieutenant A.R. Williams notes no ill feeling at the front towards the German soldier, but rather pity; he was killed in 1917, aged twenty-three.

October 16th, 1916

. . . So much is written about the war now-a-days, and so little of it strikes a right and wholesome note, – and yet it is so clear. It is nothing but an intimately personal tragedy to every British (and German) soldier concerned in the *fighting* part of it. Also it is quite the exception to note any ill feeling towards the individual German. In many cases it is impossible not to feel pity. The belief at home that the individual enemy is an incurable barbarian is simply wrong, however black his record has been in the war organisation. . . .

Germany has got to be beaten, and, in that way, since it is the only way, shown the error of her ways. *Then*, we must not only tolerate the return of the whipped child into the family circle again, but, if we sincerely want peace, not merely for our own advantage but for the sake of peace itself, we must even be prepared to lend a helping hand.

But I am rambling rather stupidly, and the noise of the 'whipping' is never far distant. . . .

D.H. Lawrence, pacifist husband of Frieda von Richthofen, and hounded from Cornwall as a suspected spy, went as far as pleading: 'Let there be an end to this German hating. . . . German victory is a lesser evil than continuation of the War.'

The poet Charles Sorley took the most extreme view, that few could have shared. He had spent the first half of 1914 in Germany after leaving school, and had fallen so much in love with it that he identified completely with his newly-adopted fatherland. 'I felt I was a German', he wrote home, 'and proud to be a German. . . . Perhaps I could die for Deutschland – and I have never had an inkling of that feeling about England, and never shall.' Even when he was already training as a soldier in the autumn of 1914 he wrote: 'I hope Germany will win.' Yet he was not uncritical of Germany when he described the war as one between 'the efficient and intolerant against the casual and sympathetic', and expressed the vague hope that as a result, 'efficiency and tolerance will no longer be incompatible'.

Sorley rebelled against the prevailing jingoistic upsurge and bourgeois complacency in general:

England – I am sick of the sound of the word. In training to fight for England, I am training to fight for that deliberate hypocrisy, that terrible middle-class sloth of outlook and appalling 'imaginative indolence' that has marked us out from generation to generation . . . Suburbia and Westminster and Fleet Street.

He continues in a mood of alienation: 'I think that after the war all brave men will renounce their country and confess that they are strangers and pilgrims on earth. . . .' Then he feels ashamed of his surrender:

> But all these convictions are useless for me to state since I have not had the courage of them. What a worm one is under the cartwheels of public opinion. I might have been giving my mind to fight against Sloth and Stupidity: instead, I am giving my body (by a refinement of cowardice) to fight against the most enterprising nation in the world.

Finally, he wryly observes that, 'All patrols – English and German – are much averse to the death and glory principle, so, on running up against one another, pass by on the other side, no word spoken' so as not to violate, for their own discomfort, 'the unwritten laws that govern the relations of combatants permanently within a hundred yards . . . until they have their heads banged forcibly together by the red-capped powers behind them, whom neither attempts to understand.'[17]

In one of his last letters before being killed in the Battle of Loos, he realizes that the process has gone too far.

18

THE INSIDIOUS PROGRESS OF BRUTALIZATION

Captain Charles Sorley (1895–1915) writes to Lieutenant A. Watts.

26 August 1915

Looking into the future one sees a holocaust somewhere . . . out in front at night in that no-man's land and long graveyard there is a freedom and a spur. Rustling of the grasses and grave-tapping of distant workers: the tension and silence of encounter, when one struggles in the dark for moral victory over the enemy patrol: the wail of the exploded bomb and the animal cries of the wounded men. The death and the horrible thankfulness when one sees that the next man is dead: 'We won't have to *carry* him in under fire, thank God; dragging will do': hauling in of the great resistless body in the dark, the smashed head rattling: the relief, the relief that the thing has ceased to groan: that the bullet or bomb that made the man an animal has now made the animal a corpse. One is hardened by now: purged of all false pity: perhaps more selfish than before. . . .

---

17 *Letters of Charles Sorley*, Cambridge University Press, 1919, *passim*.

Unreality and Reality of the Trenches

The bird stopped its song. Then it began again, a frail soliloquy, persistent in chaos
H.M. TOMLINSON (1873–1958), ALL OUR YESTERDAYS

My hands are caked in mud, my body is bathed in it, my soul is full of it.
I can hear nothing but the steady drip of water, gradually washing away
the remains of this dug-out.
CAPTAIN GRAHAM GREENWELL (15 DECEMBER 1915)

A future prime minister compares nostalgically the empty desolation of the trench scene during a lull with the shining magic of the old wars.

19

'The glamour of red coats'

Harold Macmillan (1894–1986), Grenadier Guards, to his mother.

May 13, 1916

Perhaps the most extraordinary thing about the modern battlefield is the desolation and emptiness of it all. Nothing is to be seen of war or soldiers – only the split and shattered trees. One can look for miles and see no human being. But in those miles of country lurk (like moles or rats) thousands, even hundreds of thousands of men, planning against each other perpetually some new device of death. Never showing themselves, they launch at each other bullet, bomb, aerial torpedo and shell and yet the landscape shows nothing of all this – nothing but a few shattered trees and three or four lines of earth and sandbags. . . . The glamour of red coats – the martial tunes of flag and drum – aides-de-camp scurrying hither and thither on splendid chargers – lances glittering and swords flashing – how different the old wars must have been!

A few months later he reflects on his experience of lying wounded in a trench on the Somme for nine interminable hours before being picked up: 'Bravery is not really vanity, but a kind of concealed pride, because everybody is watching you. Then I was alone and there was no need to show off any more, no need to pretend. I was frightened.'

Sergeant-Major Keeling experienced the usual transformation after a taste of the reality of war. At first, on the march up to the front, delighted with what, deceptively, appeared to him like a picnic excursion, he had a rude awakening when the shells were exploding everywhere in the firing-line and when he was wounded himself. He could not even quite find 'the tinge of joy of battle' he had imagined fighting would excite in him, because invisibly distant war machines, rather than men, were pitted against each other.

20

THE PICNIC TURNS INTO HELL

Sergeant-Major Frederick Keeling writes to Mrs Green.

27 May 1915

My first week of warfare has been a delightful picnic – two days in a splendid camp over the sea, three days in an idyllic French Flemish village, then two days of easy marching towards the firing-line. Weather delightful all the time. Since Sunday night we have been hearing the big guns in the distance. Well, we are living like fighting-cocks and enjoying a continental tour at the Government's expense. That is all that war means so far, except for the boom of the guns, which has just come to my ear again as I lie in this pleasant meadow girt with pollarded elms. We sleep in barns of straw, absolutely the best in the world. . . .

29 July

I have been in the battle and I am wounded, but not badly. We were near the firing-line then and things were warm, but the great thing to keep cool and happy is to have something to do. I could never have lived through the nine days in the trenches last time if I had not been worked to death day and night. . . . I was ordered to lead the second party which went up to support the firing-line. I led my men across the field which had been heavily shelled just before. Shells were falling everywhere. I passed several men dead or horribly wounded. I felt cheerful nevertheless, really a sort of tinge of joy of battle in spite of the hellishness of it all, though you can't get a real joy of battle in these artillery days. Then suddenly I heard a specially loud crash, and fell, seeing 'red', and thinking, 'Am I going to die? This is not so bad as I thought it would be.' I had got about four cuts on the back of the head and neck. I came back to the dressing station, a little ashamed of not going back to the firing-line. It isn't a 'Blighty',[18] I am pretty sure, so I shan't see you yet. . . .

Keeling was in fact sent home to hospital. From there he gives a vivid account of the soldiers' hardships – not a picnic any longer. Coming from a middle-class background (he was a Wykehamist), he strongly resented the young officers' privileges.

21

PRIVILEGE AND THE RELATIVITY OF HARDSHIP

Keeling makes some bitter comments to Mrs Hubbock about discrimination between officers and men.

Liverpool Merchants' Hospital, 8 Aug. 1915

This is to let you know that I am quite right again after a week in hospital and expect to be back at duty very soon. I was lucky to be knocked out so soon after my battery

---

18 Wound entitling the victim to be sent home – longed for by many soldiers.

got there. I don't think we have more than half a dozen officers left and probably half of the men in action were wiped out. It was all shell fire. I never saw a German. In the original attack which they made early in the day they used liquid fire for the first time.

God, how one will value and enjoy life if one does have the luck to survive the War! You can't think what the simple luxuries mean to one. I tasted a good bit of roast beef to-day for the first time for months. You can't imagine the rough standard of physical civilization one sinks to when one has slept on the ground almost without intermission for months, eaten and drunk out of dirty tin, chased lice or tried to chase them out of one's clothes as a matter of course every few days, and not used a hand-kerchief for God knows how long.

I don't think people realize the difference between the officers' and common soldiers' lot out here. The difference in regard to hardships endured is enormous. That is the chief thing which makes a commission distasteful to me. One does not grudge it to the company officers, but I think the subalterns get more than their share of comfort, though I daresay that their health rate entitles them to a bit more. And one does not blame the individuals; it is just the system that is obnoxious in a democratic age.

I was a bit irritated just before I got wounded at some incidents in a small town near where we were lying. Officers could get there freely; we did not get passes and could only get a limited number. Then when we got there and tried to get a simple meal, poached eggs and coffee, at a restaurant, one was put off with excuses, while all the time the young officers, not of the most attractive class, were enjoying a jolly good feed. This happened to me and also to some of my men on a separate occasion. When one had just come out of the trenches, up to which men already overloaded with their equipment had had to carry special bags of rations and whisky for officers through communication trenches with water up to their knees, one felt a bit sick. I am afraid the language that I and a Radical fellow-sergeant used about officers on our way back to the camp was decidedly 'detrimental to good order and military discipline'. However, I have known officers' rations go astray in the trenches. Some day, if I come back, I can tell you some amusing yarns about that. I will omit them now, in case the Censor reads so far. . . . [He was killed in 1916, aged thirty.]

The Prime Minister's eldest son was among these privileged junior officers but he refused the staff post into which the establishment was trying to edge him. He was a brilliant scholar (Winchester and Balliol) and an irreverent cynic whose exuberant sardonic wit grew weary in the deafening monotony of the trenches. He came to look upon war with 'an invincible pride and stiff indifference to the brutal muddle of the universe': it seemed to him 'like "Saturday night on the underground", men milling around to no obvious effect', nothing but 'pure convention, like debates in the House of Commons, the birthday honours. . . .' John Buchan said of him: 'He would destroy some piece of homely sentiment with a jest, and he had no respect for the sacred places of dull men. There was a touch of scorn in him for obvious emotion, obvious creeds.'[19]

19   J. Joliffe, *Raymond Asquith*, Collins, 1980, p. 18.

22

'Don't think I am becoming heavy or heroic'

Lieutenant Raymond Asquith (1878–1916), 3rd Grenadier Guards, was a devoted husband but seemed more at ease with Lady Diana ('Dilly') Manners, the celebrated society beauty who loved him, in expressing his moods, oscillating between impassive lucidity and lighthearted banter. He was killed leading his men into the attack in September 1916.

19 November 1915

. . .´ The trenches are more uncomfortable and less dangerous than I had been led to expect. An unpleasant feature is the vast number of rats which gnaw the dead bodies and then run about on one's face making obscene noises and gestures. Lately a certain number of cats have taken to nesting in the corpses but I think the rats will get them under in the end; though like all wars it will doubtless be a war of attrition. . . .

26 December 1915

. . . Shelling – especially in the dark – quite comes up to Christmas number standards. The odd thing is that as a method of killing people, it somehow just fails to come off – aims at a million and misses a unit almost every time, but by inches only. Red and yellow flame and tall columns of dirt and smoke and sand-bags fly into the air all round you; clods of earth fall upon your neck, the nose-cap of the shell whizzes over your head with a noise of a thousand bad harmoniums played at once by a maniac, and the most respectable soldiers look too idiotically serious for words, while the most disreputable ones shout with laughter and pour out a stream of obscene jokes. You think at first that everybody in the trench must be dead except yourself and after the thing is over you find that two men are slightly wounded.

19 January 1916

. . . Death is the only solution of the problem of life which has not so far been definitely proved to be the wrong one, and to be killed in action would gracefully set at rest many urgent and recurring anxieties.

It has seemed to me of late that my only point was being a potential corpse. Without the glamour of the winding sheet I have no *locus standi* in the world. . . . Don't think I am becoming heavy or heroic, Dilly. Nothing of the sort – I am as flippant and dastardly as ever. But I am simply balancing my accounts in a purely commercial spirit. . . .

10 July 1916

I agree with you about the utter senselessness of war. . . . I cannot see that it has a single redeeming feature. The suggestion that it elevates the character is hideous. Burglary, assassination, and picking oakum would do as much for anyone. . . .

We are in the front line now. . . . One dozes off in the day time with a pleasant humming in one's ears which makes one dream of woods and hay fields in England and when one wakes one finds that it is a covey of bluebottles quarrelling over a bit of bully beef that some blasé private has flung into the trenches.

Yesterday I saw a very handsome fly with a bottle green bodice and magenta skirt. This is the nearest I can get to a pretty woman.

5 September 1916

I was given 24 hours' leave to Amiens and whipped off there with two or three others, in young Wales' excellent Daimler on Saturday afternoon. We ate and drank a great deal of the best, slept in downy beds, bathed in hot perfumed water, and had a certain amount of restrained fun with the very much once-occupied ladies of the town. I took a particular fancy to a perfect *'femme du monde'*, with a voice as hoarse as the late Lady Westmorland's, and a skin distinctly less exhausted who entertained a dozen of us for an hour or more with talk and sweet champagne and all manner of lingeries. . . .

Such upper-class mocking contempt for sentiment contrasts with evocative feelings about Nature in a world where reality and unreality are strangely mingled. For example, birdsong made Keeling nostalgic:

Every morning when I was in the front-line trenches I used to hear the larks singing soon after we stood-to about dawn. But those wretched larks made me more sad than anything else out here. . . . Their songs are so closely associated in my mind with peaceful summer days in gardens or pleasant landscapes in Blighty.[20]

The war poet of protest, Captain Siegfried Sassoon, felt the same nostalgic love of Nature:

In the warm dusk . . . nightingales were singing beautifully . . . and the stars were showing among a few thin clouds. But the sky . . . glowed with swift flashes of the distant bombardments of Amiens and Albert, and there was a faint rumbling, low and menacing. And still the nightingales sang on. O world God made![21]

But for Rifleman Alex Bowlby the lark's song evoked the absurdity of war: 'In the lulls between explosions I could hear a lark singing. That made the war seem sillier than ever.'[22] On another occasion, when under fire from German guns, he first takes the bird-call for a German signal:

But as the bird sang on I realized that no human could reproduce such perfection. It was a nightingale. And as if showing us and the Germans that there are better things to do it opened up until the whole valley rang with song. . . . I sensed a tremendous affirmation that 'this would go on'.[23]

20 Housman, op. cit., p. 163.
21 S. Sassoon, *Memoirs of an Infantry Officer*, Faber & Faber, 1937, p. 111.
22 *Recollections of Rifleman Bowlby*, L. Cooper, 1969, p. 43.
23 Ibid., p. 139.

The next letter expresses similar feelings of a higher eternal reality. Nostalgia, alienation, life's continuity – a lieutenant, killed five months later at Loos, evokes all three when the eternal beauty of Nature calls to him louder than all the noise and confusion of war.

23

The nightingale's song was the only real thing

Second Lieutenant A.D. Gillespie tells those at home about a moonlit night in Flanders.

Billets, May 5, 1915

This day began for me about midnight, as I lay in my dug-out in the breastwork watching the plough swing slowly round. I shall remember that night; there was a heavy thunder-shower in the evening, but when we marched down it cleared away for a warm still summer night; still, that is, except for the sniper's rifles, and the rattle of the machine-guns, and sometimes the boom of a big gun far away, coming so long after the flash that you had almost forgotten to expect it. The breastwork which we held ran through an orchard and along some hedge-rows. There was a sweet smell of wet earth and wet grass after the rain, and since I could not sleep, I wandered about among the ghostly cherry trees all in white, and watched the star-shells rising and falling north and south. Presently a misty moon came up, and a nightingale began to sing. I have only heard him once before, in the day-time, near Farly Mount, at Winchester; but, of course, I knew him at once, and it was strange to stand there and listen, for the song seemed to come all the more sweetly and clearly in the quiet intervals between the bursts of firing. There was something infinitely sweet and sad about it, as if the countryside were singing gently to itself, in the midst of all our noise and confusion and muddy work; so that you felt the nightingale's song was the only real thing which would remain when all the rest was long past and forgotten. It is such an old song too, handed on from nightingale to nightingale through the summer nights of so many innumerable years. . . . So I stood there, and thought of all the men and women who had listened to that song, just as for the first few weeks after Tom was killed I found myself thinking perpetually of all the men who had been killed in battle – Hector and Achilles and all the heroes of long ago, who were once so strong and active, and now are so quiet. Gradually the night wore on, until the day began to break, and I could see clearly the daisies and buttercups in the long grass about my feet. Then I gathered my platoon together, and marched back past the silent farms to our billets. There was a beautiful sunrise, and I went to sleep content. . . .

This was written under the magic spell of the night; in day-time the war was again very real and contemplation gave way to humour.

24

THE BATTLE OF 'TURNIPS' VERSUS 'SAUSAGES'

Lieutenant Gillespie writes home in a frivolous mood.

Trenches, June 14

We had a lively afternoon yesterday, for a trench mortar battery came along to wake the Germans up. They started with 33-pounder bombs, like a big turnip with a long handle, and we watched them sailing through the air, with the handle spinning round. But out of twenty large bombs, only eight went off. Then the Germans brought out their sausage machine, and started to reply. The sausage machine throws up a long bomb like a rolling-pin, which makes a most infernal noise. We could hear the report and see them come rocketing over a tall row of trees just above our trenches, tumbling over and over in the air. I felt like a small boy at Winchester waiting for high catches in the deep field, for the sausage seemed to hang in the air above your head, while your past life rose before you like a cloud, and you wondered when the thing was going to come down, and whether it would go right over, or hit a branch and drop straight on your head; and all the time it seemed to hang there, tumbling round and round. Luckily, they all went over the fire trench where I was standing, but one sausage was rude enough to come into our company trench quarters, where it wrecked Clark's house, and very nearly spoilt the dinner. It was really very funny to see them. We replied with two smaller mortars, which showered turnips on them until their sausage machine was damaged or silenced for want of sausages. But by that time they were thoroughly angry, and had sent word to their artillery, which put more than thirty shells over our heads, and into the trenches on our left. They also showered rifle-grenades on us, to which we replied in kind, and for a while there was quite a battle with turnips, sausages, rifle-grenades, and shells all flying through the air, and bursting round about. But, in spite of all this frightfulness, no one in this company was hit. For some time, however, we all had a sausage eye, and kept looking up anxiously when a swallow passed the trees, and in the evening when three or four large bats came out, I kept on seeing them past the corner of my spectacles, and looking round anxiously for cover. . . .

The sight of the wounded at his hospital behind the lines where he worked as a Red Cross orderly, revolted a future poet laureate.

25

'I never knew I loved men so much'

John Masefield writes to his wife.

March 5, 1915

Whenever I look at these poor fellows my soul boils. Nothing else in the world matters but to stop this atrocious thing. . . . You have no idea of it, you can't even guess the stink of it, from the bloody reeking stretchers to the fragments hopping on crutches, and half heads, & a leg gone at the thigh, & young boys blinded & grey-headed old men with their backs broken. I never knew I loved men so much. . . .

But the City clerk who had enlisted at thirty-eight, saw in his hospital ward only a cosy refuge of 'extreme luxury' from the intense discomfort of the trenches: he has been through the 'hardening of experience'.

26

'And yet – one is merry there'

Sergeant Ernest Nottingham writes to his friend Charles Williams. He was killed in 1917.

27/3/16

. . . In the long ward, a cheerful contented undertone of conversation. Two fires burning and the occupants lying comfortably on mattresses or stretchers. Fed, warm, cosy. Far from shells, bullets, bombs, minnies, gas. There's the rain again. It beats furiously on the skin window-panes and on the low roof. Up there the boys stand in mud and water thro' the night. Silent the sentries on the fire steps, peering across 'no man's-land' . . . Rain, pitiless rain, soaking and numbing. And so to wear the night away. Blessed the tot of rum which unlocks quickly a man's reserves and allows him to 'carry on' . . . Happy the section with a little kindling wood . . . Here, in the warm with my three blankets to lie and listen to the rain, and see the trenches knee-deep in parts, I feel uncomfortable – and yet enjoy the extreme luxury. . . .

I know there's another world than this hard, cheerful objective life we lead – I feel it momentarily (and feel sad) at the sound of a train, or a church bell, or the scent and sight of a flower, or the green of a hedge. But not now in the ecstasy of a lark. That is inseparably connected with 'stand to' in trenches. So often from Festubert onwards have I heard him singing joyously in the early dawn. I spoke of the hardening of experience. Here's an instance. I've just come from where 50,000 bodies lie, bones and barbed wire everywhere, skeletons bleached if one takes a walk over the frightfully contested and blown up hill. Boots and bones protruding from one's dug-out walls, and yet – one is merry there. At the midnight hour one sees, nor expects to see, nothing of wraiths, or of the spirits of countless brave ones who met there a violent death!

Generally the men accepted their lot with cheerful humour and a healthy dose of cynicism. Also, it must not be forgotten that, in some ways at least, they were often better off in the trenches than they had been at home: 'They are having the time of their lives. They know that they're alive now, and they're not responsible for anything. Not a blessed obligation, except to carry a gun. No fear of the sack, no landlord. Fed, clothed, and told not to think.

Everything done for them, right down to funerals. It's ideal. Isn't that so?', writes H.M. Tomlinson, admittedly with a pinch of sarcasm.[24] The rank and file soldier's defence-mechanism in 'this hard, cheerful objective life' was bitter irony, mitigated by anti-heroic humour and humane comradeship.

A Royal College of Music scholar extols the companionship of the soldiers, 'a fixed grey-coloured nobility of mind that will last longer than hate and fury, for it is subject to no after-effects of exhaustion or lethargy of spent force'.

27

'The English virtues at their best'

Private Ivor Gurney of the Glosters writes to Marion Scott, a violinist from College.

7 August 1916

Men go one by one, some with nice blighties, some with the Eternal discharge. . . . I have an unresting imagination which never ceases to suggest danger, which when it comes does not greatly affect me. . . .

There is fun, occasionally. What there is to see, and see with joy – is men behaving coolly with white lips, or unaltered faces. Men behaving kindly to one another. Strained eyes and white faces yet able to smile. The absence of swank of a sort – among the men. The English virtues displayed at their best and least demonstrative. . .

In my dugout there is placed very prominently a photo of a place that stands for delight with all Gloster men. It means a good tea, clean air, female society, a good row on a pretty stretch of river, Beauty and leisure to enjoy it; Home and all its meaning. . .

June/July 1917

What a life! What a life! My memories of this week will be, – Blockhouse; cold; stuffy heat; smashed or stuck Tanks; A gas and smoke barrage put up by us. A glorious but terrifying sight; Fritzes shells; one sunset; two sunrises; Thirst; Gas; Shrapnel; Very H.E.; Our liquid fire; . . . Does it sound interesting? May God forgive me if I ever come to cheat myself into thinking that it was, and lie later to the younger men of the Great Days. It was damnable. . . . 'It might be me tomorrow. Who cares? Yet still, hang for a Blighty.'

Why does this war of spirit take on such dread forms of ugliness, and should a high triumph be signified by a body shattered, black, stinking; avoided by day, stumbled over by night, an offence to the hardest? No doubt there is consolation in the fact that men contemplate such things, such possible endings; and are yet undismayed, yet persistent; do not lose laughter nor the common kindliness that makes life sweet – And yet seem such boys – Yet what consolation can be given me as I look upon and endure it?. . .

24 H.M. Tomlinson, *All our Yesterdays*, Heinemann, 1930, p. 448.

Robert Graves, half Irish, half German, and commissioned in the Welch Fusiliers in 1914, was the most realistic of the amazing crop of soldier poets and writers who found inspiration in the trenches of Flanders. He spent four years at the front: despite being severely wounded on the Somme and shell-shocked at Loos, he went back to France for a third time, 'a glum, 21 year old veteran', because he 'could not stand England any longer' and thought France was 'the only place for gentlemen now'. He wrote to Edward Marsh on 12 July 1917: 'I am a sound militarist in action, however much of a pacifist in thought.'[25] He took a stoic, resigned view: 'Apart from wounds, gas and accidents of war, the life of the trench soldier could not be called unhealthy.' His view that regimental pride rather than patriotism or religion was the strongest moral force is borne out by Major Ferrers:

The lad who goes in with the proper affection for the Old Battalion and damn all else is going to come out top dog in the long run. You can't surprise him because he's too beastly ignorant to be surprised, you can't sicken him with dark or dirt or danger or disease or death or damnation because he's damned already and means to die for the Battalion anyhow.[26]

Graves's clinical descriptions are unemotional. Even forty years later the familiar trench smell still haunts his nostrils,

compounded mainly of stagnant mud, latrine buckets, chloride of lime, unburied or half-buried corpses, rotting sandbags, stale human sweat, fumes of cordite and lyddite. Sometimes it was sweetened by cigarette smoke and the scent of bacon frying over wood fires (broken ammunition boxes); sometimes made sinister by the lingering odour of poison gas.[27]

His letter relates two stories about 'cushies' with the black humour of the old hand.

28

'Pessimistic but cheerful'

Captain Robert Graves (1895–1985) writes home.

May 23, 1915

You'd be surprised at the amount of waste that goes on in the trenches. Ration biscuits are in general use as fuel for boiling up dixies, because kindling is scarce. Our

25 *Broken Images. Selected Letters of Robert Graves*, (ed.) P. O'Prey, Hutchinson, 1982, pp. 61, 64, 77.

26 J.C.M. Baynes, *Morale*, Cassell, 1967, p. 259 f.

27 *Observer*, 9 November 1958. Graves also remembered 'a certain respectful sympathy for the Fritzes – later we called them "Jerries" in envy of their capacious steel helmets.'

machine-gun crew boil their hot water by firing off belt after belt of ammunition at no particular target, just generally spraying the German line. After several pounds' worth of ammunition has been used, the water in the guns – which are water-cooled – begins to boil. They say they make German ration and carrying parties behind the line pay for their early-morning cup of tea. But the real charge will be on income-tax after the war.

May 24th

Tomorrow we return to the trenches. The men are pessimistic but cheerful. They all talk about getting a 'cushy' one to send them back to 'Blitey'. Blitey is, it seems, Hindustani for 'home'. My servant, Fry, who works in a paper-bag factory at Cardiff in civil life, has been telling me stories about cushy ones. Here are two of them.

'A bloke in the Munsters once wanted a cushy, so he waves his hand above the parapet to catch Fritz's attention. Nothing doing. He waves his arms about for a couple of minutes. Nothing doing, not a shot. He puts his elbows on the fire-step, hoists his body upside-down and waves his legs about till he gets blood to the head. Not a shot did old Fritz fire. "Oh," says the Munster man, "I don't believe there's a damned square-head there. Where's the German army to?" He has a peek over the top – crack! he gets it in the head. Finee.'

Another story: 'Bloke in the Camerons wanted a cushy, bad. Fed up and far from home, he was. He puts his hand over the top and gets his trigger finger taken off, and two more beside. That done the trick. He comes laughing through our lines by the old boutillery. "See, lads," he says, "I'm off to bonny Scotland. Is it na a beauty?" But on the way down the trench to the dressing station, he forgets to stoop low where the old sniper's working. *He* gets it through the head, too. Finee. We laugh, fit to die!'

To get a cushy one is all that the old hands think of. Only twelve men have been with the battalion from the beginning, and all are transport men except one. . . . The few old hands who went through the last show infect the new men with pessimism; they don't believe in the war, they don't believe in the staff. But at least they would follow their officers anywhere, because the officers happen to be a decent lot. They look forward to a battle because that gives them more chances of a cushy one in the legs or arms than trench warfare.

Four months before being hit by a 5.9 howitzer shell, and reported as 'died of wounds', Graves returns for his last spell in the trenches.

29

'I always enjoy trenches'

Graves to Edward Marsh.

15 March 1916

It's rather trying having to go back into trenches after a three months' holiday, especially trenches like this where the two parties are so exceedingly embittered against each other: I have to get used to all the old noises, from the crack! rockety-ockety-ockety-ockety-ockety of a rifle bullet, to the boom! . . swish . . . swish . . . Grr. . . GRR! . .

GRR! . . ROAR! of a 15 in. shell and there are a lot of new terrors since last December. The *spécialité* here is 'canisters', round, tin, barrel-shaped trenchmortars filled with about 23 pounds of the highest explosive.

About 10 or 12 times as much stuff is handed round now as when I first came out, but I always enjoy trenches in a way I must confess: I like feeling really frightened and if happiness consists in being miserable in a good cause, why then I'm doubly happy. England's is a good cause enough and the trenches are splendidly miserable: my company's firing-line averages 30 yards from the Bosches, the mud is *chronic*, there are few parts of the trench where one can stand upright without exposing oneself, and not a single canister-proof dug-out. If only it was blowing sleet and a gas attack was due tomorrow my cup of happiness would be full. We work all day and night and enjoy ourselves thoroughly, wading knee-deep through our native element, and humming the popular tune:–

> Après la guerre finie
> Et les Anglais partis,
> Toutes les mademoiselles de Béthune
> Auront bébés anglais jolis.

In August 1915 'Billie' Nevill thought war 'the greatest fun imaginable' which he would not have missed for worlds, but a year later, hardened by the experience of seeing so many of his comrades killed, he wrote: 'What a ghastly thing war is nowadays.' A wistful observer, he excelled in catching the atmosphere of trench life in every minute detail.

30

'Our Freddie'

Captain Wilfred Nevill writes home.

15 August 1915

Let us talk of Freddie. You don't know Freddie, do you? Freddie is the mouse who 'keeps' just north of our dinner table, in the wall. He's a dear little chap & diets entirely on currants & tallow & he's careful not to spoil the wick or eat the tiny dry stalks. But you must see him at 'dejeuner' or 'fif-o'clock tay', to know and appreciate him. I can always tell when it's 'Our Freddie' who's in my neck or nibbling my hair (he eats hair as one would drink coffee & liqueurs). Other mice are silly and bite string in half, or chew into air pillows or rattle paper at night. Of course it's only want of thought and I know the little dears don't *mean* any harm.

'Billie' was to become a folk hero when on 1 July 1916, the first day of the battle of the Somme, he kicked two footballs into no man's land at Montauban to launch the attack. His men dribbled them right up to the German trenches, bearing the inscriptions 'The Great European Cup-Tie Final. East Surreys v.

Bavarians' and 'No referee' (i.e. killing allowed). At twenty-one he was one of the 19,000 killed that day just outside the German barbed wire in which both foot-balls were found; they were kept as a regimental trophy at Kingston Barracks.[28]

The hazards of shell explosions sometimes created grotesque visions of death.

31

R.I.P.

Ivo Grenfell writes to his sister from Vermelles near the ruins of Loos.

29.9.1915

We have got a delightful sight in our graveyard here. From one of the graves the tombstone has been laid open by a shell, and the vault below the coffin lid has been torn off showing the skeleton of a man, a toad sitting on his chest and little brown mice are playing on his bones. R.I.P. says the tombstone.

Shortly afterwards, six days before being killed, he remarks: 'The War seems wary of its own melodrama but does not know how to give it up.'

In contrast to Ivo Grenfell's black humour tempering his horrifying experi-ence, another member of the coterie is inspired by the sight of a hand to rapturous feelings of beauty.

32

THE HAND

Duff Cooper (later Lord Norwich) writes to Lady Diana Manners whom he married in 1919.

11 August 1918

This afternoon in lovely sunlight and heat I went for a little crawl by myself and had rather fun. I found an arm sticking out of the earth. I don't know what impulse made me take off the glove. The arm had been there a long time and there was little left but the bones. The hand was beautiful – thin and delicate like the hand of a woman and the nails had grown long and even like a Mandarin's nails. How much the flesh may once have hidden the beauty of the framework you couldn't tell, but it must always have been a small hand and I think the owner must have been proud of it because gloves are not usually worn at the war. It gave me no feeling of disgust or uneasiness but rather content to find that beauty can still hang about the bones, surviving the

28 R.E. Harris, *Billie, The Nevill Letters*, MacRae, 1991, pp. 195– 203.

corruption of the flesh, and staying with the body until the bitter end of complete annihilation. The hand was raised and the fingers curved in rather an affected gesture. I wish I could have kept the glove. . . .

A fortnight later Duff Cooper glories in the beauty of a night attack:

A full moon, a star to guide us – a long line of cheering men, an artillery barrage as beautiful as any fireworks creeping on before us – a feeling of wild and savage joy. It is a picture that will hang in my gallery for ever. . . . I was the first of my company in the German trench. I boast like a Gascon but it was what the old poets said war was and what the new say it isn't. . . .

Ivar Campbell combines Robert Graves's matter of fact sense of detail with Gillespie's feeling for Nature, symbolized in the song of birds. But to him the little men in the trenches are nothing but puzzled frightened rabbits in an inhuman world which has lost all meaning.

33

'What the blankety, blankety hell is this?'
ALIENATION

Captain Ivar Campbell writes home. He was killed in 1916, aged twenty-five.

[1915]

Here is the scene I shall remember always: a misty summer morning – I went along a sap-head running towards the German lines at right angles to our own. Looking out over the country, flat and uninteresting in peace, I beheld what at first would seem to be a land ploughed by the ploughs of giants. In England you read of concealed trenches – here we don't trouble about that. Trenches rise up, grey clay, three or four feet above the ground. Save for one or two men – snipers – at the sap-head, the country was deserted. No sign of humanity – a dead land. And yet thousands of men were there, like rabbits concealed. The artillery was quiet; there was no sound but a cuckoo in a shell-torn poplar. Then, as a rabbit in the early morning comes out to crop grass, a German stepped over the enemy trench – the only living thing in sight. 'I'll take him,' says the man near me. And like a rabbit the German falls. And again complete silence and desolation . . .

The splutter of shrapnel, the red squeal of field guns, N.E.; the growl of the heavies moving slowly through the air, the cr-r-r-ump of their explosion. But in a bombardment all tones mingle and their voice is like machinery running not smoothly but roughly, pantingly, angrily, wildly making shows of peace and wholeness.

You perceive, too, in imagination, men infinitely small, running, affrighted rabbits, from the upheaval of the shells, nerve-racked, deafened; clinging to earth, hiding eyes, whispering 'O God, O God!' You perceive, too, other men, sweaty, brown, infinitely small also, moving guns, feeding the belching monster, grimly, quietly pleased.

But with eyes looking over this land of innumerable eruptions, you see no line. The land is inhuman.

But thousands of men are there; men who are below ground, men who have little bodies but immense brains. And the men facing West are saying, 'This is an attack, they will attack when this hell's over,' and they go on saying this to themselves continually.

And the men facing East are saying, 'We have got to get over the parapet. We have got to get over the parapet – when the guns lift.'

And then the guns lift up their heads and so a long, higher song.

And then untenanted land is suddenly alive with little men, rushing, stumbling – rather foolishly leaping forward – laughing, shouting, crying in the charge. . . .

There is one thing cheering. The men of the battalion – through all and in spite of that noisy, untasty day; through the wet cold night, hungry and tired; living now in mud and water, with every prospect of more rain to-morrow – are cheery. Sometimes, back in billets, I hate the men – their petty crimes, their continual bad language with no variety of expression, their stubborn moods. But in a difficult time they show up splendidly. Laughing in mud, joking in water – I'd 'demonstrate' into Hell with some of them and not care.

Yet under heavy shell-fire it was curious to look into their eyes – some of them little fellows from shops, civilians before, now and after: you perceived the wide, rather frightened, piteous wonder in their eyes, the patient look turned towards you, not, 'What the blankety, blankety hell *is* this?' but 'Is this quite fair? We cannot move, we are little animals. Is it quite necessary to make such infernally large explosive shells to kill such infernally small and feeble animals as ourselves?'

I quite agreed with them, but had to put my eye-glass fairly in my eye and make jokes; and, looking back, I blush to think of the damnably bad jokes I did make. . . .

34

PEACE BY 1930

Captain Campbell has a vision of redemption from the trenches – still an eternal fifteen years away – when a civilian will be ploughing between the lines: a powerful image of desperate longing for peace.

So in moments of despair we talk of 1930; of how our dug-outs will be nearly finished by that time; of our promotion by the wastage of lives superior, technically to our own; of Fritz, Hans, and Wilhelm growing old as they sit face to face to, though hidden from, James, Jones, and Robinson; of peace at last, when the long thin line of sandbags from Switzerland to the sea is fallen to earth, loose and untroubled; when our eyes, ourselves' and Fritz's, Hans', and Wilhelm's – grown dim and short-sighted from seeing nothing but the sky above and walls around, and a few yards away another (enemy) wall – shall gaze with silent awe upon a thing our memory shall recall to be a plough, led patiently by unmilitary horses, guided by a young and military age-CIVILIAN, ploughing between the lines.

Then, we say, we shall open our eyes, and scales will fall from them, and we shall rise up and meet, we and Hans and Fritz and Wilhelm, around that young man and his plough, and we shall plough away all memory of war and sow the seeds of perpetual peace.

But we have got to wait till 1930 for that. . . .

Gallipoli

Men live through more in five minutes on
that crest than they do in five years . . .
A radiant force of camaraderie in action
GENERAL SIR IAN HAMILTON

War is made of blood, smell, lice, filth,
shells, noise, weariness and death
CORPORAL ALEC RILEY AT HELLES

Was it hard, Achilles,
So hard to die?
NAVAL LIEUTENANT PATRICK SHAW-STEWART,
LOOKING ACROSS THE HELLESPONT TO TROY

In February 1915 an Anglo-French naval force of eighteen capital ships under Admiral de Robeck, sponsored by Churchill at the Admiralty, was sent to Gallipoli to circumvent the deadlock on the Western Front and detract attention from the appalling casualties; it was to reopen the route for war supplies to reach hard-pressed Russia through the Dardanelles and knock out Turkey – all without the aid of the Army, as both Generals French and Joffre opposed the dispatch of troops. On 18 March the forts were bombarded, marines were landed and an attempt was made to sweep the minefields at night; but the naval attack, although taking the Turks by surprise, failed to destroy the guns of the forts on both sides which protected the minefields, and led to the loss of three old battleships and crippled three others. Just when the Turks had almost run out of ammunition, de Robeck abandoned the attempt to rush the Narrows: the Army had to be called in after all. After muddles and delays, and lack of secrecy in the preparations, five divisions under General Sir Ian Hamilton landed on 25 April on the Helles and Anzac beaches.

The complacency was staggering: Hamilton, sixty-three, a charming poet from the age of chivalry, but also a seasoned soldier who had been severely wounded on Majuba Hill and recommended three times for the VC, was full of breezy optimism when he addressed his troops: 'Take a good run at the Peninsula and jump plump on – both feet together.' Kitchener had told him:

'If the Fleet gets through, Constantinople will fall of itself and you will have won, not a battle, but the War.' No more than five thousand casualties were expected. The Army was in great spirits when it sailed over from Alexandria: some took the *Iliad* with them and were looking forward to visiting Troy, while others dreamt of 'Turkish delights' in the harems of Constantinople.[29]

The new naval commander was pleased with the way the landing operations were going when he watched them through his field-glasses.

35

'Nothing was going to stop them'

Rear-Admiral Rosslyn Wemyss (1864–1933), later Admiral, First Sea Lord and Baron, writes about the Navy's part in the successful landing.

May 11, 1915

. . . The landing is practically over. All the troops and artillery are on shore, and we have put them there without a hitch, thank God. On looking back on the whole business the more amazed am I at the initial success, and I cannot help feeling proud at the manner in which the Navy have done their work. I believe now that when I began the task I thought it impossible, but I wouldn't let myself think like that: it *could* be done. And sure enough it was, and it was only when I realized that we had gained the cliffs and that we had planted ourselves on the shore that I knew how really I had doubted of success. How splendidly everybody worked!

We towed more than 90 boats by night from Tenedos to the Dardanelles and put nearly 3,000 men into them all in the dark, and nothing was missing or wrong. And so small a mistake might have spelt failure! To see those boats going in towards the beach, which we knew was so strongly fortified, like a sort of parade as the day broke, is a sight I shall never forget. Try to imagine my feelings as I was standing on the bridge of the *Euryalus* watching them. . . . Imagine the positive sickness that came over one when one saw the leading men jump out of the boats only to be shot down as they got mixed up in the barbed-wire entanglements, a feeling of sickness which changed gradually to exulting pride as it dawned upon one that *nothing* was going to stop them and that the enemy were giving way. The seamen were just as magnificent. One saw wounded men helping to pull the boats back to get more men, and never hesitating for an instant – these men without means of firing back on the enemy, only oars in their hands. I am not sure I do not think that theirs was the greatest courage. By two o'clock in the afternoon we had landed 13,000 men an hour quicker than we had anticipated. Since then we have been perpetually pouring on shore men, guns, ammunitions, stores and provisions. . . .

29 R. Rhodes-James, *Gallipoli*, Batsford, 1965.

But the impressions of two officers of the Lancashire Fusiliers (a regiment which earned six VCs) on the bullet-swept Helles Beach, which they were never to leave again, were less rosy: a mere three Turkish platoons killed or wounded 533 out of 950 landed from the *Euryalus*. The naval bombardment had not touched the well-concealed trenches of the Turks, and the corpses soon piled up on the beach in front of the barbed wire.

36

THE SEA WAS CRIMSON

Major Shaw, soon to be killed, wrote of the landing:

About 100 yards from the beach the enemy opened fire, and bullets came thick all around, splashing up the water. . . . As soon as I felt the boat touch, I dashed over the side into three feet of water and rushed for the barbed wire entanglements on the beach; I got over it amidst a perfect storm of lead and made for cover, sand dunes on the other side. . . . On the cliff was a line of Turks in a trench taking pot shots at us. I looked back. There was one soldier between me and the wire, and a whole line in a row on the edge of the sands. The sea behind was absolutely crimson, and you could hear the groans through the rattle of musketry. A few were firing. I signalled to them to advance. I shouted to the soldier behind me to signal, but he shouted back 'I am shot through the chest'. I then perceived they were all hit. . . .

37

UP THE CLIFFS

Captain Clayton, killed six weeks later, wrote about the charge through the barbed wire.

There was tremendously strong barbed wire where my boat landed. . . . There was a man there before me shouting for wire-cutters. I got mine out, but could not make the slightest impression. The front of the wire by now was a thick mass of men, the majority of whom never moved again. . . . The noise was ghastly and the sights horrible. I eventually crawled through the wire with great difficulty, as my pack kept catching on the wire, and got under a small mound which actually gave us protection. The weight of our packs tired us, so that we could only gasp for breath. After a little time we fixed bayonets and started up the cliffs. . . .

The expeditionary force remained pinned down on the shore by strong Turkish forces under General Liman von Sanders, head of the German Military Mission, who had had a month to fortify the hills above; it could not make any headway even when reinforced by the arrival of further divisions in Suvla Bay.

38

'Gott strafe . . .'

Naval Lieutenant Patrick Shaw-Stewart describes to Lady Diana Manners how war transformed the beauty of Gallipoli into desolation.

11 June 1915

Shall we ever have fun again? I suppose yes! . . . *Gott strafe* the heat, the flies, the tepid drinks, my smelly lousy growsing men. . . . Not so much the Turks, who are really very nice, nor the scenery which is admirable – but the poppies and bright birds are gone, and our end of the peninsula, which was a dream when we landed is now simply a dusty fly-blown maze of dug-outs and latrines.

Despite the grim struggle and conditions, humorous banter passed between the very close trenches on the hills, with sympathetic feelings among the Allied soldiers for 'Johnny Turk' who was throwing over grapes and sweets in exchange for cigarettes and tins. The Turks even complained in a bi-lingual note: 'Bully beef – non. Envoyez milk,' which was understandable as owing to the lack of green vegetables with the fatty meat, and swarms of green 'corpse flies' in the scorching heat, an epidemic of dysentery had broken out which killed many thousands on both sides.[30]

39

'JOHNNY TURK' THE HUMORIST

Colonel Sir Henry Darlington, 5th Manchesters (miners from Wigan), writes to his aunt.

22 May 1915

Brother Turk is a bit of a humorist, he signals washouts with a spade when our snipers miss them. We drew them all right yesterday. We rigged up a dummy and put it up, he had some shots at it and then got suspicious and stopped, and I told a man to lower the dummy, poke up a rifle on the parapet, and then shove the dummy as if it was one of our snipers; that fairly fetched the Turk and when he had quite finished we shoved the dummy right up and waggled it at them.

The Turks put their bucket up to draw our snipers, and if one fires the Turk signals the miss.

We put a bully beef tin up to represent the end of a periscope and he hit it first shot. . . . The only thing that spoils the view up in the front is the big number of dead Turks and Australians . . . the smell is appalling. . . .

30 A. Moorehead, *Gallipoli*, H. Hamilton, 1956, p. 174.

Hamilton's optimism soon gave way to an admission of failure in face of the impenetrable scientifically placed defences, and he asked Kitchener for another 95,000 men. He was promptly replaced by General Sir Charles Monro who at once recommended evacuation (Churchill punned: 'I came, I saw, I capitulated'), but even Kitchener, after first sacking him too, agreed when he came to see for himself. Meanwhile a hundred soldiers perished in a November blizzard, and the Turks under the ruthlessly brilliant young Mustafa Kemal bayonetted all defenders of the strategic Chunuk Bair which the East Lancashire Division had so bravely stormed while being shelled by their own Navy; on this ridge alone, fifty thousand died on both sides. A letter from their colonel is a moving testimony of loyal acceptance and quiet determination in face of an impossible task.

40

'It is not for us to reason why, we must go on and see it through'

Colonel Fred Hardman describes to his wife the heavy shelling they are suffering; he longs to see his little boy.

Dardanelles, May 21, 1915

My dear Wife,

Since our arrival here we have been continually under fire. . . . We have been shelled day after day in fact we have had more casualties down here than we had in the trenches. There is not a single part of the ground which is not under fire. The *Goeben*[31] drops her big shells on us and when the shrapnell comes it is a perfect inferno. Before we had time to dig ourselves in, they opened fire on us dropping as many as 20 shells to the minute. The earth seemed to tremble and rock. . . . Tonight we got into the front fire trenches: we have to cross open fields and the enemy's searchlight is playing about and star shells are being sent up, one requires to rub your nose in the ground a bit in order to avoid being seen. . . .

I was pleased to get the new photograph of our little Rex. I cannot realise my boy is so old and so big and bonny. Two great tears stood in my eyes as I looked at it for at that moment the Turks were giving one of their best displays and my seeing him again seemed so remote and so far away. However while there is life there is hope and continue to look forward with glorious expectancy of the happy day when we shall all meet again.

The British in my opinion have made the same mistake in this job as they always do by underestimating it. From the first bombardment of the forts we gave them two months before we landed troops, in the meantime, they had made this place a network of fortifications. We are attacking a position now which is nothing less than a

---

31 German battle-cruiser assisting the Turks.

Giberalter [sic], during the last month there has been enough casualties to make a record gate at Oldham Football ground and what they will be before we take the hill, God only knows, but we shall do our best. It is not for us to reason why, we must go on and see it through. . . .

I have lost one of my artificial teeth with biting dog biscuits and don't know whether I have swallowed it or not as I can't find it. We get very little rest as we have to sleep every night with our clothes and equipment on. I think I have been undressed once during the last fortnight and expect we shall be in the front trenches a week and by then I shall have to get them off with a knife. . . .

The quarters I have occupied for the last four days have been a hole two foot deep in the ground, a yard wide and two yards long, the earth being piled up on the side facing the enemy. It is not absolutely shell proof as I can not go any lower because I come to water, but when the bombardment starts I manage to hutch on one corner like a whipped dog and wait until the storm has passed, trusting to providence the while.

(Chocolate and toffee I should appreciate just now. I don't know that I can say much else. I am making the best of things, thinking of you all at home, and hoping to return some day. I have seen some terrible sights but I am getting hardened to them now. Perhaps me going through it now is saving our little Rex having to go through it in years to come. I think of you and him every night and many times during the day. . . . With deepest affection yours as long as I am my own)

Fred

The situation became increasingly hopeless. Ego Charteris expresses the general despondency on 10 September:

Gallipoli seems the last word in hell. . . . You never hear of anything but bungling and ghastly casualties. It is no fun being killed when you feel it is just hopeless waste. From generals downward everybody talks in the same strain.

After a nine-month campaign Gallipoli had to be evacuated. 410,000 British and 70,000 French troops had been landed who never got out of sight of the beaches and of whom 46,000 were killed and 220,000 wounded; vast stores had to be left behind.

Admiral Fisher, despite his pugnacity, had always been shrewd enough to recognize the lack of realism in Churchill's cherished brainchild which also had Kitchener's support. He favoured a Baltic landing instead, and was the first to warn Lloyd-George that it was futile to attempt to rush the Dardanelles without the Army. He now sent in his resignation in a rage against Churchill. Beatty had written to his wife about them: 'Two very strong and clever men, one old, wily and of vast experience, one young, assertive, with great self-satisfaction but unstable. They can't work together, they can't both run the show.'[32]

---

32 W.S. Chalmers, *Beatty*, Hodder & Stoughton, 1951, p. 179.

41

Churchill 'a bigger danger than the Germans'

Admiral Lord Fisher to Andrew Bonar Law, Leader of the Conservative Party.

May 17, 1915

Private and Personal

This letter and its contents must not be divulged now or ever to any living soul.

My dear Friend,

. . . I am absolutely unable to remain with W.C. (HE'S A REAL DANGER!) but he is going to be kept (so I go! at once, TODAY) . . . W.C. is leading them all straight to ruin. . . . A very great national disaster is very near in the Dardanelles! Against which I have vainly protested . . . W.C. is a bigger danger than the Germans by a long way. . .

There can be no doubt that the operation was an imaginative strategic move, but because of disagreement between ministers and service chiefs it was executed piecemeal and not as a combined naval and military attack right from the beginning which, with the essential momentum of surprise, would have had a very good chance of success. The Gallipoli fiasco had far-reaching consequences: Churchill was dismissed (and later left for France to take over command of the 6th Royal Scots Fusiliers), the Liberal Government fell, the crumbling Turkish resistance revived, Bulgaria was brought into the war, and Serbia collapsed. It has also been argued that the failure to relieve Russia helped precipitate the Bolshevik Revolution.[33]

---

33 J.F.C. Fuller, *Decisive Battles of the Western World*, III, Eyre & Spottiswoode, 1957.

T W O

Trench Stalemate
and War of Attrition (1916)

. . . the wind
Blowing over London from Flanders
Has a bitter taste
RICHARD ALDINGTON (1892–1962)

. . . as that Great War unmasked its ugliness . . .
EDMUND BLUNDEN (1896–1974)

Zepps over London

. . . illumined and dumb
A shape suspended
Hovers, a demon of the starry air!
. . . Poised deadly in a gleam
LAURENCE BINYON (1869–1943), 'THE ZEPPELIN'

Germany produced eighty-eight Zeppelin airships in four factories for North Sea patrol and bombing raids in the first deliberate attack on civilian morale. To counter the threat to civilians a blackout was imposed, searchlights and anti-aircraft guns installed, and fighter planes developed (but without success for another year). Altogether there were only two thousand casualties but the production of munitions was reduced by a sixth by the alarms.

1

CURIOSITY AND PANIC

VAD[1] Nurse Ursula Somervell (1891–1980) describes to her mother the Zeppelin raid on the City which hit Liverpool Street and Euston Stations and initiated a month of bombing of the East End, causing consternation.

Bethnal Green Military Hospital,
September 9th, 1915

We had a pretty terrifying time with Zepps again last night. We were waked by 10–30 by a terrific noise of bombs, aircraft, guns, etc., apparently all round us; we rushed on dressing gowns, said a prayer, and got downstairs as quickly as we could; the lights were put out just as we got to the bottom, and we were left in a herd of frightened females in pitch darkness.

The bangs were going on all round, and we were absolutely expecting to have the building about our ears any minute. I'm sorry to say I did feel pretty frightened. . . . We found Joyce's Ward Sister, who clutched on to her, and we finally all three decided to go up into her ward to see if the Night-Nurse was all right. We found all the able-bodied men and the nurse at the window, watching a Zepp, and the firing at it; but it went out of sight behind clouds just as we came up and we never saw it.

It was a perfect night – starlight with scattered clouds, and searchlights playing everywhere; everyone who saw the Zepp – and lots of nurses and orderlies and men did – say it was a wonderful sight – buff colour in the searchlight and disappearing at intervals behind the clouds. We found Joyce's men very calm and amusing and peaceful and wished we could have stayed up there, but we were soon sent down by a Night Sister. I believe the people in the streets round us were shrieking terribly all the time, but I didn't hear them then; only later when we were back in bed, we heard some hysterical woman shrieking most weirdly.

There was a tremendous glare in the sky to the West of us, which came from a big fire in Wood Street, somewhere near Liverpool Street Station I think. I believe most of the damage was done along Oxford Street, Holborn, Euston Road, and round Liverpool Street and Shoreditch, very near to us again. A lot of people were killed in a motor 'bus . . . It would have been terrifying to be out, as I believe there's fearful panic in the streets. I am afraid there must have been a great many casualties.

Goodbye my lambs; don't be anxious as I don't think they're likely to come over us again; they were practically overhead last night.

To the soldier at the front the Zeppelin raids appeared mildly disconcerting. Captain Greenwell wrote two days later:

Is it really true that those devilish Zepps have been over the Strand? I shall certainly be frightened at the prospect of coming home. What with the

---

1 Voluntary Aid Detachment, nicknamed 'Very Artful Darlings' or 'Victim Always Dies' by the soldiers (L. Macdonald, *Roses of No Man's Land*, M. Joseph, 1980, p. 75).

Zepps in London and submarines in the Channel, I shall run more risks than I ever did in the firing line![2]

The great height (up to 20,000 ft) at which the Zepps flew, their speed, the invulnerability of the envelope, and the difficulty of landing at night, defied the fighter planes until 1 April 1916 when the first Zepp was shot down over the sea by the use of incendiary darts and petrol bombs with fish hooks. Over London, the first Zepp fell to the Lewis gun of Lieutenant L. Robinson: for fifty miles the sky was 'illuminated by a vast, elongated, yellow flaming torch' and people cheered and danced with joy in the streets.[3]

2

THE FIRST ZEPP IS BROUGHT DOWN IN FLAMES

Miss Somervell to her mother.

Sept. 3rd 1916

. . . We had a most exciting time with Zepps last night when terrific firing began quite close to us. I went out onto a bridge just by the ward, and had a glorious view of a huge Zepp – apparently fairly close but not above us, so I wasn't frightened – with shells bursting all round it; it looked much larger than the last one we saw, and I could see the framework perfectly distinctly, the searchlights were so well on it; I am sure it was a Super-Zepp.

Quite suddenly the whole sky was lit up by an enormous glare and amid tremendous cheers from the Hospital and from the people all round we saw her turn right on end and fall, apparently quite slowly, and with huge flames leaping upwards, to the ground. It must have been 8 or 10 miles away (we hear this morning it was at Enfield), as we could hear very little, though there was a great hush of listening for the expected explosion as she struck the earth with her bombs; but it never came.

The Air Ace

I know that I shall meet my fate
Somewhere among the clouds above
W.B. YEATS

The Royal Flying Corps of August 1914 had only four squadrons of sixty-three aeroplanes, flown and serviced by seven hundred airmen, but expansion was rapid. The slow, ramshackle wooden boxes of those heroic days

---

2 Greenwell, op. cit., p. 48.
3 K. Poolman, *Zeppelins over England*, White Lion Publications, 1975, *passim*.

were at first too light to carry bombs and were only used for reconnaissance and artillery direction; there was no hostile action between rival airmen. The Germans soon developed the first true fighter, the Fokker monoplane 15, with a machine-gun firing through the propeller; the British reply was the de Havilland 2 and the Nieuport, used on the Somme. The horrifying sight of comrades shot down in flames resulted in 'protective callousness' which, however, could not always suppress deep guilt feelings over the burning of enemies. The epic single combats between famous air aces like Manfred von Richthofen (score: 80), Boelcke, and Voss against Mick Mannock (score: 74), James McCudden, Lanoe Hawker, and Albert Ball provided the only movement in the congealed trench desert. In 1916, the Germans started formation flying in 'circuses' and, through greater fire power and better training and discipline, gradually gained air superiority. Early in 1917, 1,270 British planes were destroyed in three months and a pilot's average life span was only eleven days.[4] He had to be very clever *and* lucky to survive in his box and the danger and self-reliance attracted the most daring.

The writer of the following extract finds gardening a good remedy for calming frayed nerves.

3

DOWN TO REAL WORK – GARDENING

Second Lieutenant Albert Ball (1896–1917) writes home.

[Spring 1916]

No flying on account of rain . . . One of our men is putting a wire round the tent, making a space of about 40 square yards. This is being turned into a garden, in which I hope to spend my spare time in the evenings.

Will you do me the great favour of sending me one packet of marrow seeds, one of lettuce, one of carrots, and a good big packet of mustard and cress. Also I would like a few flower seeds, one packet of sweet peas, and a few packets of any other flowers that will grow quickly. You will think this idea strange, but you see it will be a good thing to take my mind off my work. It will be rather a nerve pull, so I think it is best for me to forget all about it after it is over. . . .

I am at last in for the *real work*.

---

4   Alan Clark, *Aces High*, Weidenfeld & Nicolson, 1973, *passim*.

4

MUSTARD AND CRESS FOR THE MESS

I had four flights in one patrol on my Nieuport, and came off top in every flight. Four Fokkers and an L.V.G. attacked me about 12 miles over the lines. I forced the L.V.G. down with a drum and a half, after which I zoomed up after the Fokkers. They ran away at once.

Out of all the fights I only got about eight shots into my machine, one just missed my back and hit the strut. However, on my way back, the Hun Archie[5] guns hit the tail of my machine and took a piece away, but I got back and have now a new tail.

Well, my garden is going on fine, peas are now about four inches, and I had the first crop of mustard and cress in the mess yesterday. It did make the chaps laugh, but they liked it.

At nineteen Ball was *the* British air hero, an eager, tense, hard-playing public school boy who exulted at hunting whole enemy formations as a 'lone wolf' in his single-seat scoutfighter, despite crashing three times. He describes, in the characteristic terse style of airmen, his exploits which helped to bring about air ascendency over the Somme.

5

Alone against fourteen – 'good sport and good luck'

Lieutenant Ball, MC, to his parents.

[August 25, 1916]
Cheerio, dears. Really I am having too much luck for a boy. I will start straight away, and tell you all. On August 22nd I went up. Met twelve Huns.

No. 1 fight. I attacked and fired two drums, bringing the machine down just outside the village. All crashed up.

No. 2 fight. I attacked and got under the machine, putting in two drums. Hun went down in flames.

No. 3 fight. I attacked and put in one drum. Machine went down and crashed on a housetop.

All these fights were seen and reported by other machines that saw them go down.

I only got hit eleven times, so I returned and got more ammunition. This time luck was not all on the spot. I was met by about fourteen Huns, about fifteen miles over their side. My wind screen was hit in four places, mirror broken, the spar of the left plane broken, also engine ran out of petrol. But I had good sport and good luck, but

5   Anti-aircraft gun.

only just, for I was brought down about one mile over our side. I slept near the machine and had it repaired during the night.

Unlike von Richthofen, who coldly and systematically pursued his killing mission, Ball became sick of slaying:

I do not think anything bad about the Hun. Nothing makes me feel more rotten than to see him go down . . . oh, I do get tired of always living to kill. I am beginning to feel like a murderer. . . .

He was refused leave after his fourth narrow escape and given command of the new crack No. 56 Squadron. Despite his scruples, he held the record for shooting down enemy planes and gained the first triple DSO.

6

Score: 42 – I hate 'this beastly killing'

Captain Ball writes to his fiancée two days before he was killed at the age of twenty. Hit by a machine-gun on a church steeple while attacking von Richthofen's famous Jagdstaffel he was awarded a posthumous VC.[6]

May 5th, 1917

. . . You see my garden always causes a lot of sport, and when I am happy I dig in the garden and sing. I don't get much time off, but what I get is enjoyed.

Well, I made my total 40 last night, and G. Trenchard[7] rang up to say I am going to be presented to G. Sir D.H.[8] to-morrow. I am very pleased and know you will be. Oh, won't it be nice when all this beastly killing is over, and we can just enjoy ourselves and not hurt anyone. I hate this game, but it is the only thing one must do just now.

I went up on patrol and met two Albatross Scouts. I attacked the nearest and got underneath it, putting three drums of Lewis into it. The pilot was killed, and the machine crashed. I was getting ready for the second when all at once it came for me, head on. We opened fire at the same time and made straight for each other.

Well, Bobs, I thought all was up with us, and it was going to be a ramming job. But just as we were going to hit, my engine was hit by a bullet, and all the oil came into my face. For a short time I saw nothing, but when all got O.K. again, I looked down and saw the Hun going down out of control. He crashed about 400 yards from his pal.

I was attacked on the way back, but all my ammunition was used, and I only just got back before my engine gave out.

This makes my 42nd.

---

6 R. Jackson, *Fighter Pilots in World War I*, A. Barker, 1977, *passim*.
7 Major-General Sir Hugh Trenchard, Commander-in-Chief, RFC.
8 General Sir Douglas Haig.

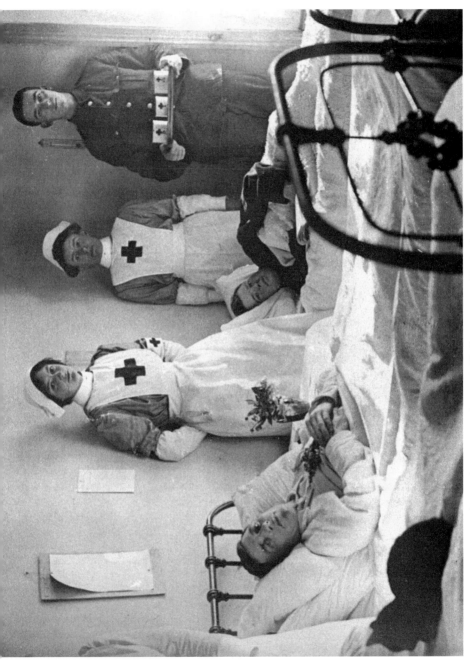

VAD nurses with patients at a hospital in Honiton, Devon. (*Allhallows Museum, Honiton*)

Admiral Jellicoe's Grand Fleet steams towards Jutland, 1916 (Royal Naval Museum, Portsmouth)

Jutland

There is something wrong with my bloody ships to-day
VICE-ADMIRAL BEATTY

We had them stone-cold and we let them go
A CAPTAIN

When Tirpitz was relieved of the command of the High Seas Fleet for his inactivity, Fisher, now also retired, wrote him a humorous letter of commiseration; it is unlikely, though, that Tirpitz would have been amused, had the letter ever reached him.

7

FISHER IN THE SAME BOAT WITH 'TIRPS'!

Admiral Lord Fisher to Admiral von Tirpitz.

March 29th, 1916

Dear Old Tirps,

We are both in the same boat! What a time we've been colleagues, old boy! However, we did you in the eye over the battle cruisers and I know you've said you'll never forgive me for it when bang went the *Blücher* and *Von Spee* and all his host!

Cheer up, old chap! Say '*Resurgam*'! You are the one German sailor who understands war! Kill your enemy without being killed yourself. *I don't blame you for the submarine business.* I'd have done the same myself, only our idiots in England wouldn't believe it when I told 'em.

Well! So long!

Yours till hell freezes,
Fisher

I say! Are you sure if you had tripped out with your whole High Sea Fleet before the Russian ice thawed and brought over those half-a-million soldiers from Hamburg to frighten our old women that you could have got back un-Jellicoed?

R.S.V.P.

The Germans planned to destroy weaker British units piecemeal without risking their inferior numbers in a big battle. The British wanted to destroy the High Seas Fleet to safeguard British command of the oceans, but proceeded with great caution – Churchill had said that Admiral Jellicoe was the only man who could lose the war in one afternoon.

Beatty was 'eating his heart out', haunted by fears he might never achieve glory in action before being 'sunk by a mine or submarine'.[9] His panache

---

9 Letter to Sir Roger Keyes (*Keyes Papers* I, p. 36 f.).

captivated seamen and the public alike, and made him the last naval hero; a love affair with the wife of a friend completed the Nelsonian connection. Such qualities, however, were out of date in a technical age in which sea battles were decided by accuracy at great distance. (It was significant that no signals existed any longer for 'Engage the enemy more closely' and 'General chase'.) With remarkable foresight, Jellicoe had warned Beatty fourteen months before Jutland not to be rushed headlong into a trap by his daredevil impetuousness.

8

A PROPHETIC WARNING

Admiral John (later Earl) Jellicoe (1859–1935), Commander-in-Chief of the Navy, to Vice-Admiral Sir David Beatty.

23 March 1915

I imagine the Germans will try to entrap you by risking their battle cruisers as a decoy. They know that the odds are that you will be 100 miles away from me, and can draw you down to Heligoland Bight without my being in effective support. This is all right if you keep your speed, but if some of our ships have their speed badly reduced in a fight with their battle cruisers, or by submarines, their loss seems inevitable if you are drawn into the High Seas Fleet with me too far off to extricate them before dark. The Germans know you very well and will try to take advantage of that quality of 'not letting go when you have once got hold it,' which you possess, thank God, but one must concern oneself with the result to the country of a serious decrease in relative strength. If the game looks worth the candle the risks can be taken. If not, one's duty is to be cautious. I believe you will see which is the proper course, and pursue it victoriously.

The High Seas Fleet ventured out on 31 May, 1916, when Admiral Scheer, under pressure of the British blockade, sent Hipper with a decoy squadron to lure Beatty's battle- and light cruiser force towards the German dreadnoughts. Beatty promptly fell for the bait and lost two of his ten cruisers to Hipper's weaker force, but he succeeded in drawing Scheer's battle fleet straight into Jellicoe's Grand Fleet which was steaming onto the scene. Yet Scheer recovered from his surprise more decisively than Jellicoe proceeded with his deployment which he had minutely prepared for twenty months.

Thirty-seven British capital ships clashed with twenty-seven German vessels (150:101 with light cruisers and destroyers) in the last massive gun battle, in foul weather conditions. British superiority in numbers, gun power and speed was balanced to a certain extent by German superiority in heavy defensive armour, the 'unsinkability' of their watertight compartmentation, the greater accuracy of their range-finders and the tendency of British shells to break up instead of penetrating.

Jellicoe's caution was against the Navy's tradition, and his belief in cen-
tralized rigid signal orders for deployment in single line-ahead battle formation, rather than fighting instructions in the spirit of the 'Nelson touch',
deprived his captains of initiative (Fisher, with Nelson in mind, had said: 'In
war, the first principle is to disobey orders'). After successfully manoeuvring
to cut the High Seas Fleet off from the German ports, Jellicoe was forced to
swerve under a brave torpedo attack by four destroyers and a suicidal ramming attempt by battle-cruisers. In poor visibility, and worried about imagi-
nary mines and submarines, he failed to intercept Scheer's two battle turns
behind his massed destroyers' smoke-screen and allowed him to escape during the night through the weakest point in the rear of the Grand Fleet; fatal-
ly, the Admiralty had not passed on the intercepted German signals about
Scheer's alteration of course to Horn Reefs.

As an admiral of ships rather than of war, Jellicoe fought 'to make a
German victory impossible rather than a British victory certain' (Cyril Falls),
but, equally, it could be argued that 'Jellicoe was right to avoid losing the
battle, even though it meant failing to win it' (Arthur Marder). Owing to
superior German gunnery ('It's NOT numbers that tell, but GUNNERY! . . .
Gunnery, gunnery, gunnery! All else is twaddle. Hit the target!', Fisher had
written to Beatty) and armour, the British losses were heavier: three battle-
cruisers and three cruisers, altogether 112,000 tons were sunk with over 6,000
men; the Germans lost only one old battleship, one battle-cruiser and four
light cruisers, altogether 62,000 tons with over 2,500 men. But the Navy was
left in possession of the North Sea and the Germans never risked battle
again, apart from an abortive attempt to lure the Grand Fleet into a submarine ambush.[10]

Prince Albert served, as his father King George V had done for fifteen
years, as a naval officer, from 1913–17, and, aged twenty, took part in the
Battle of Jutland in the battle-cruiser *Collingwood*. Always plagued by sea-
sickness, he found himself in the sick-bay with indigestion after a 'heavy
soused mackerel supper' when the action-alarm sounded and instantly
roused him: 'Out of his bunk leaps 'Johnson' [the Prince's nickname in the
Navy]. Ill? Never felt better! Strong enough to go to the turret and fight a
prolonged action? Of course he was,' wrote Lieutenant Tait to the Prince of
Wales.

The *Collingwood* came under heavy torpedo attack, one passing ahead and
one astern, while they saw the *Black Prince* and the *Defence* sink and the
Invincible wrecked. Then suddenly, the battle-cruiser *Derfflinger* appeared
out of the mist and fired three salvoes at 8,000 yards before it withdrew into
the mist again when the *Collingwood*'s guns had set its after-turret on fire.

---

10 D. Macintyre, *Jutland*, 1957; G.M. Bennett, *Jutland*, 1964, and *Naval Battles of the First World
War*, 1968; O. Warner, *Great Sea Battles*, 1963; P.M. Kennedy, *Rise and Fall of the British Naval
Mastery*, 1976; A. Pollen, *The Great Gunnery Scandal*, 1980; S. Roskill, *Beatty*, 1980.

They also caused Hipper's flagship *Lützow* to burst into flames; after rescuing their admiral and crew, the Germans blew it up with a torpedo. The *Collingwood*, however, was never hit, which made Prince Albert feel sorry that 'she has nothing to show she has been in the fight'.[11]

9

A FUTURE KING IN THE BATTLE OF JUTLAND

Acting Sub-Lieutenant Prince Albert (later King George VI, 1895–1952) sends the Royal Family an account of his first action.

I was in A turret and watched most of the action through one of the trainer's telescopes as we were firing by the Director, when the turret is trained in the working chamber and not in the gun house. At the commencement I was sitting on the top of A turret and had a very good view of the proceedings. I was up there during a lull, when a German ship started firing at us, and one salvo 'straddled' us. We at once returned the fire. I was distinctly startled and jumped down the hole in the top of the turret like a shot rabbit!! . . . It seems curious but all sense of danger and everything else goes except the one longing of dealing death in every possible way to the enemy. . . .

My impressions were very different to what I expected. I saw visions of the masts going over the side and funnels hurtling through the air etc. In reality none of these things happened and we are still quite sound as before. No one would know to look at the ship that we had been in action. It was certainly a great experience to have been through and it shows that we are at war and that the Germans can fight if they like. . . .

Oh, if only they would come out again and we could meet them, but this time in the early morning, we should have better light and more daylight to deal with them. In a war on such a scale as this of course we must have casualties and lose ships & men, but there is no need for everyone at home to bemoan their loss when they are proud to die for their country. They don't know what war is, several generations have come and gone since the last great battles. . . .

The *Southampton*, flagship of Commander Goudenough's Light Cruiser Squadron, was the first to spot Scheer's battle fleet, and soon came under heavy fire from the German ships. By nightfall, its gun crews had been virtually wiped out and the upper deck was strewn with dead and wounded.

11 J.W. Wheeler Bennett, *King George VI*, Macmillan, 1958, p. 94 ff.

10

A LUCKY ESCAPE

Naval Lieutenant Stephen King-Hall tells his parents that he took 'continuous notes' in the heat of battle.

HMS *Southampton*

We were in action at night with one armoured cruiser and three Light cruisers at a range of 1500 yards! Sounds quite archaic, doesn't it, but my word, you get it pretty hot at that range. Our casualties were extremely heavy, over 70 per cent of the personnel on the Upper Deck were hit. I myself had a complete gun's crew knocked out round me, and was actually standing in flames for a fraction of a second, and got out of it all with singed eye-brows and slightly burnt clothes!

About 30 seconds later, a searchlight was hurled down on us where I was superintending the putting out of a fire aft (we had three big fires). The searchlight missed me by inches. We expected to blow up any minute, but as things happened, we actually drove them off in confusion.

I'll tell you all about the whole show, which I saw from start to finish, and took continuous notes of, when we meet. We were at Action Stations for 23 hours. It was a remarkable experience.

A flotilla of eight destroyers, led by the *Nestor* under Commander Bingham, ran into a German battle squadron: after bravely attacking with all its twenty torpedoes, sinking two torpedo boats and damaging the *Seydlitz*, the *Nestor* found itself within point-blank range of the German 12-inch guns and was quickly sunk. Bingham, who gained the VC for his gallantry, was picked up by the Germans and wrote the following letter from captivity four days later.

11

THE END OF THE *NESTOR*

Commander E.B.S. Bingham writes to his wife from a German prison camp.

[We] were left like little lambs directly in the path of the oncoming High Seas Fleet. There we lay for a few awful moments, the enemy masses looming up nearer [and] nearer and not a friend in sight. It was a relief when the shells arrived. I cleared away the boats. I could not retaliate, my guns were too small. Then the shells came, salvoes of enemy projectiles. I knew it was only a matter of a few minutes so I gave the order, 'Every man for himself'. . .

We took to the boats and shoved off clear. [The *Nestor*] sank a few seconds after, stood up bows in the air, then dived stern first. We gave three cheers as she went down and then sang 'Tipperary' and 'The King'. [Later] a division of German destroyers came along and picked us up, 75 out of 83, who spent the rest of the battle like rats in a hole [below decks under guard] quite sure that British destroyers would come up and sink us. It tested our loyalty to the utmost to wish it so at the expense of our own lives. Can you picture our feelings every time the alarm gong rang and their guns barked? [However] the room was nice and warm, we were given food and wine, the [German] officers were very kind to us and nature came to my rescue and I slept!

The Somme

. . . misty light
Shrouds Thiépval Wood and all its worst . . .
EDMUND BLUNDEN

The line goes up and over the top,
Serious in gas masks, bayonets fixed,
Slowly forward – the swearing shells have stopped –
Somewhere ahead of them death's stopwatch ticks
PETER PORTER, 'SOMME'

What passing bells for those who die as cattle?
Only the monstrous anger of the guns.
Only the stuttering rifles' rapid rattle
WILFRED OWEN, 'ANTHEM FOR DOOMED YOUTH'

During the ten-month battle for Verdun, Falkenhayn attempted to bleed the French army into submission. Pressed to relieve it, Haig launched his murderous offensive on 1 July 1916 on a fifteen-mile front north of the Somme in Picardy, confident it would achieve a breakthrough to Bapaume and Cambrai and win the war. But after a solid week's barrage from over fifteen hundred guns, pouring out one-and-a-half million largely ineffective shells mixed with gas, the Germans emerged unscathed from the safety of their forty-foot deep dug-outs; with their machine-guns set up in concealed hill positions, they meted out death to the 110,000 British soldiers who were slowly advancing in dense shoulder to shoulder waves, weighed down by 66 lb packs, yet marching rigidly upright as if on parade: 21,000 were killed and 40,000 wounded, the worst loss on any day of any army on the Western Front, while German casualties were only 6,000.

No attempt had been made before launching the offensive to test the enemy defences by patrols or to attack under cover of darkness: the generals in control had no first-hand knowledge of conditions at the front and, in any case, regarded severe casualties as inevitable. It seems even more surprising that, in view of the many battles won in the past, both by the British Army and the Navy, through fast concentrated fire, Haig and other generals were so slow in appreciating the devastating effect of the machine-gun, forty times quicker than the rifle, on even the bravest attackers:

A consumptive machine gunner, too scared in an attack to bolt, can sit in a lucky hole in the ground and scupper a company of the best as they advance. Courage isn't what it used to be. The machine runs over us and we can't stop it.[12]

Despite this horrible setback to blindly optimistic expectations, Haig stubbornly persisted in the offensive until November, with British casualties reaching 420,000 for very little progress. Kitchener's amateur volunteer army was decimated, but the professional Germans were equally exhausted by similar losses and succumbed to the French counter-attack at Verdun.

The gun barrage, described below, was a significant feature of the First World War; its drawback, however, was that it churned up the ground so badly that it became almost impassable for the attackers.

12

FROM CINEMATOGRAPH TO PLUM & APPLE JAM

Major Alan Brooke (later General Lord Alanbrooke, 1883–1963) describes an attack on the Somme in terms of a dreamlike filmshow returning to cosy normality.

Yesterday we arrived just in time to see in the distance one of our attacks on Coutalmaison; it was a wonderful sight. To begin with the heavy Artillery were pounding the village, great columns of smoke and brick dust were flying up into the air, some of them three times as high as the ruins of the chateau. The whole village was wrapped in a cloud of smoke, lit up by flashes of bursting shell. This went on for some time, and then the shrapnel barrage became intense, rows of little puffs of smoke and the ground whipped up into dust by the shrapnel bullets, and away in the distance we could see our infantry advancing in lines towards the village. One felt as if one was in a dream, or that one was watching some extraordinary cinematograph film, and that it could not all be true.

You could see the German shells bursting in amongst our lines and men fall down, but the remainder seemed to move on as if nothing were happening. . . . The ground all round went up in spurts of dust, and the whole party went down like ninepins. I thought they had all been wiped out, I watched through my glasses and saw them gradually crawl into some shell holes and carrying on a bombing match with the German garrison of that trench.

12 Tomlinson, op. cit., p. 481.

The noise was unimaginable and in the midst of it all, the infantry was moving about in and out of the captured German trenches, some of them comfortably huddled up in a corner of the trench, sleeping; others peacefully boiling a little tea in their cooking pots and smearing plum & apple jam with a clasp knife on ration biscuits; others again quietly reading some penny novel.

But what appeared to Brooke 'a wonderful sight' from his bird's eye view of the drama was harrowing agony to the infantry on the ground.

Captain Graham Greenwell, who later remembered the war years as 'among the happiest', must have forgotten about the Ovillers trench.

13

'It reduces men to shivering beasts'

Captain Greenwell tells his wife he will never again look on warfare as fine or sporting.

Skyline Trench, Ovillers,
August 17, 1916

You won't be able to conceive the filthy and miserable surroundings in which I am writing this note – not even if you were accustomed to the filthiest slums in Europe.

I am sitting in the bottom of an old German dug-out about ten or twelve feet under the earth with three other officers and about ten men, orderlies and runners; the table is littered with food, equipment, candle grease and odds and ends. The floor is covered with German clothing and filth. The remains of the trench outside is blown to pieces, and full of corpses from the different regiments which have been here lately, German and English. The ground is ploughed up by enormous shell holes; there isn't a single landmark to be seen for miles except a few gaunt sticks where trees once were. The stench is well-nigh intolerable, but thank God I have just found the remains of a tube of frozacalone Bridge sent out, which I have rubbed under my nose. Everyone is absolutely worn out with fatigue and hunger. . . .

I shall never look on warfare either as fine or sporting again. It reduces men to shivering beasts: there isn't a man who can stand shell-fire of the modern kind without getting the blues. The Anzacs are fine fellows, but they say Gallipoli was a garden party to this show.

August 25

. . . If only people at home could imagine a tenth of the vileness of this part of the world that figures so gloriously in all our cold official communiqués!

August 26

. . . Your dear anxious letter about my 'wound' arrived in the trenches with a parcel containing – oh! sacred joy! a Fuller's cake and some Haversack chocolate which dropped like manna from Heaven in our midst. The cake reposed – a veritable Snow Queen – among the variegated litter of the German dug-out which was my headquarters. . . .

No wonder there were some soldiers who could not adapt themselves.

14

A MISFIT

Captain Greenwell draws for his wife the portrait of one who could not take it.

La Houssoye, October 25, 1916

. . . My poor schoolmaster is absolutely miserable and depressed. He knows literally nothing about soldiering, has never done any bayonet fighting, bombing, musketry or even drill for the last six months and they have no right to send him out. He is a victim of chronic neuritis, has a sad lack of sense of humour and can only express his horror and detestation of the whole business and his opinion that he and most of us will all be dead in a fortnight. In vain do I point to my longevity, in vain tempt him with five-course dinners, in vain lure him on with unlimited booze. Cards do not distract him: a lively argument on the subject of Socialism may possibly fix his wandering attention for a while, but he soon relapses into a morbid state of self-pity and recalls the long tale of his woes. In fact I felt so sorry for the boy that I spoke to the C.O. about him this morning and he has been sent to see the doctor. His kit alone was a monument of stupidity, containing a folding bath, an enormous eiderdown quilt, a Gladstone bag, enormous woollen bedstockings and, crowning folly, a Dayfield body-shield of steel weighing the Lord knows what and quite useless.

The tragic agony suffered in the Somme offensive by a British Army resigned to sacrificing their lives, produced some of the most poignant war letters ever written, deeply moving in their sincerity, faith and – banality.

15

'Tell Dad and Daisy not to worry about me'

Miss K.E. Luard, matron of a casualty clearing station, tells about the cheerful letter to his mother a Yorkshire lad had dictated to her a few days before he died.

[Barlin, June 1916]

. . . I never told you about Bob, the very badly wounded boy from Yorkshire. He has a weary painful existence, but he dictated me this letter to his mother:

'Dear Mother – This is to tell you I am doing grand – the wound in my side is healing fine'. (It isn't; it is a colotomy and also has a broken rib sticking out of it.) 'You are well looked after here – it is as good as being at home – bar kin – You live on the best of everything. I had chicken and jelly for dinner to-day. And there is a gramophone and the best of company. Tell Dad and Daisy not to worry about me at all. I hope I shall soon be with you all.

Your loving son, Bob.'

I said, 'Well, you've told her all the nice things, Bob, what about all the nasty things?' He looked me deliberately in the face and said, 'And what are the nasty things, Sister?' And he has very bad nights, a racking cough from the rib, a helpless right arm lying on a cushion, a septic wound through his cheek which gives him a horrible taste in the mouth, and the broken rib and the colotomy.

16

'Time presses'
A FAREWELL LETTER

Second Lieutenant John Engall writes to his parents on the eve of the attack in which he was killed, aged twenty.

30th June, 1916

My dearest Mother and Dad,

'I'm writing this letter the day before the most important moment in my life – a moment which I must admit I have never prayed for, like thousands of others have, but nevertheless a moment which, now it has come, I would not back out for all the money in the world. The day has almost dawned when I shall really do my little bit in the cause of civilization. Tomorrow morning I shall take my men – men whom I have got to love, and who, I think, have got to love me – over the top to do our bit in the first attack in which the London Territorials have taken part as a whole unit. I'm sure you will be very pleased to hear that I'm going over with the Westminsters. The old regiment has been given the most ticklish task in the whole of the Division; and I'm very proud of my section, because it is the only section in the whole of the Machine Gun Company that is going over the top; and my two particular guns have been given the most advanced, and therefore most important, positions of all – an honour that is coveted by many. So you can see that I have cause to be proud, inasmuch as at the moment that counts I am the officer who is entrusted with the most difficult task.

I took my Communion yesterday with dozens of others who are going over to-morrow; and never had I attended a more impressive service. I placed my soul and body in God's keeping, and I am going into battle with His name on my lips, full of confidence and trusting implicitly in Him. I have a strong feeling that I shall come through safely; but nevertheless, should it be God's holy will to call me away, I am quite prepared to go; and I could not wish for a finer death; and you, dear Mother and Dad, will know that I died doing my duty to my God, my Country, and my

King, I ask that you should look upon it as an honour that you have given a son for the sake of King and Country. . . .

I wish I had time to write more, but time presses. . . .

I fear I must close now. Au revoir, dearest Mother and Dad.

Fondest love to all those I love so dearly, especially yourselves.

Your devoted and happy son,

Jack

17

'Somewhere the Choosers of the Slain are touching'

Captain T.M. Kettle writes to his brother the day before he was killed.

September 8th, 1916

. . . If I live I mean to spend the rest of my life working for perpetual peace. I have seen war and faced modern artillery, and know what an outrage it is against simple men. . . .

We are moving up to-night into the battle of the Somme. The bombardment, destruction and bloodshed are beyond all imagination, nor did I ever think the valour of simple men could be quite as beautiful as that of my Dublin Fusiliers. I have had two chances of leaving them – one on sick leave and one to take a staff job. I have chosen to stay with my comrades.

I am calm and happy but desperately anxious to live. . . . The big guns are coughing and smacking their shells, which sound for all the world like over-head express trains, at anything from 10 to 100 per minute on this sector; the men are grubbing and an odd one is writing home. Somewhere the Choosers of the Slain are touching, as in our Norse story they used to touch, with invisible wands those who are to die. . . .

The Progress of Bloodlust

I killed and killed with slaughter mad;
Killed till all my strength was gone
ISAAC ROSENBERG (1890–1918)

I saw stab
And stab again
A well-killed Boche
This is the happy warrior,
This he
SIEGFRIED SASSOON (1886–1967)

The letters which follow relate the contrasting reactions to insidious and relentless brutalization as the war grew more desperate. The first writer protests against the glorification of war, and extols the beauty of comradeship, in the same spirit as that of the private who wrote from his squalid trench:

> To live amongst them who would give their last fag, their last bite, aye, even their last breath if need be for a pal – that is comradeship, the comradeship of the trenches. The only clean thing borne of this life of cruelty and filth. It grows in purity from the very obscenity of its surroundings.[13]

18

'War is an obscenity'

Captain Theodore Wilson tells Mrs Orpen that war is not romantic poetry but dirty tragedy. He was killed in 1918, aged twenty-nine.

May 3rd 1916

. . . We've just had a very trying day, as the Hun has bombarded us rather violently. . . . I wish I could see you, and tell you a little of what I think of war.

It is utterly peaceful now. Evening, with birds singing their hearts out, larks over the fields, lilac in the gardens of the poor ruined farms round us, a wonderful sea of brilliant yellow turnip-flower which smells like meadow-sweet, swallows flying high and happy – and, higher still, a little resolute yellow-white fly of an aeroplane, watching, watching, and moving with a sort of calm certainty through the shrapnel which is bursting round it. That is very far and unreal. The shells burst silently, in snow-white puffs of smoke, which remain for ten minutes or so unchanged by wind or rain in those still places. It is as though some huge hand dabbed the blue canvas with little fanciful flakes of white. Then, many seconds later, you hear the bang of the shell, and the whine of fragments through the air – very faint and elfin. It is as I say, unreal, and not terrible, somehow, to us on the green earth here.

But every now and then there comes a sound like a steam-saw cutting through thin wood and moving towards you with great speed. It ends suddenly, far off, in thunder. At any minute it may end in thunder close at hand. It is merely an interesting phenomenon to those new comers who haven't yet seen the work a shell can do. To the rest who *have* seen, it is a terrible and fiendish thing, which one must keep so to speak, masked – which one mustn't talk too much of! I saw a man to-day, for instance – No. One can't describe it. Only the memory of things like it makes one see this Spring evening's beauty through a sort of veil of obscenity, as a madman may see beauty. For mangled bodies are obscene whatever war-journalists may say. *War* is an obscenity. Thank God we are fighting this to stop war. Otherwise very few of us could go on.

Do teach your dear kids the horror of responsibility which rests on the war-maker. I want so much to get at children about it. We've been wrong in the past. We have

---

13 J. Ellis, op. cit., 1976, p. 202.

taught schoolboys 'war' as a romantic subject. We've made them learn the story of Waterloo as a sort of exciting story in fiction. And everyone has grown up and soaked in the poetry of war – which exists, because there is poetry in everything, but which is only a tiny part of the great dirty tragedy. All those picturesque phrases of war writers – such as 'he flung the remnants of his Guard against the enemy', 'a magnificent charge won the day and the victorious troops, etc. etc.', are dangerous because they show nothing of the *individual* horror, nothing of the fine personalities smashed suddenly into red beastliness, nothing of the sick fear that is tearing at the hearts of brave boys who ought to be laughing at home – a thing infinitely more terrible than physical agony.

I can't explain it all without getting into a sort of confounded journalese swing of words, but you'll understand. It isn't death we fear so much as the long-drawn expectation of it – the sight of other fine fellows ripped horribly out of existence by 'reeking shard', as a great War-journalist says who spoke (God forgive him) of 'a fine killing' in some battle or other.

Meanwhile there are the compensations of a new sort of comradeship, of new lights on life, of many new beauties in humanity. I hope I shall come through it alive, though it's doubtful. I hope I shall be a much, much better sort of person for it all though that is a selfish sort of aspect of a huge drama like this. . . .

Anyhow there is always God. That stays firm. And if He *is Love*, it must all be working out somehow, but how sad He must be sometimes, when even a little little heart like one's own nearly bursts with pity. Don't think me overwrought or sentimental – unduly so at any rate – I am sticking things very well really. Only to you who understands so well, it is a relief to pour out a little of all one feels.

To strike horror into their enemies' ranks, the Germans invented the 'flammenwerfer' early in 1915. A year later, the British retaliated with a flame projector of their own which produced an eighty foot roaring jet lasting thirty seconds and searing everything within range.

19

TOO GENTLEMANLY AND SENTIMENTAL TO ADOPT GERMAN 'FOUL AND HELLISH METHODS'?

Second Lieutenant Engall describes a 'liquid fire drill' to Miss N. Locke.

9th April 1916

I see no harm in telling you what happened this morning. We went to see a demonstration of the liquid fire as used by the Boches up at Ypres some time back. Well, I'd imagined that it would be something pretty dreadful, but my thoughts were nothing compared to the actual thing. I can imagine nothing more calculated to strike absolute dread and horror into men's hearts than this liquid fire, when encountered for the first time. It's nothing short of Hell. Just imagine being in a trench and seeing great searching roaring flames, greater and more deadly than any flames produced by a burning building. Is it any wonder then that a man, ignorant of what to do, should lose his nerve when he sees this fire, roaring like a furnace, coming rapidly towards him, belching forth clouds of smoke, behind which he knows there are hundreds of human devils advancing to turn him out of his position?

It is devils who invent and use things like this whom we are fighting – fighting with our gloves on, in as clean and gentlemanly a way as is possible in war. And yet, although the Germans deserve the worst we can give them, I think I should be sorry if we adopted their foul and hellish methods. But then, like the country I belong to, I'm too sentimental.

Two months later, Engall is puzzled how he can find pressing the trigger 'absolutely heavenly', and chuckles over the hell the Germans must be going through in the barrage he 'gloried in'.

20

'YOUR MEEK AND GENTLE OLD JACK' HAS BECOME BLOODTHIRSTY

Lieutenant Engall describes his transformation to Miss Locke.

3rd June 1916

The last few mornings I've been getting up with the lark at a quarter to two, in order to indulge in a little pastime known as 'Peppering Peter' – in plain English, I've been popping off my little M.G. just an hour's strafe at night and another one first thing in the morning. I tell you, it's 'some' feeling to sit behind a gun and pop off at Brother Fritz. It bucks you up no end. And then, when you've shut him up, you feel that the war is practically won. It's absolutely great. I never realized I could be so bloodthirsty. And aren't the men in the front line pleased when you stop Brother Fritz's M.G.s – well, not slightly! When I opened fire for the first time, they nearly fell on my neck and kissed me, because they had been having hell, Boches firing M.G.s with absolutely no return at all. And the feelings of the man who presses the trigger – well, it's absolutely heavenly, and makes a real man of you. And to think that these should be the feelings of your meek and gentle old Jack. Ah, well! this fearful war is responsible for lots of dreadful things. . . .

The night before last I saw the most wonderful sight I have ever seen in my life. . . . We were on the way back from the front line when, with a sound that made us nearly all jump out of our skins, our artillery started to strafe on the Boche. Every gun in France seemed to be firing, and the sky was lit up almost as bright as day by the flashes of the guns in front of us and the blinding light of the shells bursting right behind us. For a solid hour and a half it seemed as though hell itself had been let loose. Not for a second did the guns slacken, and the noise was so deafening that you couldn't possibly speak to one another. German flare-lights were going up all along the line, showing that he'd his wind up with a vengeance. I simply stood and gloried in it. The Hun must have had a warm time. I thought of the warm time he's given me during the past few days, and I'm afraid I chuckled over the hell he must be going through at the time. It did me no end of good, and I thought perhaps after all we might win the war before long. . . .

Robert Graves recalls[14] that prisoners were frequently killed, either in revenge for a fallen friend, or out of 'military enthusiasm', or in fear of being overpowered, or in jealousy of a prison camp in 'Blighty', or simply out of impatience with escorting them: no questions were asked. Captain Greenwell wrote in July 1916: 'Feelings run a bit too high to make the unwounded prisoner's lot a happy one. A whole crowd who came towards our own trenches with their hands up were mown down by their own machine guns as well as ours.'[15]

The following extract shows how the initial heroic ideals of the subaltern evaporated in disillusion and doubt under the brutal impact of sordid reality and the growing awareness of bestial instincts.

21

'Primitive passion for slaughter let loose'

Second Lieutenant Donald Hankey writes to his sister about the inevitability of bloodlust, shortly before being killed.

July 12, 1916

'It is a sweet and honourable thing to die for one's country' – It is, however, not 'sweet' nor can it ever be a source of satisfaction, to have experienced the blood lust, to have killed for one's country and gloried in it. Yet that is an experience which comes to almost every survivor at one time or other. I can imagine nothing more horrible than suddenly to feel the primitive passion for slaughter let loose in one. . . .

Some of these sensitive young officers worried deeply about the morals of 'mopping up' and 'being more Prussian than the Prussian' in order to beat him at his own game.

22

'We shall become all that we hate'

Captain J.E. Crombie writes to a friend about this predicament, shortly before being killed, aged twenty.

March 3, 1917

As for the morals of the war, they are horrible. Perhaps they are a little worse than we are, but the point is that by fighting we have hopelessly degenerated our own morals.

14 R. Graves, *Goodbye to All That*, Cassell, 1957, p. 153.
15 Greenwell, op. cit. p. 119.

For instance, listen to this. Without going into details, for 'mopping up' a captured trench i.e. bombing out the remaining inhabitants, you have parties of nine men specially equipped. When you come to a dug-out, you throw some smoke bombs down, and then smoke the rest out with a smoke bomb, so that they must either choke or come out. Now when they come out they are half blinded and choked with poisonous smoke, and you station a man at the entrance to receive them, but as you have only got a party of nine, it would be difficult to spare men if you took them prisoners, so the instructions are that these poor half-blinded devils should be bayoneted as they come up. It may be expedient from a military point of view, but if it had been suggested before the war, who would not have held up their hands in horror?

The fact is, that if we decide to beat the German at his own game, we can only do it by being more Prussian than the Prussian; if we hate all that is Prussian, we shall become all that we hate. If we do win, it is only an argument for the Prussian, that if he had been a little more Prussian he would have won, and he will probably strive to be more so the next time, which is the very thing we wanted to avoid, and it can only be prevented by our keeping our top-dog attitude to him.

It's absolutely Gilbertian, but I don't think we will make the German a pacifist except by example, and we have given him back his own example, only rather more efficiently. But, the question is, what else could we do? If we did not fight, we admitted the superiority of his example, as it showed us that he could conquer us, and that by conquest he could force on us his principles. It is an extraordinary tangle when you think of it.

And I am sorry to be pessimistic, but I doubt if it will have helped us to find God. Among the millions actually fighting it seems only to have increased the drunkenness and vice – perhaps some among those at home, anxious for dear ones fighting, may have learnt to rely on Him. It is wonderful to think of Peace, and all this ghastliness ended.

The War with the Turks

On the straight bar of Sinai ahead the low sun was falling,
its globe extravagantly brilliant in my eyes, because I was dead-tired of my life,
longing as seldom before for the moody skies of England . . .
for weakness, chills and grey mistiness,
that the world may not be so crystalline clear,
so definitely right and wrong.
I began to wonder if all established reputations were founded, like mine, on fraud.
T.E. LAWRENCE, SEVEN PILLARS OF WISDOM

In the Middle East, 250,000 soldiers under Lieutenant-General Sir Archibald Murray were guarding the Suez Canal against Turkish attacks. In the spring of 1916 they advanced through the Sinai Desert towards El Arish, laying railway tracks and water pipes. On 4 August they beat off an attack by Anatolian crack troops under the German general Kress von Kressenstein in the over-hot sand dunes of the Romani Desert, twenty miles west of the Suez Canal. Three thousand prisoners were taken, but half the Turkish infantry, marching more easily on the burning sands than their pursuers on horseback, escaped after a fierce fighting retreat.

23

THE BATTLE FOR THE SUEZ CANAL

A lance-corporal describes how 'Johnnie Turk' was defeated in the Romani Desert.

6th August 1916

... The Turks attacked on the night of 3rd–4th, and we retired just a little according to the General's plan – just to let Johnnie Turk get enough rope to hang himself with – and then the Turkish attack reached its culminating point about 6 a.m. on the morning of the 4th; just when Johnnie thought everything was going A.1. we counter-attacked. I never saw troops so surprised in my life as those Turks were when we advanced to the attack; they got utterly demoralized; some turned to run, but were shot down, and the ones who stayed fired a few wild shots, which went high overhead, and then threw up their hands before we could get anywhere near them with the bayonet.

We made our presence felt on his main position about 9 or 10 a.m., and shortly after that time he began to yield, slowly at first, and making desperate efforts to resume his offensive, but it was useless and cost him very dearly. The really desperate fighting lasted for nearly 24 hours, and then he suddenly gave way, and we broke into his main position everywhere and then he started his retreat in earnest: we pursued for two days and then the cavalry took the whole line of pursuit, harassing him and inflicting heavy losses on him, back to his base. He was a much wiser and sadder enemy.

He left his base with 18,000 men, and got back with 9,000; in addition we captured a vast amount of guns, machine guns, rifles, ammunition of all kinds, stores and a complete field Hospital. The engagement showed that the Turks were out-generalled and outfought and I think their hope of ever conquering Egypt is shattered for ever. They may try again, but I doubt it.

Yes, the news from all fronts is splendid; it makes me bite my nails when I read it, and think what I'm missing; it makes me feel sometimes that I am shirking. Just imagine me – a regular soldier – melting to nothing in the barren desert, and all that fighting going on. I suppose it is necessary to have someone here, but I find it very galling. Of course don't think I'm squealing, my time may come later.

Meanwhile in the Mesopotamian campaign for the protection of oil installations, Major-General Townshend had been forced to surrender Kut el Amara with over ten thousand men, after holding out bravely for five months of isolation in face of superior Turkish forces. The garrison had been reduced to eating their horses and mules, pies made of rooks and starlings they shot were highly prized, and they smoked old tea leaves mixed with ginger. All relief attempts, the last by Lieutenant-General Gorringe, got stuck in the knee-deep mud of the roads and suffered severe casualties from the blockading Turks. More than half of the British prisoners succumbed during the fifty-day death march to Mosul through starvation, thirst, sunstroke and disease, and the survivors were decimated by Turkish brutality and pestilence in their airless dungeons; only 837 returned at the end of the war.

24

'All UP now'
THE SIEGE OF KUT

Captain W.C. Spackman gives his family a day-to-day account of the final stages.

5th April 1916

Getting near the end now . . . If Gorringe fails to get thro' in the next ten days I shall have to prepare to march to Mosul! (heard relief guns!)

13th

Things are beginning to get rather desperate now. We only get five ounces of bread each daily. The only thing left to eat with it is anchovy sauce, with about one and a half lbs. of horse or mule, eked out with herbs. All eat grass, the only thing that has kept off scurvy. Our bread *finishes* on 21st but we could hold on a bit after that on mule and grass I suppose. We eat a lot of sparrows nowadays as a sort of change.

16th

The latest idea is to keep us going by food dropped by aeroplane. But as they would have to drop at least 15,000 lbs. a day to keep us going, I fancy it is just to help us hang on a few extra days. We are now decidedly on the lean side.

27th

All U P now, which is a terrible pity. I don't know what sort of terms we shall get, if any. Townshend & staff went up river this morning to arrange terms.

29th

We blew up our guns (about 40) today and burnt everything of a military value. I fired my revolver into the prisms of my beautiful binoculars, and then smashed my revolver with a sledge hammer & burnt my saddlery. The Turks marched in at noon and took over the place. . . .

Major-General Maude restored British fortunes when he captured Baghdad on 11 March 1917, only to die of cholera. Murray was replaced by General Sir Edmund Allenby ('The Bull') who took Jerusalem on 9 December as 'a Christmas present for the British people'.

At the same time, the legendary and controversial archaeologist-guerrilla leader T.E. Lawrence was spinning his romantic intrigues with the Arab sheiks and, suddenly emerging from the desert with his Bedouin camel troops, descended on Aqaba and disrupted the Hejaz railway line. Posing as the champion of Arab independence, he instigated the Arab revolt against the Turks as a deliberate fraud, based on his 'conviction that Arab help was necessary to our cheap and speedy victory in the East, and that better we win and break our word than lose'.[16] The following letters give two contrasting versions of one of his famous

16   T.E. Lawrence, *Seven Pillars of Wisdom*, J. Cape, 1940, p. 24.

train-bashing raids. In the first, addressed to an admirer in the Army, he adopts the heroic posturing of a schoolboy in 'Buffalo-Bill' language (he dubbed himself once 'a bag of tricks'), while in the other, written to a scholar friend, he drops the martial mask and reveals a horrified sensibility near breaking point.[17]

25

LAWRENCE OF ARABIA: HEROIC FUN OR UNNERVING NIGHTMARE?

Colonel T.E. Lawrence (1888–1935) to Major Stirling.

[September 1917]

The last stunt was the hold up of a train. It had two locomotives, and we gutted one with an electric mine. This rather jumbled up the trucks, which were full of Turks, shooting at us. We had a Lewis, and flung bullets through the sides. So they hopped out and took cover behind the embankment, and shot at us between the wheels, at 50 yards. Then we tried a Stokes gun, and two beautiful shots dropped right in the middle of them. They couldn't stand that (12 died on the spot) and bolted away to the East across a 100 yard belt of open sand into some scrub. Unfortunately for them, the Lewis covered the open stretch. The whole job took ten minutes, and they lost 70 killed, 30 wounded, 80 prisoners, and about 25 got away. Of my 100 Howeitat and two British NCO's there was one (Arab) killed, and four (Arab) wounded. . . . My loot is a superfine red Baluch prayer-rug. I hope this sounds the fun it is. The only pity is the sweat to work them up and the wild scramble while it lasts.

26

T.E. Lawrence to E.T. Leeds.

The last stunt has been a few days on the Hejaz Railway, in which I potted a train (oh, the Gods were kind) and lost all my kit, and nearly my little self. . . . I'm not going to last out this game much longer: nerves going and temper wearing thin. . . . I hope when the nightmare ends that I will wake up and become alive again. This killing of Turks is horrible. When you charge in at the finish and find them all over the place in bits, and still alive many of them, and know that you have done hundreds in the same way before and must do hundreds more if you can.

---

17 I am indebted to Desmond Stewart's *T.E. Lawrence* (H. Hamilton, 1977, p. 179 f) for quotation and interpretation of the two letters.

T H R E E

From Failure to Victory (1917–18)

Only authentic England is in France . . .
Not many elsewhere now, save under France
WILFRED OWEN

Front and Home – Two Nations

'Don't talk patriotic' –
They went on in stubborn despair
with their sentimental songs and cynical talk
and perpetual grousing
RICHARD ALDINGTON, 'DEATH OF A HERO'

War has no fury like a non-combatant
C.E. MONTAGUE, 'DISENCHANTMENT'

April 1917 was the worst month of the war: Nivelle failed in his much-vaunted offensive on the Aisne which was preceded by the British attack at Arras in which 142,000 were killed, and large sections of the French army were in open mutiny, eventually quelled by Pétain. Peace negotiations, initiated by the German Secretary of State, Kühlmann, Emperor Charles of Austria, President Wilson, and the Pope, came to nothing, and the March Revolution in Russia threatened to end the war in the East.

A quarter of the British merchant fleet (423 ships of 849,000 tons) was sunk in renewed unrestricted submarine warfare, aiming to starve Britain out of the war before the United States, who had declared war on 2 April, could save her. The replacement rate was only 10 per cent, and not more than six weeks' supply of wheat was left in stock. The convoy system, imposed by Lloyd George on a violently opposed Admiralty, later reduced these losses to 1 per cent, with the aid of aerial reconnaissance and depth charges. At home queues had started for food and fuel, and prices were soaring;

rationing was introduced later. Strikes for higher wages and status flared up in the factories and mines, and an annual average of four million working days were lost in the middle of a desperate war.

Paradoxically, soldiers in the trenches were less discontented but felt, for the first time in British history, that the whole nation, and not only the young men, should be conscripted. Popular demand for conscription to rope in the 'slackers' had already grown in 1915, although there were more volunteers coming forward than could be equipped. Conscription was finally introduced in January 1916 for single men and in May for the married; paradoxically, recruitment dropped severely, because compulsion produced so many claims for exemption. To replace the men, about two million women were gradually absorbed in munition factories, in the WAAC, WRNS and WRAF, and in the nursing, police and transport services.

In the following letter Fisher thunders against the new prosperity of the working class while the rich are being fleeced, and, at the same time, against the uneconomic class-ridden use as servants of soldiers who ought to be fighting.

1

CHOCOLATES FOR THE POOR AND GROOMS FOR THE STAFF

Admiral Fisher to Admiral Jellicoe.

30.5.1916

. . . The poor have never been so rich! The mass of pianos and chocolates bought by the working classes is now prodigious, and boys of 15 are getting actually three pounds a week! While the rich are, by the end of this year, going to drop 75% of their income into the pockets of – well! I won't call anyone names! And our Allies are fleecing us, never to be repaid! And only 400 British war vessels kept in the Mediterranean! And a quarter of a million of able-bodied British fighting men in France occupied as servants and grooms instead of being in the trenches. Half a million British soldiers in the trenches – four and a half million of British soldiers in the rear somewhere! Are we much better on the sea? But I refrain!

Profiteering and high wages at home upset the soldiers on leave: 'The English either volunteer for this hell or else sit down and grow fat on big money at home. The contrast between the two fates is too great,' wrote Sergeant-Major Keeling.[1] The next letter expresses in detail this outraged resentment felt by the soldier at the front.

---

1 Keeling, op. cit. p. 271.

2

'What wonderful people are our infantry!'

Lieutenant-Colonel Rowland Feilding writes to his wife that he feels ashamed of civilians earning huge wages and striking for more, and thinks they ought to be conscripted too.

Curragh Camp [Belgium], December 14th, 1916

. . . What wonderful people are our infantry! And what a joy it is to be with them! When I am here I feel – well, I can hardly describe it. I feel, if it were possible, that one should never go away from them; and I contrast that scene (at 1s. 1d. a day) with what I see and hear in England when I go on leave. My God! I can only say: 'May the others be forgiven!' How it can be possible that these magnificent fellows, going home for a few days after ten months of this (and practically none get home in less), should be waylaid at Victoria Station and exploited, and done out of the hard-earned money they have saved through being in the trenches, and with which they are so lavish, baffles my comprehension. It is unthinkable . . .

I can never express in writing what I feel about the men in the trenches; and nobody who has not seen them can ever understand. According to the present routine, we stay in the front line eight days and nights, then go out for the same period. Each Company spends four days in the fire-trench before being relieved. The men are practically without rest. They are wet through much of the time. They are shelled and trench-mortared. They may not be hit, but they are kept in a perpetual state of unrest and strain. They work all night and every night, and a good part of each day, digging and filling sandbags, and repairing the breaches in the breastworks; – that is when they are not on sentry. The temperature is icy. They have not even a blanket. The last two days it has been snowing. They cannot move more than a few feet from their posts: therefore, except when they are actually digging, they cannot keep themselves warm by exercise; and when they try to sleep, they freeze. At present, they are getting a tablespoon of rum to console them, once in three days.

Think of these things, and compare them with what are considered serious hardships in normal life! Yet these men play their part uncomplainingly. That is to say, they never complain seriously. Freezing, or snowing, or drenching rain; always smothered with mud; you may ask any of them, 'Are you cold?' or 'Are you wet?' – and you will get but one answer – always with a smile – 'Not too cold, sir,' or 'Not too wet, sir'. It makes me feel sick. It makes me think I never want to see the British Isles again so long as the war lasts. It makes one feel ashamed of those fellow-countrymen, earning huge wages, yet for ever clamouring for more; striking, or threatening to strike; while the country is engaged upon this murderous struggle. Why, we ask here, has not the whole nation, civil as well as military, been conscripted?

The curious thing is that all seem so much more contented here than the people at home. The poor Tommy shivering in the trenches, is happier than the beast who makes capital out of the war. Everybody laughs at everything, here. It is the only way.

Christmas dinner in a shell hole at Beaumont Hamel, 1916. *(Imperial War Museum, London)*

"SITUATION REPORT."

Enemy ration party seen on the skyline at 5-15 p.m.

"Bong Jour, Alf! Have you changed your socks to-day? If not, why not?"

A. E. FRA$

"Our 'Tommies' are always cheerful.

From the "DAILY LI

Sketches from the *Fifth Gloucester Gazette*, 'A Chronicle, serious and humorous of the Battalion while serving with the British Expeditionary Force', 1917. *(Reproduced by courtesy of the Gloucestershire Regiment Museum)*

Not every officer felt so deeply for his men. Captain Greenwell is not concerned with the contrast between the poor Tommy in the trenches and the war profiteer at home: what counts for him is only his own enjoyment which he finds in the excitement of war.

3

'It's a gay life'

Captain Greenwell writes home.

La Maisonette Trenches, March 2, 1917
. . . I shall take care to be over forty in the next year. But we never know what is good for us and I can imagine myself sitting at home fifteen years hence bitterly regretting the days when I was a Captain in the Army, free, with plenty of money and sport and with no worries about food or habitation. After all, it's a gay life sometimes and full of change. . . .

Savy, November 17
I am once more persuaded that military life is full of excitement and romance. It is something to be able to spend one's youth gloriously in France, Flanders, Italy, Egypt and Palestine visiting the scenes of victories and defeats of one's ancestors instead of living at home and being hustled round the Continent once a year via Cooks. . . .

[Shortly before being demobilized] Maglio, December 26, 1918
. . . it will be hard to leave the regiment after so many years. . . . Could you ever have guessed how much I should enjoy the war?

When the 'rape of little Belgium' had rallied the nation reluctant to go to war, propaganda began to manipulate public opinion by a hate campaign. Notions of Britain, 'the embodiment of courage, heroism, and resolution', gloriously defending freedom, justice, democracy and Christianity against the 'Evil Hun' were painted in black and white. Atrocity stories were fabricated to intensify jingoism – 'the passion of the spectator, not of the fighter' – aliens were hounded, German music was banned, and dachshunds stoned. 'England was beastly. Envy, hatred, malice and all uncharitableness, fear and cruelty born of fear . . . only in the trenches were chivalry and sweet reasonableness,' wrote Charles Edmonds; returning on leave, he could not understand the 'war-madness' which the soldiers at the front did not feel.[2] There was only a tiny number of people at home who opposed the general trend.

After the introduction of conscription, a small pacifist lobby supported the conscientious objectors to war service (16,500, as against 60,000 in the Second

---

2 C. Haste, *Keep the Home Fires Burning,* Allen Lane, 1977, *passim.*

World War), braving the indignant contempt of the vast majority of patriotic citizens and the penalties of the authorities. In a letter to the *Nation* after the outbreak of war, Bertrand Russell had attacked the fostering of 'the instincts of hatred and blood lust against which the whole fabric of society has been raised' and blamed national pride and greed for this transformation.[3] In the winter of 1915/16 his open appeal to President Wilson to act as peace mediator in the prevailing stalemate appeared in the American press: speaking 'in the name of reason and mercy', he ranted against 'the fury of national passion', stirred up by fear, and 'the ferocity that always attends it', leading to 'terror and savagery', and extolled the soldiers' desire for peace in their 'despair of ever achieving military decision'.[4]

4

CONSCIENTIOUS OBJECTION

Bertrand (Earl) Russell (1872–1970) writes in the depth of despair to his lover, the actress Colette O'Niel (Lady Constance Malleson).

Guildford, December 28, 1916

How can love blossom among explosions and falling Zeppelins and all the surrounding of our love? It has to grow jagged and painful before it can live in such a world. I long for it to be otherwise – but soft things die in this horror, and our love has to have pain for its life blood.

I hate the world and the people in it. I hate the Labour Congress and the journalists who send men to be slaughtered, and the fathers who feel a smug pride when their sons are killed, and even the pacifists who keep saying human nature is essentially good, in spite of all the daily proofs to the contrary. I hate the planet and the human race – I am ashamed to belong to such a species – And what is the good of me in this mood?

Bertrand Russell continued agitating for his convictions and went to prison in 1918. He wrote from there:

War develops in almost all a certain hysteria of destruction – self-destruction among the more generous, but still destruction. We have to stand out against this hysteria, and realize that Life, not Death (however heroic) is the source of all good.[5]

---

3 Bertrand Russell, *Autobiography*, Allen & Unwin, 1968, vol. II, p. 42 f.
4 Ibid., p. 28 f.
5 J. Vellacott, *Bertrand Russell and the Pacifists*, Harvester Press, 1980, p. 250. During the Second World War Bertrand Russell's attitude changed, in recognition of the necessity of overcoming the totalitarian evil by force. He wrote to Gilbert Murray from America: 'I find I cannot maintain the pacifist position in this War. . . . I admire English resistance with all my soul but hate not to be part of it. . . . My views in this war are quite orthodox.' (Russell, op. cit., p. 247 ff)

5

'The weight of the general view'

Brigadier John Charteris (1877–1946), Haig's Chief Intelligence Officer, writes home.

September 7, 1915

. . . We had a visit from some extremist pacifist Labour 'Leaderettes' – quite pleasant, nice fellows, hugely ignorant about anything outside their own little shows. Their visits do a great deal of good. I do not think any of them go back without amending their views. They come here thinking we soldiers revel in bloodshed and bully the men. They find we loathe war as much as they do, that men and officers are comrades, not enemies, and the whole atmosphere of comradeship and good will and determination to win impresses them. One cannot help sympathizing with these Labour pacifists even when one disagrees with them. To them war is simply senseless slaying: they cannot conceive any cause in which employer and employed can be united. Their highest ideal is increased personal comfort for their own class; they measure contentment in terms of well-filled bellies and full pockets. It is all so human and natural. You cannot argue against their view for they would not understand the arguments: you can only let them feel the weight of the general view out here. . . .

One of the official war artists sent out in 1917 was the painter William Orpen, the 'Samuel Pepys of the Western Front'. He created a complete tapestry of visual documents and also gave a haunting description of the wasteland of war he found:

The whole country is obliterated for miles and miles. Nothing left at all except shell holes full of water. You pick your way between them, or jump at times; miles and miles of bodies rifles steel Helmets gas Helmets, German and English, and shells and wire, all white with mud, one feels the horrors the water in the shell holes is covering – and not a living soul anywhere near, a truly terrible peace in the new and terribly modern desert. . . .[6]

In contrast another war artist, the painter Paul Nash, discovered by a striking process of sublimation, in the same devastated battlefields, what he called 'the full poetic potentialities of modern warfare'. (As an official RAF artist in the Second World War he was less emotive.) He wrote of the 'incongruity between hell of blasted earth' and 'manifestations of unconquerable Nature'.[7]

But pacifist propaganda found no common ground of understanding in the front-line climate of comradeship resigned to a cruel fate.

6 B. Arnold, *Orpen*, J. Cape, 1981, p. 316.
7 Lieutenant J. Engall wrote: 'No artist could ever paint a picture of war as it really is, because an artist cannot depict noise – noise, I think, is 75% of war.' (Housman, op. cit., p. 109).

6

'Oh! These wonderful trenches'

Paul Nash (1889–1946) pictures to his wife Nature's victory over devastation.

March 7, 1917

I came upon a bank where real French violets grew, you know, those dark ones that have such an intoxicating smell. . . . Flowers bloom everywhere. . . . The dandelions are bright gold over the parapet, and nearby a lilac bush is breaking into bloom; in a wood passed through on our way up, a place with an evil name, pitted and pocked with shells, the trees torn to shreds, often reeking with poison gas – a most desolate and ruinous place two months back, to-day was a vivid green, the most broken trees even had spouted somewhere and, in the midst, from the depth of the wood's broken heart poured out the throbbing song of a nightingale. Ridiculous incongruity! One can't think which is more absurd, the war or nature; the former has become a habit so confirmed, inevitable, it has its grip on the world just as surely as spring and summer. Thus we poor beings are doubly enthralled.

Here in the backgarden of the trenches it is amazingly beautiful, the mud is dried to a pinky colour and upon the parapet and through the sandbags even the green grass pushes up and waves in the breeze, while clots of bright dandelions, clover, thistles and twenty other plants flourish luxuriantly, brilliant growths of bright green against the pink earth. . . . The birds sing all day in spite of the shells and shrapnel. I have made three more drawings all of these wonderful ruinous forms which excite me so much here. . . . I feel very happy these days, in fact I believe I am happier in the trenches than anywhere out here. It sounds absurd but life has a greater meaning here and a new zest and beauty, is more poignant. I never feel dull or careless, always alive to the significance of nature. . . .

April 6

. . . Oh! These wonderful trenches at night; at dawn; at sundown! Shall I ever lose the picture they have made in my mind. Imagine a wide landscape, flat and scantily wooded, and what trees remain, blasted and torn, naked and scarred, and riddled. The ground for miles around furrowed into trenches, pitted with yawning holes in which the water lies still and cold or heaped with mounds of earth, tangles of rusty wire, tin plates, stakes, sandbags, and all the refuse of war. In the distance runs a stream where the stringy poplars and alders lean dejectedly, while further a slope rises to a scarred bluff, the foot of which is scattered with headless trees standing white and withered, hopeless without any leaves, done, dead. As shells fall on the bluff, huge spots of black, brown, and orange mould burst into the air amid a volume of white smoke, flinging wide incredible debris while the crack and roar of the explosion reverberates in the valley. . . . As night falls the monstrous land takes on a strange aspect. The sun sinks in a clear evening and smoke hangs in the narrow bars of violet and dark. In the clear light the shapes of the trench stand massy and cold, the mud gleams whitely, the sandbags have a hard, rocky look, the works of men look like a freak of nature, rather, the landscape is so distorted from its own gentle forms nothing seems to bear the imprint of God's hand, the whole might be a terrific creation of some malign friend working a crooked will on the innocent country-side. . . . As the dark gathers the horizon brightens and again vanishes as the Vèry lights rise and fall shedding their weird greenish glare over the land and in acute contrast to their lazy flight breaks out the agitated knocking of the machine guns as they sweep the parapet. . . . At intervals we send up Vèry lights and the ghastly face of No Man's Land leaps up in the garish light, then as the rocket falls the great shad-ows flow back shutting it into darkness again.

Knights of the Air

Laughing through clouds . . . Cities and men he smote from overhead
RUDYARD KIPLING

In 1917 the war in the air grew more intense as the effectiveness of the aero-plane was rapidly improved. The airmen alone were facing the enemy in close single combat with the chivalry of a bygone age; they hated the machine rather than the German in it. In their often very short lives they had a taste of excite-ment, self-reliance and comparative luxury among an élite of fellow knights.

But knight errantry was soon to be superseded by cavalry-like formation tactics. By 1918 Britain had the largest air force, consisting of 22,000 planes and 300,000 airmen, with an independent section carrying out raids on the Rhineland and the Ruhr. The Germans had already begun to bomb England: their largest raid on London, at noon on 13 June 1917 by thirty planes, caused 580 casualties, including 120 schoolchildren, and was then regarded as the ultimate horror.

7

'TWO LITTLE SAUSAGES' OVER HUNLAND

Captain W.E. Molesworth describes how he brought down his first observa-tion balloon.

60 Squadron R.F.C., April 1917
. . . Still more excitement! I tackled my first balloon yesterday, and consider it even more difficult than going for a Hun; at least, I think one gets a hotter time. We had received orders a week ago that all balloons *had* to be driven down or destroyed, as they were worrying our infantry and gunners during the advance. . . .

We all went off individually to the various balloons which had been allotted to us. I am glad to say most of us managed to do them down. I personally crossed the trenches at about 10,000 feet, dropping all the time towards my sausage, which was five or six miles away. It was floating in company with another at about 3,000 feet, and reminded me of that little song, 'Two Little Sausages'.

I started a straight dive towards them, and then the fun began. Archie got quite annoyed, following me down to about 5,000 feet, where I was met by two or three strings of flaming onions,[8] luckily too far off to do any damage. Then came thousands of machine-gun bullets from the ground – evidently I was not going to get them without trouble. I zigzagged about a bit, still heading for the balloons, and when within 200 yards opened fire. The old Huns in the basket got wind up and jumped out in their parachute. Not bothering about them, I kept my sight on one of the balloons and saw the tracer going right into it and causing it to smoke.

By this time the second balloon was almost on the floor. I gave it a burst, which I don't think did any damage. The first sausage was in flames, so I buzzed off home without meeting any Huns. On the way back a good shot from Archie exploded very near my tail, and carried away part of the elevator.[9] Don't you think this is the limit for anyone who wants excitement? I must say I prefer it to the infantry, as one gets decent food, and a comfortable bed every night, if you are lucky enough to get back. . . .

8

THE LONELINESS OF THE SCOUT PILOT *

June 1917

There is no doubt that scout pilots have the most exciting experiences while flying over Hunland, and it sometimes happens that these experiences may be their last. . . . However, we do not think of these sort of things in the air, but instead, we are filled with the spirit of confidence in our machines, and the ever-present thought that the best way to defend is to attack.

There is the feeling of joy about it all which is sometimes mixed with loneliness. You are flying between a huge expanse of earth or sea below, merging into the vast spaces of the heavens above. The continuous drone of the engine in front of you and the whistling of the wind through the wires all add to this sense of loneliness, while the bracing air, and the knowledge that you have some of the finest machines and companions in the patrol, make you feel that flying is absolute perfection.

9

HOW TO KEEP COOL IN A HEAT WAVE

June 1917

The heat is simply terrific, and the only ways of keeping cool are flying or sitting under the trees in the orchard. We spend most of the day, when not in the air, in multi-coloured pyjamas, some lads even going so far as to fly in them.

---

8 A number of balls of fire fastened together and shot up into the air in order to fall over the attacking machine and bring it down in flames.
9 The tailplane which is used to direct the machine up or down.

Another awfully good way of keeping cool is to dig a hole about a foot deep and three feet long and cover it with a ground sheet, pegged down at the corners, so as to make a bath. You lie in this with a book and a cooling drink by your side, and if you are lucky enough to escape the bombardment of mud, stones, and various other missiles which are thrown at you by the more energetic and lively spirits in the camp, you can really enjoy yourself. These baths have been such a success that we decided to dig a small bathing-pool about twenty feet square by three feet deep. When we got this going the whole population of the nearest village had to come and watch us. This was rather disconcerting, as we used to bathe *tout à fait nude*. Most of the chaps managed to rig up something in the way of a bathing-dress by buying various articles of clothing in the neighbouring village – I was forced to content myself with a type of female under-garment, which seemed to cause great amusement amongst the ack-emmas.[10] The village maidens were highly delighted, and thought it quite the thing, now that we were decently clad, to watch us at our aquatic sports.

10

'New grids: the Huns got pukka wind-up'

August 1917

The new grids[11] are a great success, and we have been hard at work training and doing line patrols. Three of us, led by our famous 'Hun-strafer', used them over the lines for the first time. As a rule, we only fight in flights, but on certain occasions we volunteer for a 'circus', that is a mixed formation generally composed of the best pilots in the squadron.

Our numbers were not overwhelming this time, but we know that the Huns had got pukka[12] wind-up by the way they disappeared when we arrived on the line, so we felt quite confident in taking on twice as many as ourselves. Of course, we were all out for trouble, as we wanted to show what the new machines could do. As soon as our leader spotted a formation of Huns, he was after them like a flash. I think there were seven of them, but we were all much too excited to count. Suddenly they saw us coming, and tried desperately to escape, but our leader got into his favourite position, and the rear Hun hadn't a ghost of a chance. The next instant he was a flaming mass.

We simply had it all over the Boche for speed and, as we had the height, they could not possibly get away. I picked my man out as he was coming towards me, and straight at him, opening fire with both guns at close range. He suffered the same fate as his companion.

A burning machine is a glorious but terrible sight to see – a tiny red stream of flame trickles from the petrol tank, the long tongues of blazing petrol lick the sides of the fuselage, and, finally, a sheet of white fire envelops the whole machine, and it glides steeply towards the ground in a zig-zag course, leaving a long trail of black

10 Air mechanics.
11 SE5s.
12 Genuine, real (from Hindustani).

smoke behind it, until it eventually breaks up. There is no doubt that your first Hun in flames gives you a wonderful feeling of satisfaction. I can well imagine what the big-game hunter must think when he sees the dead lion in front of him. Somehow, you do not realise that you are sending a man to an awful doom, but rather your thoughts are all turned on the hateful machine which you are destroying, so fascinating to look at, and yet so deadly in its attack.

Passchendaele

I died in hell (they called it Passchendaele) . . .
I fell into the bottomless mud, and lost the light
SIEGFRIED SASSOON, 'MEMORIAL TABLET'

On 7 June, 1917, General Sir Herbert Plumer (a pot-bellied image of Colonel Blimp but one of the best generals) blew up the German hill stronghold on the Messines Ridge by setting off nineteen mines dug 100 ft underneath; in three hours the whole ridge was taken together with seven thousand prisoners.

11

ZERO HOUR

Lieutenant-Colonel Feilding describes to his wife the success of the initial surprise attack and attributes it to the business methods of the offices of the Empire.

Rossignol Wood, June 8th, 1917
Yesterday morning (the great day) I got up and went out at three o'clock. The exact moment of the assault which had been withheld by the Higher Command, as is usual, till as late as possible, had been disclosed to us at 3.10 a.m.

I climbed on to the bank of the communication trench, known as Rossignol Avenue, and waited. Dawn had not yet broken. The night was very still. Our artillery was lobbing over an occasional shell; the enemy – oblivious of the doom descending upon him – was leisurely putting back gas shells, which burst in and around my wood with little dull pops, adding to the smell but doing no injury.

The minute hand of my watch crept on to the fatal moment. Then followed a 'tableau' so sudden and dramatic that I cannot hope to describe it. Out of the silence and the darkness, along the front, twenty mines – some of them having waited two years and more for this occasion – containing hundreds of tons of high explosive, almost simultaneously, and with a roar to wake the dead, burst into the sky in great sheets of flame, developing into mountainous clouds of dust and earth and stones and trees.

For some seconds the earth trembled and swayed. Then the guns and howitzers in their thousands spoke: the machine-gun barrage opened; and the infantry on a ten-mile front left the trenches and advanced behind the barrage against the enemy.

The battle once launched, all was oblivion. No news came through for several hours: there was just the roar of the artillery; – such a roar and such a barrage has never been before. Our men advanced almost without a check. The enemy – such of them as were not killed – were paralysed, and surrendered. In Wytschaete Village they rushed forward with their hands up, waving handkerchiefs and things. And no one can blame them. The ordeal through which they have been passing the last fortnight must have surpassed the torments of hell itself. . . .

I have been thinking to-day of the saying – that the battle of Waterloo was won on the playing-fields of Eton. That remark wants revision now. You must for the 'playing fields of Eton' substitute the 'offices of the Empire'. From the offices have been introduced business methods which are essential to the complicated operations of nowadays. The Staff work yesterday was perfect. What a contrast to the time of Loos!

Passchendaele, or the Third Battle of Ypres, opened on 31 July. Here, in 1915, the Germans had used chlorine gas for the first time, and the British, retaliating a few months later, had had it blown back in their faces; here, in the too narrow offensive of Loos, sixty thousand casualties had been suffered, 'a useless slaughter of infantry' according to the Official War History. And now, Haig, believing he could defeat the Germans single-handed, drove his army into the most futile horror of the war – the swamp created by the combination of torrential rain and destruction of the drainage system by a ten-day bombardment by four million shells: 324,000 British soldiers fell there in the next three months, wading up to their waists in mud,[13] their tanks and guns getting stuck and clogged up, while the Germans sprayed them with murderous machine-gun fire from their concrete pill-boxes or suffocated them with mustard gas. A four-mile advance to the ruins of Passchendaele was all that was achieved by this senseless massacre, staged by a remote GHQ ignoring reality (Major-General Fuller called it an 'inexcusable piece of pig-headedness') – and even that was soon lost again.[14]

---

13 'Ground? There wasn't any. The very earth itself was skinned. It had no hide. It would not support. Its raw dark body was rotten, an expanse of wet entrails and decomposition. . . . The land was dead, like its people.' (Tomlinson, op. cit., p. 473 f).

14 Major Alan Brooke, the brilliant CIGS of the Second World War, remarked that Haig 'spoke in the rosiest terms of our chances of breaking through . . . to my mind quite impossible. I am certain he had never seen the ground for himself.' (D. Fraser, *Alanbrooke*, Collins, 1982).

12

'I sat down in the mud and cried'

Private Jack Sweeney to his fiancée Joy Williams.

Somewhere in the mud [November 1917]
. . . I was wet to the skin, no overcoat, no water sheet, I had about three inches of clay clinging to my clothes and it was cold, I was in an open dugout and do you know what I did – I sat down in the mud and cried, I do not think I have cried like I did that night since I was a child. . . .

If only the people of England could have seen what I saw yesterday they would not grumble about the air raids. . . . I saw motor lorries sunk in the mud over the wheels, also horses with just part of their heads showing above the swamp, also two tanks which were in the Push and were buried – the men who were still in them will never be able to tell the tale of the fight but they were heroes. And the dead – a lot have been buried in the bogs. The Somme was bad enough but this is a thousand times worse.

There are men now in the trenches full of water who are nearly dead, they are fast dying of cold they go sick see the doctor go back and try to stick it until they get relieved. . . . Some of them find that they are too ill to walk back and they have to stop for a rest and may be hit by shrapnel and taken on the stretcher to the dressing station, that is if we have any brave stretcher bearers who are willing to risk their lives – it is every man for himself on this road, you just go forward, there is no place to take cover and it is terrible. I have thanked God for sparing me. . . .

A GHQ officer who visited the front also broke into tears when he saw for the first time the hell of Passchendaele. A company commander in the Guards voices the outrage felt at the front about the Londoners' grumble over air raids.[15]

13

'Seeing what the soldier has to put up with . . .'

Captain (later Colonel) Alex Wilkinson to his sister Sidney; wounded later and in hospital, he avoided 'suffering from acute depression for evermore' by seeing 'the humorous side of this war' and 'trying to extract what fun [he] may out of it'.

---

15 Herbert Read also criticized Londoners: 'They simply have no conception whatever of what war really is like and don't seem to be concerned about it at all. They were much more troubled about a few paltry air raids. They raise a sentimental scream about one or two babies killed when every day out here hundreds of the very finest manhood "go west".' (*Contrary Experience*, Faber & Faber, 1963, p. 97).

16.7.1917

About the air raids, to judge by the papers, the majority of people seem to be entirely demoralised. After there has been an air raid over London it is difficult to believe there is still a war on out here. Columns and columns of what we consider to be entire nonsense are written on the subject & there is an entire omission of any other war news. One reporter had the impertinence to say that 'under the circumstances cheerfulness would have been as offensive as panic'! He should see the British soldier undergoing a nice bombardment, possibly a little more unpleasant than bombs dropped from aeroplanes – cheerfulness is never found to be offensive. Such drivel I have seldom read and the idea that London should be guarded by hordes of aeroplanes is preposterous. I cannot believe that the war will be won by rendering London immune from aerial attack. Whereas we cannot have too many aeroplanes out here.

In fact most of us out here are not very well pleased with the attitude of Londoners. Seeing what the soldier has to put up with, we think that people at home might show a little more fortitude when they get a mild insight into the realities of war. There are many women whom it will not harm to realise that this war is not quite the joke they thought it was.

A harassed CCS matron describes the terrible number of casualties.

14

THE CASUALTY CLEARING STATION IS FULL UP

Miss K.E. Luard, RRC, Matron of Brandhoek CCS, tells how they were working under shellfire.

[July 31, 1917]

. . . We have been working in the roar of battle every minute since I last wrote, and it has been rather too exciting. I've not had time to hear any details from any of our poor abdominals, but the news has been good till this evening; thousands of prisoners – and Ypres choked with captured guns and ammunition, and some few miles (?) of advance. . . .

Everything has been going at full pitch – with the 12 Teams in the Theatre only breaking off for hasty meals – the Dressing Hut, the Preparation Ward and Resuscitation and the four huge Acute Wards, which fill up from the Theatre; the Officers' Ward, the Moribund and the German Ward. That, and the Preparation and the Theatre are the worst places. Soon after 10 o'clock this morning he began putting over high explosive. Everyone had to put on tin-hats and carry on. He kept it up all the morning with vicious screams. They burst on two sides of us, not 50 yards away – no direct hits on to us but streams of shrapnel, which were quite hot when you picked them up. No one was hurt, which was lucky, and they came everywhere, even through our Canvas Huts in our quarters. Luckily we were so frantically busy that it was easier to pay less attention to it. The patients who were well enough to realise that they were not still on the field called it "a dirty trick". They were not gas shells, thank Heaven.

It doesn't look as if we should ever sleep again. Apparently gunners and soldiers never do: it is difficult to see who can in this area. . . . And there was a moment about tea-time when I thought the work was going to heap up and get the upper hand of us, but the C.O. stopped admitting for an hour and sent them on lower down, which saved the situation. . . .

But to the public school subaltern, one of the lost generation which perished in Flanders (their average life expectation was a mere three weeks), the stark reality of war appears infinitely more worthwhile than the sordid triviality of life in peacetime.

15

HONEST SAVAGERY BETTER THAN SELFISH COMMERCIALISM

Lieutenant Henry Jones, Tanks Corps, writes to his brother, comparing the exhilaration of attack to that of a big school match; four days later he was killed, aged twenty-seven.

July 27th, 1917

. . . Have you ever reflected on the fact that, despite the horrors of the war, it is at least a big thing? I mean to say that in it one is brought face to face with realities. The follies, selfishness, luxury and general pettiness of the vile commercial sort of existence led by nine-tenths of the people of the world in peacetime are replaced in war by a savagery that is at least more honest and outspoken. Look at it this way: in peacetime one just lives one's own little life, engaged in trivialities; worrying about one's own comfort, about money matters, and all that sort of thing – just living for one's own self. What a sordid life it is! In war, on the other hand, even if you do get killed you only anticipate the inevitable by a few years in any case, and you have the satisfaction of knowing that you have 'pegged out' in the attempt to help your country. You have, in fact, realised an ideal, which, as far as I can see, you very rarely do in ordinary life. The reason is that ordinary life runs on a commercial and selfish basis; if you want to 'get on', as the saying is, you can't keep your hands clean.

Personally, I often rejoice the War has come my way. It has made me realise what a petty thing life is. I think that the War has given to everyone a chance to 'get out of himself', as I might say. Of course, the other side of the picture is bound to occur to the imagination. But there! I have never been one to take the more melancholy point of view when there's a silver lining in the cloud.

Certainly, speaking for myself, I can say that I have never in all my life experienced such a wild exhilaration as on the commencement of a big stunt, like the last April one for example. The excitement for the last half-hour or so before it is like nothing on earth. The only thing that compares with it are the few minutes before the start of a big school match. Well, Cheer-oh!

In complete contrast the poet Herbert Read, a pacifist in 1914 who regarded war as nothing but imperialist rivalry and hoped that international working-class action would stop it, found himself in the OTC and soon commissioned in the Green Howards. He observed that 'one week in the trenches was sufficient to strip war of its lingering traces of romance' left from the Boer War, and that Ypres was nothing but 'primitive filth, lice, boredom and death'. With 'no hatred of the enemy, the whole business became fantastically unreal, a monstrous nightmare from which one could not awake', as 'apart from uniforms Germans and English are like as two peas: beautiful fresh children . . . magnificently brave . . . and massacred in inconceivable torment'. Among the ideals of warfare, like 'austerity, endurance, gaiety, fearlessness, fatalism', Read the intellectual thinks comradeship with the common soldier was foremost in overcoming horror and hardship, and making the army tolerable to him:

I begin to appreciate, to an undreamt of extent, the 'simple soul'. He is the only man you can put your money on in a tight corner. Bombast and swank carry a man nowhere out here. In England they are everything. Nor is the intellect not a few of us used to be so proud of of much avail. It's a pallid thing in the presence of a stout heart.[16]

A few weeks after writing this in a letter to a female student he had known at university, Herbert Read gives her a graphic description of a night raid and of his fraternization with a German prisoner.

16

NIGHT RAID

Captain Herbert Read (1893–1968) to a girlfriend.

1 August 1917

Well, the 'stunt' is over, so now I can tell you something about it. I, along with another officer, was detailed to get as many volunteers as we could from our company and, on a certain dark and dirty night, to raid the enemy's trenches, kill as many as possible and bring back at least one prisoner for identification purposes. Out of a possible 60 we got 47 volunteers. . . . That was a jolly good start. We had about a fortnight to make our plans and rehearse. This we set about with enthusiasm – everybody was keen. Our plans were made with all the low villainous cunning we were capable of. We two officers had to discover the weak points in the enemy's wire, the best routes thither and as much of the enemy's habits as we could.

This went on until the fateful night arrived. Picture us about midnight: our faces were blackened with burnt cork, everything that might rattle was taken off or tied up. We armed ourselves with daggers and bombs and various murderous devices to

16 Ibid., p. 97.

blow up the enemy's wire and dugouts – and, of course, our rifles and revolvers. The raid was to be a stealth raid and depended for its success on surprise effect. So out thro' our own wire we crept – our hearts thumping but our wills determined. We had 540 yards to traverse to the objective. The first half were simple enough. Then we began to crouch and then to crawl – about a yard a minute. Suddenly, about 150 yards from the German trenches, we saw and heard men approaching us. We were following one another in Indian file. They seemed scattered to the right and left as far as we could see. In a moment all our carefully prepared plans were thrown to the winds. New plans had to be made on the spur of the moment. Our position was tactically very weak. My fellow-officer began to crawl carefully back to reorganize the men into a defensive position, leaving me in front to deal with the situation if necessary. I could now see what was happening. The Huns were coming out to wire and were sending out a strong covering party to protect the wirers from surprise. This party halted and took up a line in shell-holes about 20 yards from us. Then some of them began to come forward to reconnoitre. We lay still, looking as much like clods of earth as we possibly could. Two Boche were getting very near me. I thought we had better surprise them before they saw us. So up I get and run to them pointing my revolver and shouting 'Haende hoch' (hands up), followed by my trusty sergeant and others. Perhaps the Boche didn't understand my newly acquired German. At any rate they fired on me – and missed. I replied with my revolver and my sergeant with his gun. One was hit and shrieked out. Then I was on the other fellow who was now properly scared and fell flat in a shell-hole. 'Je suis officier!' he cried in French. By this time there was a general fight going on, fire being opened on all sides. In a minute or two the guns were on and for five minutes it was inferno. The real object of the raid was achieved – a prisoner and a valuable one at that had been captured. So I began to make my way back with him whilst the other officer organized covering fire. In another five minutes we were back in our own trenches. . . .

We had to take him down to Brigade – an hour's walk. It was a beautiful early morning and everything was peaceful and the larks were singing. In our broken French we talked of music. He played both the violin and the piano and we found common enthusiasms in Beethoven and Chopin. He even admired Nietzsche and thenceforth we were sworn friends. He wrote his name and address in my pocket-book and I promised to visit him after the war if ever I came to Germany. By the time I handed him over to the authorities at the Brigade we were sorry to part with each other. And a few hours previously we had done our best to kill each other. . . .

Londoners were shocked to hear the boom of the guns on the other side of the Channel and to suffer air raids, mostly by single planes. Altogether in the war, 208 Zeppelins and 435 planes raided southern England, dropping 300 tons of bombs and killing about 1,500 people. These raids which seem to us insignificant after the experience of the Second World War, caused a considerable stir at the time and an outcry for retaliation. When the RAF was founded as an independent service on 1 April 1918, its first commander, Major-General Sir Hugh Trenchard, was planning large-scale bombing raids on German cities, but these were prevented by the Armistice.

17

LONDON LIFE IN 1917

F.S. Oliver tells his brother in Canada how he was woken by the roar of the guns in Flanders at the big dawn attack of 31 July.

August 1st, 1917

. . . Then a door began banging dully at irregular intervals and I thought I couldn't get to sleep till I had shut it. But it wasn't a door at all; it was the guns in Flanders – as plain as plain could be – what air there was being from the east. So as I couldn't stop the guns, or shut them off, I just lay awake. Then shortly after dawn there were more much more violent detonations – two of them I actually *felt* and not merely heard. Then shortly the market motors began running and I heard no more.

It was a curious sensation; for of course one felt, on hearing the big noises just after dawn, that the big attack had begun.

September 5th

. . . Last night I was dining in Portland Place with a couple of friends and left a few minutes before midnight to walk home. Everything was very quiet in the streets and I heard an aeroplane quite distinctly. I didn't think much of that because it is a common enough occurrence; the only thing that struck me was that it was singularly loud, much louder than I had ever heard an aeroplane before. There was a little fleece of cloud in the sky so that, although there was a bright moon, I could see nothing of the object itself. The next thing I knew was that there were some shots – not artillery fire – but obviously something in the nature of machine-gun shots, being exchanged in the air, for one saw little 'Stars' very high up in the sky. It was obvious that there was a fight between aeroplanes going on up there. Then I heard some big noises which I thought were guns rather far off, but which were, in fact, bombs rather close by. Then the big guns north of Regent's Park opened fire once or twice. After that there were a few more of the bomb sounds, but remote, and the throbbing noises gradually died away. I took refuge in an archway while the sky was lit up over my head, that is to say, for about a couple of minutes; then I walked home where I found the maids in their nightgowns and wrappers. It seemed over, so we all went to bed.

About a quarter to one I heard an aeroplane again. It became gradually much louder than I had ever heard before. Then there were a series of loud explosions and the guns in Hyde Park began to fire. I don't know how long the noise of the aeroplane went on, but I think it must have been for a full five minutes. Whether it was one plane or a string of several – one following another – I cannot say. If it was one it must have been circling round. It dropped a big bomb a little more than a quarter of a mile from us, which apparently killed a cook in the Edgware Road, and broke a certain number of windows. It fell as nearly as possible equal distances from Paddington Station and the Great Central Station. . . . It gives you a sort of impression how we live in these days.

It sometimes occurs to me to wonder if you, at the other side of an ocean and a continent, can form an adequate picture of the lives of your friends and relations over here; of a London whose wheeled traffic, I suppose, must have been reduced by about two-thirds; whose nights are dark and sometimes almost as silent as the country; where nearly all the necessaries of life, except air and water, have to be bought in the most sparing quantities, and have to be paid for on the average at something more than twice the old prices; where at any public place you are allowed no more than two tiny lumps of sugar (together not much more than half the size of the old-fashioned lump); where coal, coke, matches, and everything of that nature have to be husbanded as if they were heaps of gold.

Of course, the result of this is not by any means all bad. I never knew till last summer what a delicious thing a potato was, that is, when I couldn't buy any; not did I ever realise the transcendent luxury of white bread. The stuff you get from the baker really automatically rations the consumer because it is so abominable now as to destroy any greediness which may still lurk in our natures.

'Lions led by Donkeys'?

Reading the Roll of Honour. 'Poor young chap,'
I'd say – 'I used to know his father well;
Yes, we've lost heavily in this last scrap'
SIEGFRIED SASSOON, 'BASE DETAILS'

Sublime, benevolent, but somehow inexpert
C.E. MONTAGUE, 'DISENCHANTMENT'

French generals and English politicians were the bugbears of the Army leaders. Sir William Robertson, Chief of the Imperial General Staff, the only private ever to rise, after eleven years in the ranks, to Field Marshal, raves against both; incomprehension and irritation were mutual.

18

THEY ARE PECULIAR AND DEPLORABLE

General William Robertson (1860–1933), later Field Marshal and Baronet, to General Sir Douglas Haig.

January 5, 1916
. . . As a whole, the French Commanders and Staff are a peculiar lot. Now and again in some respects they are quite good, but on some occasions they are most elementary and impracticable. The great thing to remember in dealing with them is that they are Frenchmen and not Englishmen, and do not and never will look at things in the way we look at them. I suppose that they think that we are queer people. It is a big business having to deal with Allied Commanders, and one has to keep oneself very much in check and exercise great tolerance. . . .

It is deplorable the way these politicians fight and intrigue against each other. They are my great difficulty here. They have no idea how war must be conducted in order to be given a reasonable chance of success, and they will not allow professionals a free hand. . . . It is all very unsettling and takes up much of my time in talking and explaining what these people cannot understand and sometimes do not wish to understand.

But who were the war leaders against whom Captain Siegfried Sassoon MC (called 'Mad Jack' for his daring exploits) and other war poets revolted so bitterly? 'War is hell and those who institute it are criminals,' he wrote and defied the military authorities over what was felt to be their betrayal in prolonging the war unnecessarily, a war of which Lieutenant Engall had written in 1916: 'Ask a British Tommy why he is fighting out here, and sure as eggs are eggs he'll say "Jiggered if I know"'. It was widely held that British soldiers, in the words of General Hoffmann to Ludendorff, were 'lions led by donkeys' – staff officers wearing the 'red badge of Funk' who (with the notable exception of General Gough), rarely went near the front-line, and directed their murderous offensives from the comfort of distant French châteaux. Sassoon satirized such generals in his famous poem, 'The General':

> 'Good-morning; good-morning!' the General said
> When we met him last week on our way to the line.
> Now the soldiers he smiled at are most of 'em dead,
> And we're cursing his staff for incompetent swine.
> 'He's a cheery old card,' grunted Harry to Jack
> As they slogged up to Arras with rifle and pack.
> But he did for them both by his plan of attack.

Leaders in the 'popular tradition of heroic infallibility and amateurish good humour' tended to be ignorant of military theory; with complacent optimism and a stubborn refusal to recognize reality they pitted 'bravery, perfect discipline and absolute conviction of right and wrong and the existence of God' against the most scientifically trained army in the world.[17]

Lloyd George, in his *Memoirs*, calls the Third Battle of Ypres 'one of the greatest disasters of the war . . . illustrating the unquenchable heroism that will never accept defeat and the inexhaustible vanity that will never admit a mistake . . . who would rather a million perish than that they as leaders would own that they were blunderers', distilling a 'spell of synthetic victories' at GHQ. He wanted to sack Haig although he was, no doubt, a considerable improvement on French who lacked intellect and endurance. Haig, though, had once failed his Staff College exam and had become a captain

---

17 Alan Clark, *The Donkeys*, Hutchinson, 1961, p. 20.

only at the age of thirty-eight, before climbing rapidly as a socialite, marrying Queen Alexandra's maid of honour and gaining the King's personal confidence. Yet even he asserted that 'Cavalry will have a larger sphere of action in future wars', 'Artillery only seems likely to be effective against raw troops', and 'The machine gun is a much over-rated weapon – two per battalion is more than sufficient'.[18] But Haig was no doubt right when he uttered his guiding strategic principle: 'We cannot hope to win until we have defeated the German Army', and he remained adamant that 'It is in the great battles of 1916 and 1917 that we have to seek for the secret of victory in 1918'.

The question is whether, in order to bleed and exhaust the German war machine, such horrifying sacrifices had to be accepted as inevitable, or whether some protection for the advancing infantry could have been provided earlier by better scientific insight and up-to-date tactics, rather than relying on the emotive tradition of 'pluck' in the playing-field 'spirit'. With a 'profound streak of stubborn pride in himself, his army and his country . . . he made the facts of the situation fit his ambition' when he noted in his diary on 26 May 1917: 'Great Britain must take the necessary steps to win the war by herself.'[19] His faith in God was behind his faith in himself: 'I feel every step in my plan has been taken with divine help', he had written, echoing Cromwell, before the Battle of the Somme. But although he exacted enormous sacrifices from his soldiers, he held them 'in tremendous affection' and wanted to be loved by them in turn.

19

HAIG AND HIS TROOPS

General Sir Douglas Haig (1861–1928) (later Earl and Field Marshal) expounds his feeling for the troops to his wife; after the war he devoted himself wholly to the welfare of ex-servicemen and founded the British Legion.

April 13, 1917

Your dear letter has just reached me. I am delighted to think that *you* only believe what I write to you. You are quite right – these papers publish a lot of untruths – or at any rate only publish what suits their policy! . . .

I am very glad to hear from you that those serving under me have an affection for me. As you know, I don't go out of my way to make myself popular, either by doing showy things or by being slack in the matter of discipline – I never hesitate to find faults, but I have a tremendous affection for those fine fellows who are ready to give

18 Quoted by A. Clark.
19 C. Barnett, *Swordbearers*, Eyre & Spottiswoode, 1963, p. 242.

their lives for the Old Country at any moment. I feel quite sad at times when I see them march past me, knowing as I do how many must pay the full penalty before we can have peace. . . .

There have been arguments against the detraction of Haig and his generals: John Terraine[20] has pointed out that the 'literature of disenchantment', published at the peak of anti-militarism around 1930, expressed the feelings of only a small minority, and Corelli Barnett[21] has also turned against the streams of books churning out what he calls an unrepresentative literary folk memory of the War – clichés about callous slaughter in futile offensives; he thinks the First World War was 'a profoundly complex predicament not to be explained by simple tales of horrors and scapegoats'. The controversy continues over whether Haig's (and Nivelle's) offensives were reasonable, and whether the war could have been won in 1917.

In the early morning mist of 20 November, General Sir Julian Byng's Third Army launched a surprise attack against the Hindenburg Line in front of Cambrai (for the first time without preliminary bombardment), supported by 381 tanks, 1,000 guns and 300 planes. The initial sucess was striking: a large breach was opened by the tanks and coordinated infantry (although 65 were lost and 114 broke down).[22] But the rejoicing in London, after the dismal Passchendaele news, soon turned into disappointment when, owing to the inexplicable failure to bring up reserves in time to relieve the tired units and exploit the advantage gained, it was soon lost again by a German counter-attack; recriminations led to an enquiry.

20

CRUCIFYING SCAPEGOATS DOES NOT MAKE FOR EFFICIENCY

General Sir Henry (later Lord) Rawlinson (1864–1925), Commander of the Fourth Army, protests to Lord Derby, Minister of War, against the enquiry.

27 January 1918
. . . The fuss they are making at home, both about the Cambrai affair and the higher command out here, I confess, alarms me. Mercifully the army takes little interest in neither, for they feel sure that Wullie and D.H.[23] are strong enough to withstand the

---

20 Introduction to Greenwell, op. cit.
21 *Encounter*, May 1978, p. 66 f.
22 The 'landships', Colonel Swinton's momentous invention to counter the machine-gun, were commissioned by the Navy under Churchill's sponsorship in face of Army opposition. The first thirty-two surprised the Germans at Flers on 15 September 1916, despite their defects and inept handling; their first massed use at Cambrai heralded a new age of land warfare.

mud that is being thrown at them.

People talk of a surprise, a panic, and of officers running about in pyjamas. Do you realize that the Germans have been doing exactly the same for the last two years at the Somme, Arras, Vimy, Messines and in Flanders? They do not try to make scape-goats, but accept the inevitable, learn their lessons and try all they can to do better next time. We, on the other hand, hold enquiries, examine officers and men, agitate in the House of Commons, in order to crucify someone because our line was pressed back on a wider front than usual. It is not making for efficiency to turn our soldiers' minds out here on the enquiries regarding the past, when they ought to be straining every nerve to prepare for the future. The British public and the House of Commons must get accustomed to the Cambrais, for I should not be surprised if we had several more of them this year. We are going to have a pretty hard time, but, whatever it may produce, it will be less unpleasant than 1914. . . .

Victory and Disillusionment

> *Walked eye-deep in hell*
> *Believing in old men's lies, then unbelieving*
> *Came home, home to a lie,*
> *Home to many deceits,*
> *Home to old lies and new infamy*
> EZRA POUND

> *So we have won through. What now?*
> HERBERT READ, 'MEDITATION OF THE WAKING ENGLISH OFFICER'

Churchill's vision of the danger of what was in store was, as usual, accurate. He sensed that a major German offensive was bound to come in the spring of 1918, in a last desperate gamble to win the war before the arrival of a large American army.

21

CHURCHILL'S WARNING

Winston Churchill, Minister of Munitions, urges Lloyd George, with charac-teristic emphatic energy, to take immediate action to relieve the manpower shortage in the Army.

19 January 1918

23 Generals William Robertson and Douglas Haig.

My dear Prime Minister,

I do hope you are not closing your mind to these facts. . . . I don't think we are doing enough for our Army. . . . We are not raising its strength as we ought. We ought to fill it up at once to full strength.

It is wrong to give them to the Navy in priority to the Army. . . . The imminent danger is on the Western Front, and the crisis will come before June. A defeat here will be *fatal*. . . .

You know how highly I rate the modern defensive compared with offensive. But I do *not* like the situation now developing, and I do not think that all that is possible is being done to meet it. . . . Men at once – at all costs from Navy, from Munitions, from Home Army, from Civilian Life. Stint food and commercial imports to increase shells, aeroplanes and tanks. Wire and concrete on the largest possible scale.

A good plan for counter blows all worked out beforehand to relieve pressure at the points of attack when they manifest themselves.

If this went wrong – everything would go wrong. I do not feel sure about it. The Germans are a terrible foe, and their generals are better than ours.

Ponder, and then *Act*.

Yours always,
Winston

The great offensive Churchill had warned against came as soon as March: the Germans, reinforced by their armies no longer needed in Russia, attempted to knock out the Allies on the Somme by employing new tactics of surprise, movement and ruthlessness. One hundred and ninety-one German divisions attacked 163 Allied ones and soon infiltrated through the forward lines with merciless frightfulness. Even hospitals were bombed, foreshadowing the next war.

22

THE PLUCK OF THE GIRLS

Marguerite McArthur, with the YMCA in France describes an air raid; she was soon to die, aged twenty-six.

May 26, 1918

. . . We were sitting peacefully in the salon, writing letters, and planned to go early to bed, when we heard the sound of guns, and realised a raid was on. It was soon after 10, and almost at once we heard the loud sound of German engines, apparently overhead. . . . For two hours or more pandemonium reigned. The crash of bombs shook the house, guns thundered incessantly, machine-guns clattered, we heard shrapnel pattering on the roofs, and the sudden shiver of masses of broken glass. Twice at least the crash seemed to be just over the house, and I remember thinking that we shall not get through with our lives. There was nothing we could do – part of the time we played the piano. . . . We knew they were trying for the station, which is pretty close to us. I do not remember feeling really very nervous. The big crashes made us jump, and my heart was in my mouth once or twice, but I did not feel afraid of what seemed likely to happen. . . . It must have been an awful time in the camps and hospitals. In one tent every man was killed except one who was standing up! There was no shelter anywhere. At the hospitals men worked rescuing the wounded, carrying stretchers through a hail of shrapnel, with bombs bursting close by. The nurses' rest hut was blown in, one sister being killed outright and two mortally wounded; amidst the horror of it all shone the glory of great courage. Light-duty patients risked their lives to drag the orderlies from the burning huts – 32 of them died in the attempt. They spoke, too, of the Ambulance Girls – 'the pluckiest of the lot' – out in the thick of it, picking up wounded. . . . And the men's anxiety for the women they knew was wonderful. Everywhere they were asking: 'Are the Y.M.C.A. ladies all right?'

General Gough's Fifth Army, which had recently taken over the French extreme left wing, was unprepared for the impact, and collapsed. In two days a forty-mile breach was opened between the Allied armies; the Passchendaele losses had had a demoralizing effect. The Germans threatened to lay siege to Paris and cut off the BEF from the Channel ports. They crossed the Marne to within forty miles of Paris and drove the British back to Arras, taking 80,000 prisoners and nearly 1,000 guns. Pétain thought all was lost, and Haig, in face of 300,000 British casualties, issued his famous Order of the Day: 'With our backs to the wall and believing in the justice of our cause each one of us must fight to the end.' It sounded impressive at home but was mocked by the soldiers. Marshal Foch took over supreme command and stemmed the German onslaught with the help of 500,000 British soldiers, withheld up to then by Lloyd George in fear that they might be sacrificed in another Passchendaele: they were now sent over from England where conscription had been raised to the age of fifty, and further reinforcements were rushed over from Palestine and Salonika. Twenty-seven U.S. divisions had also arrived just in time, and were reinforced at the rate of 300,000 men per month. The Germans had exhausted their reserves in the big push and could not exploit their gains: they fell back to the Hindenburg Line.

Meanwhile, five British divisions under General Sir Herbert Plumer had been moved to Italy after the Caporetto disaster to reinforce the crumbling Italian front. They had a fairly quiet time until 15 June when five Austro-Hungarian divisions suddenly attacked the two British on the Asiago Plateau.

23

THE LAST AUSTRIAN OFFENSIVE REPULSED ON THE PIAVE

Captain Greenwell describes the attack.

Carriola, June 17, 1918

We have had a very strenuous time and the regiment was in the thick of it. We never thought the enemy would actually attack on our front. A bombardment did start at 3 a.m. just as I was going to bed and was the most intense I have ever known in the worst days of the Somme or Ypres; they shelled at the most intense pitch for four and a half hours without stop and continued it for miles behind the lines, even dropping shells right back over the mountain range on to the plain. The woods were devastated and the trees crashed down, while most of our guns were silenced pretty successfully by high concentration of gas shells. The tear gas or lachrymatory shells filled the whole of the place with a reeking mist.

At about 7.30 a.m. the beggars were seen coming over at us all along the line. They very soon penetrated our flanks and began to take us in the rear. However, once we saw what was up we rallied the remainder of the regiment, cooks, pioneers, servants, orderlies and God knows what, rushed them up and counter-attacked the enemy out of our front line. Then they again came on and drove us back, as we were by then absurdly weak and no supports had been sent up at all.

But we brought them to a stop about a thousand yards away behind our front line and they never got any further. They were simply slaughtered in thousands and the Division got almost 1,000 prisoners. By noon they were completely fought out and began giving themselves up.

Our men were simply magnificent. The attack has been smashed all along the line though the enemy were five or six to one. . . . I'm afraid that you must have been very anxious, especially with the beastly newspapers talking about 'fearful odds' and 'desperate fighting'. But once the bombardment was over everyone was quite happy and more than ready to deal with the Austrians, though once or twice things did look a little blue.

The early war years seemed already lost in remote memories and peace was unimaginable; people were torn with doubts and anxieties. On 7 September 1915 Brigadier Charteris had written:

Will there be another war after this one? . . . It will be a chastened world for a few years after the war – a world of less wealth, less luxury, less selfishness. Yet human memories are short. In ten years' time, the suffering will be forgotten. There will be new rivalries, new hates and probably new wars.[24]

His expectation that the victors would turn pacifist and the defeated not be deterred from starting another war was to prove only too true.

24 Charteris, op. cit., p. 109.

24

WHAT WILL PEACE BE LIKE?

Brigadier Charteris writes home in a philosophical mood.

August 4, 1918

It is the 4th anniversary of the war. We began with a service out of doors. A bishop from home officiated. It was all very impressive, but I fancy very few of us had their minds on the service. It let loose such a flood of memories, of hopes and of disappointments, all the host of one's friends who have been swept away in this avalanche of horrors, of one's own escapes – all the might-have-beens. I think that none of us dared, or wished, to look forward. Fate has played such strange tricks with us during these last four years. Yet as one looks back, I do not think our success was ever really imperilled except in the first few months. After them, we might not win, but we could not lose. I do not believe that the danger this year was ever as great as in 1914. It looms larger in our minds, because it is closer. 1914 is almost forgotten. One thinks of it only on anniversaries.

It is hard to picture the world at peace, and almost impossible to imagine oneself living in it. Will all our minds be obsessed with memories of war? Will those of us who survive it all, live our lives in a world that will forget? Will any of us have the strength to throw it all aside like a bad illness, and live healthy lives and think healthy thoughts again? One thing is sure. The dread of war will be with us so long as we live, like the fear of the plague, or even of death. And that, I think, will be strongest with those who win. I can well imagine the vanquished losing their dread of war in their dislike of the stigma of defeat.

On 8 August, Rawlinson's Fourth Army gained the finest British victory of the war, at Amiens: in a surprise attack, supported by 456 tanks, they advanced twelve miles, took 21,000 prisoners and shattered German morale. Ludendorff called it 'the black day of the German Army' and advised his government to sue for peace: 'The War must be ended'. Two months later he resigned.

However, in the following letter Rawlinson still does not seem to have been converted to the momentous British invention of the tank, and extols the infantry against such innovations as tanks and planes.

25

TOWARDS THE HINDENBURG LINE

General Rawlinson tells General Sir Henry Wilson, CIGS, not to 'waste man-power in tanks and aviation'.

August 29th [1918]

Things are going very well and we have the Boche seriously rattled. The confusion in his ranks here is appalling; I have never seen it so bad since the early days of the

Somme battle. He has very few reserves at his disposal and does not know where to throw them in on the very wide front on which we are pressing him. . . .

The position now is very favourable. We are up to the Somme, and shall soon drive back the enemy at least to the Hindenburg Line, if not beyond it. All you have got to do is to keep our infantry up to strength and not waste man-power in tanks and aviation. They won't win the war for you as the infantry will. We cannot beat the Boche without infantry. Tanks, aeroplanes, etc., are great helps, but they cannot and will not win the war for us by themselves, so do not let Lloyd George think they will, and persist in developing them at the expense of the infantry.

By autumn 1918, one million U.S. troops had arrived with hundreds of tanks; in a general offensive Foch reoccupied Northern France and Belgium. Germany, exhausted by the blockade and demoralized by Allied material superiority, was broken: the Armistice was signed before any foreign soldier had stepped on German soil.

A cry for revenge went up and Admiral Beatty, giving vent to his frustration, wrote to his wife: 'The only thing is to sail into their poisonous country and wreck it and take what we want and put the fear of God, Truth and Justice into them, represented by the British Tommy'.[25] As dashing, vain and ostentatious as Nelson (but snobbish, arrogant and ungenerous) and also worshipped by the Navy, Beatty felt cheated of the glorious victory he craved. With Nelson's superiority in gunnery, armour and experience it could have been his, if he had been facing a less competent adversary – but the time for naval heroes like Nelson had gone.[26]

The poet Herbert Read expressed his disenchantment about the prevailing mood of revenge.

26

THE NATIONAL TEMPER IS FOR REVENGE

Herbert Read writes critically to a girlfriend.

10 November 1918

The war, I am glad to say, is over – much to some people's disappointment. I have been fairly disgusted these last few weeks. I do not think the national temper is anything to be proud of. Christian sentiments being out of fashion or obsolete, I thought we might at any rate have exercised the Englishman's renowned sense of fair play – of not hitting a man when he is down. No. That is another damned hypocrisy exposed. We only do that when it pays. At present it will pay most of us to leave

25 Chalmers, op. cit., p. 342.
26 P.M. Kennedy reviewing S. Roskill, *Beatty*, 1980, in *The Times Literary Supplement*, 2 January 1981.

Germany incapacitated for foreign trade, etc., for a century. League of Nations? 'Damned idealistic rot. Can't imagine why we let a dreamy bloke like Wilson dictate to us. What I say: Give 'em a taste of what they gave little Belgium. Burn their villages, stick their babies, and rape their women. And now for a strong Army & Navy and keep the old flag flying.'

Do you realize that that is the way the average Englishman is talking just now?

Lloyd George, announcing the peace terms in the Commons, expressed the hope that all wars would thus come to an end. In total 745,000 Britons had died in the war and 1,600,000 had been wounded (nearly 30 per cent of the men under forty-five), and Britain's naval and commercial predominance was over.

London exploded in a three-day binge of wild rejoicing but the soldiers in France, though relieved, were sober and perplexed: the war had gone on for too long and they were by now beyond caring.

27

'For peace I don't care'

Captain Wilkinson, writing to his sister, rejoices that the war had not ended before he had 'a really good battle'; in another letter he boasted of 'fathering the three articles of loot I really wanted: a long automatic pistol, a Zeiss glass and an Iron Cross'.

12.11.18

The jolly old war has come to an end at last, and a very good end too. For peace I don't care one bit, but I am exceedingly glad that we have won. That is the point. And thank heavens I had a really good battle before the end. I would not have missed it for anything in the whole world. . . . By the time we come home most people will have forgotten us. I suppose the storm truppen in London are tremendous lions now, being cheered to the echo. And they are welcome to it.

I am a bit short of socks. If you could make me four pair & send them out I would love them. . . . We would like to celebrate the occasion a little, but we have not the means. . . .

A junior officer wrote: 'England was beastly in 1918. . . . Envy, hatred, malice and all uncharitableness, fear and cruelty born of fear, seemed the dominant passions. . . . Only in the trenches were chivalry and sweet reasonableness to be found.'[27]

Major Alan Brooke who 'felt little triumph and less hatred' was 'filled with gloom' watching the Armistice revelry: 'that wild evening jarred in my

27 C.E. Carrington, *Subaltern's War*, 1929, p. 188.

feelings'. A month earlier he had contemplated the desolation of Lens from a heap of stones where once the church had stood:

One could spend days there just looking down picturing to oneself the tragedies that have occurred in every corner of this place. If the stones could talk and could repeat what they have witnessed, and the thoughts they have read on dying men's faces I wonder if there would ever be any wars.[28]

The soldiers had grown fond of the honesty, selflessness, and camaraderie of the trenches and were apprehensive of the competitive 'other Nation' of humbug ruled by money.

28

DISILLUSIONMENT AFTER DEMOBILIZATION

Colonel Feilding explains to his wife why life was better in the trenches.

Ferfay, Pas de Calais. February 3rd, 1919
The raging desire still continues to be demobilized quickly. Nevertheless, I feel pretty sure that, for many, there will be pathetic disillusionment.

In the trenches the troops have had plenty of time for thought, and there has grown up in their minds a heavenly picture of an England which does not exist, and never did exist, and never will exist so long as men are human.

After all, there was a good deal to be said in favour of the old trench life. There were none of the mean haunting fears of poverty there, and the next meal – if you were alive to take it – was as certain as the rising sun. The rations were the same for the 'haves' and the 'have nots', and the shells fell, without favour, upon both.

In a life where no money passes the ownership of money counts for nothing. Rich and poor alike stand solely upon their individual merits, without discrimination. You can have no idea, till you have tried it, how much pleasanter life is under such circumstances.

In spite – or partly perhaps because of the gloominess of the surroundings, there was an atmosphere of selflessness and a spirit of camaraderie the like of which has probably not been seen in the world before – at least on so grand a scale. Such is the influence of the shells!

The life was a curious blend of discipline and good-fellowship; wherein men were easily pleased; where there was no gossip; where even a shell when it had just missed you produced a sort of exultation; – a life in the course of which you actually got used to the taste of chloride of lime in tea.

In short, there was no humbug in the trenches, and that is why – with all their disadvantages – the better kind of men who have lived in them will look back upon them hereafter with something like affection.

28 Fraser, op. cit., p. 79 f.

War Requiem: Wilfred Owen and 'the pity of war'

There had been years of Passion – scorching, cold
And much Despair, and Anger heaving high . . .
And the pensive Spirit of Pity whispered, 'Why?'
THOMAS HARDY, 'AND THERE WAS A GREAT CALM', 11 NOVEMBER 1918

In conclusion, we can relive the whole range of deep feelings about the First World War in the letters of Wilfrid Owen, the most profound of the 'poets of protest': from heroic idealism to 'seventh hell' and 'Sodom and Gomorrha', from exultation to resignation. He detested politicians and preachers and loved serving soldiers. Christianity was for him not in patriotism nor in the Church but only in suffering humanity: 'My subject is War, and the pity of War'. Although he wrote before the Somme offensive: 'There is a fine heroic feeling about being in France and I am in perfect spirits,' expressing what so many eager volunteers felt when they arrived at the front, two weeks later his views had changed completely.

29

'I have suffered seventh hell'

16 Jan 1917, Betrancourt on the Somme
My own sweet mother,

I can see no excuse for deceiving you about these last four days.
I have suffered seventh hell.
I have not been at the front.
I have been in front of it.
I held an advance post, that is, a 'dug-out' in the middle of No Man's Land.

We had a march of three miles over a shelled road, then nearly three along a flooded trench. From that we came to where the trenches had been blown flat out and had to go over the top. It was of course dark, too dark, and the ground was not mud, not sloppy mud, but an octopus of sucking clay, three, four and five foot deep, relieved only by craters full of water. Men have been known to drown in them. Many stuck in the mud and only got on by leaving their waders, equipment, and in some cases their clothes.

High explosives were dropping all around out, and machine guns spluttered every few minutes. But it was so dark that even the German flares did not reveal us.

Three quarters dead, I mean each of us three quarters dead, we reached the dug-out, and relieved the wretches therein. I then had to go forth and find another dug-out for a still more advanced post where I left 18 bombers. I was responsible for other posts on the left but there was a junior officer in charge.

My dug-out held 25 men tightpacked. Water filled to a depth of one or two ft., leaving four ft. of air.

lfred Owen photographed in uniform by John Gunston. *(Imperial War Museum, London)*

An old gun position in Sanctuary Wood in the Ypres sector, 25 October 1917. (*Imperial War Museum, London*)

One entrance had been blown in and blocked.
So far, the other remained.
The Germans knew we were staying there and decided we shouldn't.
Those 50 hours were the agony of my happy life.
Every ten minutes on Sunday afternoon seemed an hour.
I nearly broke down and let myself drown in the water that was now slowly rising over my knees.

Towards six o'clock, when, I suppose, you would be going to Church, the shelling grew less intense and less accurate: so that I was mercifully helped to do my duty and crawl, wade, climb and flounder over No Man's Land to visit my other post. It took me half an hour to move about 150 yards.

I was chiefly annoyed by our own mad guns from behind. The seeng-seng-seeng of the bullets reminded me of Mary's canary. On the whole I can support the canary better. In the Platoon on my left the sentries of the dug-out were blown to nothing. . . . I kept my own sentries half way down the stairs during the more terrific bombardment. In spite of this one lad was blown down and, I am afraid, blinded. . . .

I am now as well, I suppose, as ever.

I allow myself to tell you all these things because *I am never going back to this awful post*. It is the worst the Manchesters have ever held; and we are going back for a rest. . . .

As in his poems, Wilfred Owen expresses in Biblical images his outrage at the contrast between the world of soldiers at the front and that of the civilians at home.

30

SODOM AND GOMORRHA

19 January

They want to call No Man's Land 'England' because we keep supremacy there. It is like the eternal place of gnashing teeth; the Slough of Despond could be obtained in one of its crater-holes; the fires of Sodom and Gomorrha could not light a candle to it – to find the way to Babylon and the Fallen. It is pockmarked like a body of foulest disease and its odour is the breath of cancer. I have not seen any dead. I have done worse. In the dank air I have *perceived* it, and in the darkness, *felt*. Those 'Somme Pictures' are the laughing stock of the army – like the trenches on exhibition in Kensington. No Man's Land is like the face of the moon chaotic, crater-ridden, uninhabitable, awful, the abode of madness. To call it 'England'! I would as soon call my House Krupp Villa, or my child Chlorina-Phosgena. . . . The people of England needn't hope. They must agitate. But they are not yet agitated even.

After being evacuated with shell shock from the action at Fayet, Wilfred Owen writes to his brother from the 13th Casualty Clearing Station.

31

EXULTATION

14 May

. . . The sensations of going over the top are about as exhilarating as those dreams of falling over a precipice, when you see the rocks at the bottom surging up to you. I woke up without being squashed. Some didn't. There was an extraordinary exultation in the act of slowly walking forward, showing yourselves openly.

There was no bugle and no drum for which I was very sorry. I kept up a kind of chanting sing-song: keep the Line straight!

Not so fast on the Line!

Steady on the Line!

Not so fast!

Then we were caught in a Tornado of shells. The various 'waves' were all broken up and we carried on like a crowd moving off a cricket-field. When I looked back and saw the ground all crawling and worming with wounded bodies, I felt no horror at all but only an immense exultation at having got through the Barrage. We were more than an hour moving over the open and by the time we came to the German Trench every Boche had fled. But a party of them had remained lying low in a wood close behind us, and they gave us a very bad time for the next four hours. When we were marching along a sunken road, we got the wind up once. We knew we must have passed the German outposts somewhere on our left rear. All the time the cry rang down 'Line the Bank'. There was a tremendous scurry of fixing bayonets, tugging of breach-covers and opening pouches, but when we peeped over, behold one solitary German, haring along towards us, with his head down and his arms stretched in front of him, as if he were going to take a high dive through the earth (which I have no doubt he would like to have done). Nobody offered to shoot him, he looked too funny; that was our only prisoner that day!

Did I tell you that on Easter Sunday evening we brought down a Hun Plane, I took the aviator's handkerchief as a souvenir! It is not permitted to take anything belonging to the machine. . . .

Wilfred Owen went back to the front in September 1918 as a company commander and gained an MC. One week before the Armistice, he was machine-gunned when leading his men over the Sambre Canal. This is his last letter.

32

'It is a good life'

31 October 1918

Dearest mother,

I will call the place from which I'm now writing 'The Smoky Cellar of the Forester's House'. So thick is the smoke in this cellar that I can hardly see by a candle 12 ins.

away, and so thick are the inmates that I can hardly write for pokes, nudges and jolts. On my left the Company Commander snores on the bench. . . . At my right hand, Kellett, a delightful servant, radiates joy and contentment from pink cheeks and baby eyes, listening with his right ear to a merry corporal, who appears at this distance away (some three foot) nothing [but] a glance of white teeth and a wheeze of jokes.

Splashing my hand, an old soldier with a walrus moustache peels and drops potatoes into the pot. By him, Keyes, my cook, chops wood; another feeds the smoke with the damp wood.

It is a good life. I am more oblivious than alas! yourself, dear Mother, of the ghastly glimmering of the guns outside, and the hollow crashing of the shells.

There is no danger down here, or if any, it will be well over before you read these lines.

I hope you are as warm as I am; as serene in your room as I am here; and that you think of me never in bed as resignedly as I think of you always in bed. Of this I am certain you could not be visited by a band of friends half as fine as surround me here.

Ever Wilfred

The First World War had a much stronger impact on English views of war than any other, partly because it came so suddenly after a century of only rarely disturbed imperial peace, partly because it called for such terrible sacrifices. The wastage of the lives of the generous young men, ready to die in the 'obscenity' of the Flanders trenches, stirred up violent emotions which produced a generation of war poets and marked the beginning of a fundamental reassessment and a painful transformation of attitudes to war. In its final stages, the war foreshadowed an even more horrifying prospect of total war on whole populations by totalitarian regimes, made possible by the perfection of the engines of war through modern technology.

In an atmosphere of hatred, the claims of revenge ('Hang the Kaiser! Make Germany pay!') were understandably stronger than the sober recognition, found in some of our letters, that only wholehearted reconciliation could safeguard peace in the future: the seeds of the Second World War were sown at Versailles, not so much because the terms were harsh, but because they were modified too little to encourage the Weimar Republic and not enforced at all when Hitler swept them contemptuously away.

D-Day, 6 June 1944. (*Imperial War Museum, London*)

PART TWO

THE SECOND WORLD WAR

'Hitler kept us waiting'

First there will be fortitude – the power of
enduring when hope is gone . . .
There must be patience, supreme patience . . .
There must be resilience under defeat . . .
A manly optimism, which looks at the facts
in all their bleakness and yet dares to be confident
JOHN BUCHAN (1875–1940), THE GREAT CAPTAINS

The issues were clear cut in the Second World War: the German attacks on Poland, Norway, Belgium, Holland, France, Britain, the Balkan countries, and finally the Soviet Union, carried out with systematic ruthlessness and cruelty to the civilian populations, made it a true People's War. In contrast to the First World War, conflict broke out owing to an imbalance, and not an excess, of preparations, caused by Allied dissension and lack of resolution.

The British people in particular had come to dislike all violence and to believe in decency and kindness, and the possibility of solving all international conflicts by a fair-play compromise, in which they would act as a benign umpire. The expansionist imperial stance had increasingly given way to the love of a quiet life at home, on an island isolated from the self-assertive struggle of other nations.

For fifteen years the Armed Forces had been neglected, and mechanization of the Army and expansion of the Air Force had been left until it was almost too late. Nazi propaganda, backed by threats, found it easy to play on English guilt feelings over Versailles and readiness to accept even the most extreme claims with sympathy and to indulge in wishful thinking that good-will could be bought by wholesale concessions. The result was, understand-ably, an ignominious and fatal, though popular, appeasement policy, based on an ignorant and complacent misjudgement of the cynical and nihilist Nazi mentality.

Treaty obligations to small nations, an adapted version of the Schlieffen Plan, and, after 1941, the same Grand Alliance, were points of resemblance to the First World War, but the global extension of the conflict and the final occupation and division of Germany, as well as the defeat of the two Axis partners, Italy and Japan, who had been on the Allied side before, were dif-ferences. The mass-production of war machines of great precision also made the Second World War much more destructive, especially to civilians, although set battles of attrition only occurred in the Soviet Union.

Instead of the patriotic exultation and idealism ('war to end war') that characterized the outbreak of the First World War, there was a grim and sober determination to finish a job that had to be done, without indulging in any illusions; the division between fighting men and civilians tended to dis-appear and everybody shared the toil and danger of the war together. In face of much greater provocation, there was little of the sense of shock, perplexi-ty, and indignation which marked the First World War and this dispassion-ate outlook made it possible to arrive at an infinitely more sensible post-war settlement. Imperial posturing and hero worshipping had gone for ever.

The letters which follow illustrate the changes in social patterns and in attitudes to war; their factual exactitude and fluency of style reflect the effect of mass education, often at the expense of the power of personality, convic-tion, and evocative feeling.

PRELUDE

The Spanish Civil War, 1936–9

I fell on a black Spanish hillside
Under the thorn-hedge, fighting for a dream
SIDNEY KEYES (1922–43)

The Spanish Civil War provided the testing ground for the approaching conflict in that new methods of warfare could be tried out in action. It began with the first airlift in history, of General Franco's forces from Morocco, and continued with massed tank assaults, coordinated with the dive-bombers of the German Kondor Legion. It also showed that terror bombing of the civilian population, as in Madrid, far from breaking morale, actually hardened the determination to resist.

Franco was supported by 40,000 Italians and 10,000 German élite troops, while 15,000 French, 1,500 American and 1,000 British volunteers fought for the Republicans, side by side with many Soviet specialists. The young poet John Cornford became the folk-hero of the English Left: as leader of the Communist students at Cambridge, he rushed to Spain to join the POUM[1] militia and fight for his convictions. While Julian Bell, son of pacifist parents, drove an ambulance and found war 'a lesser evil balanced against some kind of peace' and life 'perpetually entertaining and better than most I've lived', Cornford tried to stir up his impassive, complacent compatriots with lines like:

> O understand before too late
> Freedom was never held without a fight

and

> England is silent . . . soon
> Here too our freedom's swaying in the scales.

---

1 Partido Obrero de Unificación Marxista.

Writing to his girlfriend who admired foremost his 'cold, gritty, loveless, cynical' intellect,[2] he unfolds a remarkable insight into the attitudes of a militant idealist of the Left in the thirties. Getting away from the security of his bourgeois home means freedom to him, yet he feels homesick with 'the same loneliness and isolation as the first term in a new school' and is anxious to achieve equality with his comrades in the baptism of fire. The haphazardness of action has rarely been described so vividly; like George Orwell in *Homage to Catalonia*, he captures the whole atmosphere on the Republican side of the Aragon front.

1

'I shall fight like a Communist if not like a soldier'

John Cornford (1915–36) to Margot Heinemann; he was killed in December, too naive to recognize (as Orwell did) that he was a pawn in a sectarian power struggle.

[Aragon front, autumn 1936]

Darling,

. . . Why I am here? You know the political reasons. There's a subjective one as well. From the age of 17 I was in a kind of way tied down, and envied my contemporaries a good deal their freedom to bum about. And it was partly because I felt myself for the first time independent that I came out here. . . .

At the moment I am on top of a hill at the front in Aragon. A complete circle of rocky mountains, covered with green scrub, very barren, with a few fields in between. Two kms. away a village held by the enemy. A grey stone affair with a big church. The enemy are quite invisible. An occasional rifle shot. One burst of machine gun fire. One or two aeroplanes. The sound of their guns sometimes a long way off. And nothing else but a sun so hot that I am almost ill, can eat very little, and scarcely work at all. Nothing at all to do. We lie around all day. At night two hours on the watch . . . How long we are going to be here I don't know. And so I am not only utterly lonely, but also feel a bit useless. This loneliness, and not yet having been under fire, means that inevitably I am pretty depressed. It's inactivity that just eats at my nerves. . . .

Going into action. Thank God for something to do at last. I shall fight like a Communist if not like a soldier. . . .

I came out with the intention of staying a few days firing a few shots, and then coming home. Sounded fine, but you just cannot do things like that. You cannot play at civil war, or fight with a reservation you don't mean to get killed. Having joined, I am in whether I like it or not. And I like it. Yesterday we went out to attack, and the

2   H.D. Ford, *A Poet's War*, Oxford University Press, 1965, *passim*.

prospect of action was terribly exhilarating. But in the end we went back without doing anything. But I am settling down and beginning to feel happy. I think I'll make a good fighter, and I'm glad to be here. So I'll probably be here for two months. There is a 70% chance of getting back uninjured and 90% of getting back alive; on the whole, worthwhile – and even if it wasn't, I'd have to stay. . . .

Altogether I've passed the worst days of mental crisis, though all the physical hardship is to come. But I think I'll bear up. For days I've been shoved from place to place, lost and anxious and frightened, and all that distinguished me personally from a unit in the mass obliterated; worried, home-sick, calm, hungry, sleepy, uncomfortable in turn – and all my own individuality submerged. Now I am beginning to adapt. Probably I'll be swept off my feet again when the first action starts. . . .

What is new is the complete feeling of insecurity, but most workers have it from the day they leave school. Before there has been the background of a secure and well-provided home. Now that is no longer here, I stand completely on my own. And I find that rather difficult at first. But I shall manage.

Yesterday I watched from the tiled roof of our hut the aerial bombardment of Perdiguera. The planes circling slowly and high above; then you would see a huge cloud of dust rising, beginning to float away, and then, seconds later, the sound of the crash. The comrades with me on the roof were shouting with delight as each bomb landed. I tried to think of the things in terms of flesh and blood and the horror of that village, but I also was delighted. . . .

Yesterday for the first time I was under fire. We marched all night through the mountains in the rear of the enemy. Then the advance began. We were soon crouching in the vineyards a few hundred yards from the village [Perdiguera], and for the first time I heard shots whistling overhead. It was then our total lack of discipline made itself felt. I began to understand the planless nature of the attack. I began to collect the completely unripe grapes in my hands and suck the juice out of them. It didn't do much to relieve thirst, but it left a clean acid taste in the mouth. Then I saw the group which had taken the houses on the left come pouring back and take shelter. All this time I couldn't see any of the enemy, and so confined myself to shooting at doors and windows. Then quite suddenly we heard the noise of enemy planes. We crouched quite still among the vines. Apparently the planes didn't notice us. They confined themselves to bombing the other side of Perdiguera, where we were attacking. But after the bomardment our forces were completely dispersed – not out of cowardice, no one was in the least frightened, but simply through lack of leadership. In the end it was decided to retreat. Then suddenly bullets began to whistle very close – zip-zip-zip. We sprinted up the fields in short bouts, bent double with the bullets all around us. We marched back across the fields to the hills. My throat was utterly dry, so thirsty I could not swallow, and hungry and very weary because the heat of the sun was colossal. We reached the top, and in spite of the fiasco I was beginning to feel better. At least I felt equal to the others, when, before, I had felt rather like a sham soldier. When we reached the first outpost we learned that five men had been killed. Then home, past the big amphitheatre round the stagnant village pond with its green reeds, past the bare strip of earth which was a football ground, and back into Llecinena.

I think the days spent in the village alone were the hardest I have yet spent in my whole life. The same loneliness and isolation as the first term in a new school. All the revolutionary enthusiasm was bled out of me. I simply counted the hours until it is time to go back. But I am beginning to find out how much the Party and the International have become flesh and blood of me. Even when I can put forward no rational argument, I feel that to cut adrift from the Party is the beginning of political suicide.

To-day I found with interest but not surprise the distortions in the P.O.U.M. press. The fiasco of the attack on Perdiguera is presented as a punitive expedition which was a success. . . .

From the 'Phoney War' to Dunkirk (September 1939–June 1940)

Eerie the hush in England ere the storm:
Still skies, the stillness heralding disaster
MARTYN SKINNER

In August 1939, amid feverish preparations, tension had mounted so much that it came as a great relief when war was at last declared: everybody had their gasmasks and black-out paper ready and three-and-a-half million children, and some mothers, were evacuated from London and other cities to the countryside. All hospitals were standing by for the hundreds of thousands of air-raid casualties which were expected to result from a knock-out holocaust the Germans were then quite incapable of inflicting. There was no cheering and dancing this time – only gloomy, determined apprehension.

2

HOW WAR CAME: THE EVACUATED CHILDREN ARRIVE

An English housewife to a friend in America.

Heathfield, Sussex, September 14, 1939
Looking back over the last two or three weeks – all days before the 3rd of September were so grimly alike, days of waiting and anxiety and inactivity – no one would settle down to the ordinary things of life.

I do remember the 26th of August. The situation was beginning to look terribly grave. Mr Greenwood urged, in the House, the immediate evacuation of children. We were asked to use the telephone for important messages only, and to telegraph only in cases of emergency. I had procured rolls of black paper from Harrods and lined the heavy curtains. George, as an Air Warden, was being called up by people who had neglected to get respirators, and he was out delivering them. It was nothing to hear him calling up Headquarters: 'Gas masks required – so many of various sizes and 8 baby small and 14 baby helmets.' I don't think I could ever hear 'baby gas masks' mentioned without a cold feeling in the pit of my stomach.

The week beginning August 27 is really a blank in my mind; each day the news became graver. It was like a serious illness in the house when nothing seems normal and meals were practically non-existent. Before the evacuated children came, George had not had two bites before the telephone went, and he was called, as the children were arriving, so he dashed off to help to distribute them in the neighbourhood.

The children had arrived in Heathfield by train where they had a medical examination; they were then driven to the Broad Oak School in buses – about 90 children the first day and 80 and their mothers the second. George told me that as the coach stopped at the school house, and the children with their little parcels and gas masks climbed down, one small boy darted across the road calling 'look at the flahs' and with his dirty little hands seized a big bunch of stinging nettles.

I shall never forget those little girls grasping their meagre possessions with their gas masks over their backs – their eager and dirty faces – Hazel's little shoulders showing through her ragged blouse and the tattered lining of the baby's coat. I wanted them to get a feeling of being at home before dark and George and I unpacked their luggage as well as we could through the tears in our eyes. We knew what the contents of those cases were going to be for we had listened night after night to instructions over the radio to the evacuated children – 1 tooth brush, 1 comb, 1 nightgown, 1 change of underclothing, if possible, soap, towel – and these were so neat, so poor, and I visualized the mother who had packed them, laying each ragged little garment in with aching heart.

Then Sunday the 3rd of September came. We had all heard of the important announcement that was to be made at 11 o'clock. I shall never forget the grave tone of Mr Chamberlain. We were at war. . . .

By the time the cumbersome French mobilization machinery had at long last safely installed the Army in the defensive warren of the Maginot Line,[1] and the five divisions of the British Expeditionary Force, with sixty tanks and four fighter squadrons, had taken up their allotted sector of the front, the Blitzkrieg in Poland was over: Hitler, who had gambled on Allied inertia and slowness, could now replenish the Western Front which had been lightly held by a mere twenty-three divisions against five times their number. The Germans prepared for the conquest of France, while the Allies, greatly relieved that the expected terror attack had not taken place, remained inactive and indulged in speculative wishful thinking that the economic blockade, or some fortuitous event, would lead to Germany's collapse.

---

1   D. Chandler has aptly called it 'the supreme rationalization of the trench systems of the First World War, transformed into steel and concrete' (*Art of Warfare*, Hamlyn, 1974, p. 218).

The War at Sea

Death is a matter of mathematics.
It screeches down at you from dirty white nothingness
And your life is a question of velocity and altitude,
With allowances for wind and the quick, relentless pull of gravity . . .
BARRY AMIEL

Meanwhile, the German U-boats and magnetic mines were reaping a terrible
harvest: many millions of tons of shipping were lost in the first nine months
of the war. The next letter gives a graphic description of what it was like to
be torpedoed and what feelings an army officer would experience.

3

'My manners never deserted me'

A young officer of the Royal Engineers to his aunt in London.

December 1939

Most of us on board ship were invalids, I had been in bed for eight weeks, and was
still unable to walk. The 17th October found us about 200 miles from land in the
Atlantic. After lunch I played a game of chess with the ship's doctor, an old
Scotsman. I remember he sat studying the board for two or three minutes, then –
'Aye, y've got ma rook,' and he advanced a pawn. I leant forward to take the piece,
but my hand never reached it, for there was a sudden crash and the chessmen went
flying across the deck. We had been torpedoed; the impossible had happened.

I found myself on my feet for the first time in eight weeks, and they gave beneath
me and I fell flat on my face, half in and half out of the saloon. My life-belt was under
my chair and I put it on. As I did so I saw a great red sheet of flame with smoky
edges hanging in the sky above our stern. I once more struggled to my feet, just in
time to be thrown over by the second torpedo which hit us amidships. Somebody
said, 'put your arm around my neck', and we all trooped off. My boat station was
Starboard 5. There was a companionway over No. 3 hatch, and it was here that the
second torpedo had struck us. There was a deep yawning hole. Hanging by one hand
to the corner of a tarpaulin and swinging over this abyss with kicking legs was a little
girl. She and two others had been playing on top of the hatch – the other two had
been killed. I saw a soldier pull her to safety. Byt this time our boat's complement
had collected, and we waited anxiously for its appearance. . . .

The *Yorkshire* was listing to starboard and something seemed to be wrong with the
lifeboat. And then, at last, our boat came down. God, but we were pleased to see it!
Some women started to get in and I waited on the steps wishing desperately that I
could do something; it was wretched just sitting on those steps – no good to anyone
and not much good to myself. The waves seemed to me to be nearer the deck, and in
truth they were, for suddenly the sea seemed to gather itself together and come

aboard us in a rush; a great green, smooth-backed wave surged over the side. Those standing around the boats were either swept overboard or trapped between the two decks; those of us who were still on our feet struggled up the companionway and down to the port deck.

I staggered to the side on watery legs, straddled the taffrail, and looked down. There was a boat in the water and several ropes leading down to it. These were the lifelines fastened above to the boat deck. Halfway down one of those ropes was a woman in yellow, clinging to it like a monkey to a stick. A man with a red face was in the boat trying to help her in; he looked up; his mouth was open and his eyes looked like saucers. The woman got off the rope and I slid down it. It must have been a twelve-foot drop and the lifeboat was jumping to the swell. But my arms felt strong, and I landed right in the middle and scrambled to the side. Several more people came down. Then somebody shouted: 'Trim the boat.' We all echoed his words but nobody did anything. And then in a desperate voice the same person shouted: 'Cast off, for God's sake, she's going.' The *Yorkshire* reared her bows into the air and slid backwards to the bottom. And we were still tied to her . . .

I remember being pinned between the gunwale of the lifeboat and a rope which was held taut across my chest. The davits were within a few feet. Beneath me was a tangled mass of ropes, oars, iron, and foaming water. I saw the red-faced man disappear into this turmoil, and then I was in it myself. There was a roar of rushing water, which almost but not quite obliterated the noise of screaming. . . . The water brought me back, if not to earth, at any rate to a realization of the imminence of death, and I started to struggle for life. I did not go deep: it never became dark, but was always frothy. Hard things swept by me. I groped upwards with my hands, and kicked with my feet. I remember thinking rather numbly: 'Suppose they will see it in the The *Times*. And then to my intense surprise I was on the surface, spluttering, but otherwise feeling remarkably well.

The first thing that struck me was that the sun was shining, and that the great ship had completely disappeared. . . . I came up within a foot of a life raft and caught hold of it. Somebody was close to me in the water. Looking back, I am more and more amazed by the unreality of the whole affair. I remember being seriously worried as to the propriety of scrambling on top of this raft. I was not '*au fait*' with ocean etiquette. For all I know, good Riflemen ought to hang on to the side. However, my scruples cannot have been very serious, for the next moment I was established on top. Then somebody with a dead white face and bleeding forehead came up beside me. I helped him on to the raft and he was horribly sick. His trousers had been sucked off. He said he was a cabin steward.

I know one is supposed to feel pretty grim perched precariously on a raft in the middle of the Atlantic, but I didn't. I have seldom felt better. I suppose the realization that one wasn't dead was such an inexpressible relief that anything else seemed trivial by comparison. I felt rather like one does on coming to after laughing gas: I had the giggles. My manners, I am proud to say, never deserted me: I remember asking my companion whether he could find it in his goodness to forgive me if I made so bold as to relieve myself. . . .

There were two other rafts, each with two men on them, quite close; otherwise we could see nothing except the other ships of the convoy making off as hard as they could. It was only then that I remembered that they were forbidden to pick us up. We should have to wait until warships arrived – perhaps for many hours. I stopped giggling. And then a lifeboat appeared, threw us a rope, and we made fast. We were then towed about for two hours. They picked up a poor woman who was clinging to a piece of wood, and an unconscious man who was starfished on a hatch board. He was covered with engine oil and had a great bloody eye. . . .

At length we were joined by four other lifeboats which were towed by a small motor boat. Somebody shouted at me from one of these boats: 'Have you seen my wife?' And then, and not till then, so selfish is man, did I realize how lucky I was to have no one to ask after. . . . It soon got dark, and our optimism waned with the light. The sea looked cruel as death, and the swell seemed more formidable, the wind increased a little and began to break the tops of the swell. It was pretty cold and my wretched pyjamas were not much protection. Almost everybody was seasick. Their moans of misery made a fitting background to the scene. Some of us sang. 'Speed Bonny Boat' and 'Loch Lomond' were inevitable if inappropriate choices, and they must have sounded dismal, but they warmed us up.

And then we saw a light – only a pin-point – but definitely a light. It was a long way away, but by God, it looked good! We had some flares and these we lit. . . . We strained our eyes and tried to think that the light was coming nearer. We watched it for an hour or more, and then it faded out of sight.

It is extraordinary how much that feeble light had meant to us. While it was there, we had forgotten the intense discomfort. But as soon as it disappeared the world suddenly became a darker and a colder place, and I, for one, felt for the first time the vastness of the ocean. How could any ship hope to find us? It seemed impossible. Everybody got sick again. I was feeling by this time that I really didn't mind terribly if I was drowned, if only the damned boat would stop bucking about for half a minute.

Then I think I must have slept, for when I looked up again there was the light, but this time it was bigger and closer. By God, it was a good sight! It was a ship, and coming towards us. Not a moan from anyone now. In a minute we were all cracking jokes and shaking hands. The steward and I thumped each other on the backs, and when the next flare went up I saw that his face was wreathed in smiles. Soon we could see the navigation lights, and in another minute a signal was ordering us to come to the starboard side. Quite soon we were alongside, and it is impossible to describe the wonderful feeling that the ship gave us. She was an American freighter and I have never heard anything so sweet as the sound of those American voices, as the crew leant over the side and hailed us: 'How y're making out, you fellas?'

The *Independence Hall* was bound for New York. She had, by the grace of God, 80 beds in the hold. There were over 300 of us in that hold; the crew of another torpedoed ship had already been picked up. We were as tight as sardines in a tin, all mixed together in an indescribable hotch-potch of black and white bodies. But nothing mattered; everything was heaven. We talked most of the night: I think all of us were a little chary of closing our eyes. I know that I was for one. Whenever I tried to sleep I saw the *Yorkshire* slipping back, saw the staring eyes and open mouth of the red-faced man as he disappeared beneath that foaming mass of tangled ropes and wreckage. . . .

The sinking of the aircraft-carrier *Courageous* in September, and of the battleship *Royal Oak* in October by an incredible penetration of the defences of Scapa Flow, were deeply felt blows struck by submarines. Convoys, extended right across the Atlantic, were the answer to this threat, together with an improvement in the technique of submarine detection; degaussing with electrically charged cables neutralized the equally deadly magnetic mines.

4

'Close up and keep station'
A CONVOY GETS THROUGH

A merchant captain describes the sinking of a German submarine to George Johnston.

[undated]

We were bound from Montreal with industrial chemicals and plane parts. Soon after leaving we received instructions regarding our course and the position where we were to assemble to await the arrival of other merchant ships and the naval escorts. We butted north-east in a rising gale with bad visibility and an ugly sea. On the following night, soon after sun-down, the air became thick with radio signals. There seemed to be ships everywhere, all asking for positions and instructions and details of the convoy. By midnight we had reached the rendezvous – or at least what I thought was the rendezvous, for we had been making a course by dead reckoning in lousy weather. The noise of ships all around indicated that my reckoning couldn't be far out. Soon afterwards a small rangy destroyer whipped by close alongside, throwing it green right over her forward turret and rolling like a pig. Her signal lamp winked at us: 'What ship is that?' We told them and they gave us our position in the convoy and asked us to steam on such-and-such a course at nine knots. The destroyer washed away. God, what a life those boys had, week in and week out in the worst weather in the world.

I remained on the bridge all night. Although we couldn't see them – every ship was blacked out – there must have been ships everywhere, all washing around in the driving squalls and big seas. It's a wonder to me we don't lose half our merchant ships in collisions during the forming-up of convoys, but the destroyers looked after us. With the first streak of dawn we could see the 22 ships – passenger liners, freighters, timber droghers and a couple of tankers – bulking blackly in the grey light. We began to form up in position. There were three destroyers. One of them made a flag signal: 'Speed nine knots; course so-and-so.' A few minutes later another signal: 'Close up and keep station.' The ships were rolling and kicking quite a lot. A stiff easterly wind was whipping the top of a nasty swell.

Just at dusk a freighter was torpedoed: smoke and steam billowed into the air. A gigantic smoke ring spiralled slowly upward. The ship sank within about four minutes. The destroyers were on the spot immediately. Great columns of water were thrown up as depth-charge after depth-charge exploded. The merchant ships were scattering and zigzagging at full speed. The destroyers apparently had the position of the submarine fixed by their A.S.D.I.C.[2] equipment for they continued to hunt over one patch of torn water. The crew of the sunken ship had got to rafts tossed overside from the destroyers. My second mate yelled to me that he could see the periscope ahead of the destroyers but I couldn't see it. The destroyers were jumping themselves now at the crash of the depth-charges.

---

2   Allied Submarine-Detection Investigation Committee (1917) which developed a special kind of hydrophone, giving the direction and distance of a submarine but not its depth.

A little later a big column of steam belched from the water, and this time all of us could see the cigar-shaped hull of the submarine break the surface with a hell of a splash. The Germans came to the deck and dived overboard. About ten seconds later the submarine stood on its nose, spun slowly and dived down. Most of the ships in the convoy hoisted signals of congratulation to the destroyers. It certainly was the slickest piece of work I've ever seen. The only answer from the leading destroyer was: 'Speed –, course –; close up and keep station.'

On 13 December the pocket battleship *Graf Spee*, a surface raider which had sunk or captured nine merchant ships, was challenged near the River Plate by three light cruisers under Commodore Harwood which opened fire. The *Graf Spee*, with its eleven inch guns, first inflicted heavy damage on the *Exeter* (eight inch guns) but was prevented from finishing her off by the gallant attacks from the *Achilles* and *Ajax* with only 5.9 inch guns; the latter had both turrets and its topmast shot off. Although not greatly damaged, the *Graf Spee* sought refuge in Montevideo harbour and – rather than face the heavy British reinforcements the Germans believed to be waiting for them – scuttled herself on the 17th; in fact, there were only two light cruisers outside and the capital ships arrived two days later. Captain Parry wrote on the 20th about Captain Langsdorff: 'Poor devil! We've just got the news that he's shot himself. I feel sorry for him.' In the following letters he scoffs at BBC news.

5

THE BATTLE OF THE RIVER PLATE

Captain (later Admiral Sir) Edward Parry (1893–1972) of HMS *Achilles* to his father.

27th December 1939

Some of the BBC accounts of our action with the *Graf Spee* have been absurd. It makes one distrust all the other dope they hand out. . . .

I had sent our sailors away to breakfast, and was about to go down for my bath, when a ship was reported. I watched her come over the horizon. I am not sure which of us first exclaimed 'My God! It's a pocket battleship'. . . . The *Spee* opened fire first, and concentrated on the *Exeter*, who bore the brunt of the action. . . . We finally retired from the dreadfully close range of four or five miles. Why we weren't hit more, I can't imagine. This ship had no direct hits at all, but was peppered with fragments from shells which must have burst on hitting the water very near us. . . . There was a terrific souvenir hunt directly the action was over. The one fragment which penetrated the bridge structure knocked me over. The shock numbed my leg and prevented my feeling anything. A jolly lucky escape!

At first one felt awfully frightened – at least I did – and whenever one saw the enemy's guns go off, one wondered where the shells would land. . . . After a bit one got over one's terror; and when I was hit, I felt more surprised to see my leg bleeding than anything else. . . . We finally retired under a smoke screen. The enemy still looked quite undamaged; and although I had distinctly seen some of our shells hit them they had bounced off without doing much harm. The rest of Wednesday we spent in chasing them. . . .

The next few days gave us a very anxious time – and all the claims of a British victory struck us as very premature. Whether he believed all the B.B.C. stories of what was waiting for him outside, one doesn't know. If so, it was good propaganda, I suppose. But at the time it struck us as no better than a pious hope. Anyhow I didn't get my clothes off till after he blew himself up; not did I leave the bridge at all during the dark hours. . . .

The last act was exciting. We had an aircraft watching her; and what a relief it was when she reported a heavy explosion on board, then that she was still afloat with a heavy list. By this time both *Ajax* and ourselves had every available man on deck; and the cheers as the two ships passed one another was terrific and most thrilling. It was nearly dark by this time; and as we steamed towards Montevideo we could see a dull red glow in the sky. . . . After midnight we turned away at a distance of two or three miles from the wreck which was blazing away merrily. And then I think every available man, including myself, had their first good sleep for some days. . . .

We were just as surprised to find ourselves so much in the limelight, as we were at the *Graf Spee*'s 'inglorious end' (a jolly good Winston-ism!). It was also very pleasant to hear our little squadron referred to as 'the three cruisers whose names are on everyone's lips'. . . .

Italy declared war on 10 June 1940. The Italian fleet and air force in the Mediterranean were numerically greatly superior to the British forces there – six battleships to four, nineteen cruisers to eight, fifty destroyers to twenty, and six hundred bombers to barely one hundred – yet they were loth to give battle. Admittedly the British had the aircraft carrier *Illustrious* whose torpedo bombers were to knock out half the Italian fleet in November at Taranto: air power increasingly dominated naval battles and commanded the sea.

On 9 July 1940, off Calabria, five light cruisers under Admiral Sir John Tovey bravely challenged the Italian fleet, although they were severely outgunned. When the battleship *Warspite* (Admiral Sir Andrew Cunningham) came to their rescue by hitting the *Giulio Cesare*, the Italians disappeared behind a smoke-screen, trying to lure the British within range of their shore-based planes and submarine barrage, without risk to themselves owing to their greater speed. The Italian planes dropped hundreds of bombs indiscriminately on the British as well as the Italian fleets, without, however, hitting either of them – except one unlucky hit on the *Gloucester* which killed the captain.

The commander of one of the cruisers exaggerated enemy losses in his elation – a feature of the whole war, particularly in aerial combat (official British claims were sometimes nearly double, and German ones up to triple, the actual figures). It was an understandable combination of wishful thinking in the heat of battle and an attempt to boost morale.

The *Graf Spee* after scuttling herself, 17 December 1939. (*Royal Naval Museum, Portsmouth*)

Dunkirk beach scene, 1940. *(Royal Naval Museum, Portsmouth)*

6

'BOO' TO THE ITALIAN FLEET

A naval commander to a friend in America.

July 20, 1940

My, but we have had *some* fun lately. Your newspapers will have told you of the inglorious retreat of the Italian fleet when we said 'boo' to them. It was a lovely party, and I am allowed to tell you something about it, as the censorship has been lifted a wee bit.

We were at sea moving to cover the passage of one of our convoys from Malta when we heard that the whole Italian fleet was at sea. I guess they didn't hear that we were, too. Our fleet air arm quickly got them under observation and there seemed just a wee chance that we could intercept them. We set off at speed and, although we were bombed continuously, we kept going. At about 4 p.m. on the 9th, to our delight we sighted four of their cruisers. Our C.-in-C. detached our little bunch and told us to go and bite them.

We dashed off, but had not gone far when nine more large cruisers, two battleships and between 20 and 30 destroyers appeared over the horizon. It looked like the end of our small squadron. However, we kept pressing in through a hail of bricks [shells]. We had just started to let our guns rip when the C.-in-C. hove in sight. He saw how overweighted we were and ordered us to retire on him for support. We were not sorry to, although we were getting in some pretty good shooting. So we joined C.-in-C. and he sent us in again under the support of his big guns.

He took on the battleships and, while we were rushing in, he scored a lovely hit on the forecastle of one of them. All their cruisers were taking a crack at us and were shooting unpleasantly near. Then we started in. We quickly hit one of their big cruisers, and a destroyer laid a smoke screen to hide her so we let the destroyer have a packet, too, and got a hit. She, too, then disappeared into the smoke. Their battleships, in the meantime, got worried, and with a destroyer escort making smoke, they turned and ran. Their destroyers made an ineffective torpedo attack which was never pressed home. Our destroyers were sent in to counter-attack and were a lively sight as they sped along in perfect formation with their guns blazing. By the time they were through to the other side of the smoke, the enemy had gone. We went around the end of the smoke to cut off any retreat on Taranto, but all we found was perfect visibility and a clear horizon. We pushed right on into sight of the Italian coast but it was no use. In the meantime, all the available aeroplanes were dropping eggs around us to no effect and we took a useful toll of them.

We believe the Italians had two big ships hit and two destroyers and one submarine sunk.[3] With their overwhelming superiority in numbers and speed, they should have wiped us out but, thank God, they could not stand up to being hit and ran away instead. Although bombed continuously, we got our convoy through and reached port safely.

---

3   Only the *Cesare* was hit and no destroyer or submarine was sunk.

This job is not a rest cure, and when censorship lifts, I've a few more tales to tell. I am as fit as a fiddle and full of the joy of spring.

Early in 1940 the ghost of Gallipoli returned: a plot was hatched to send an Anglo-French expeditionary force of 100,000 to aid the Finns against the Soviet Union, and take Narvik and destroy the Swedish iron-ore mines on the way. Not surprisingly, the Norwegians and Swedes would not cooperate, and the even more fantastic French plan to bomb Baku was, mercifully, turned down by Britain. Fortunately, the Finns surrendered in March, and as soon as Chamberlain had announced in his naive delusion that Hitler had 'missed the bus', the German blitzkrieg was let loose on Norway, Belgium, Holland and France.

Ten panzer divisions, backed by one parachute and one air portable division, in close liaison with Stuka dive-bombers, had been fashioned by General Guderian on Captain Liddell Hart's[4] and Colonel Fuller's ideas of a mechanized élite army, with Hitler's backing in the face of General Staff opposition. The Germans were facing numerically more than equal Allied forces whose tanks, though heavier and in larger numbers, were, with the exception of a single armoured division, strung out ineffectually in 1918 style; the *Luftwaffe*, on the other hand, was greatly superior both in quality and numbers. The 'impossible' surprise thrust through the Ardennes Forest, bypassing the Maginot Line, and the rapid exploitation of the breach it created by relentless pursuit and deep penetration cut the arteries behind the Allied forces in a new mobile warfare against the traditional static defence line: it was *'Achtung! Panzer!'*, Guderian's up-to-date manual of 1937, versus the 'continuous fortified front' of 'peaceful and defensive France', based on ossified French General Staff doctrine, adhering to the very principle of immobility (*'contre-motorisatrice'*)!

The first surprise move by the Germans had been into Norway on 9 April to safeguard their Baltic flank and the vital supply line of Swedish iron ore against imminent Allied attack. Forestalled in his plans, Churchill talked of Hitler having been 'provoked' into committing a 'strategic blunder'. But the speed and daring of the German invasion of Norway secured Trondheim, Narvik and Oslo, before the numerically superior Anglo-French forces, with insufficient equipment, training and air cover, could be landed by an overcautious Admiralty. The slow, overland pincer movement from Namsos and Andalsnes towards the lightly held key city of Trondheim got stuck in the snow and was abandoned after a fortnight. The frustration caused by the muffed Allied counter-strokes and the reluctance of the Admiralty to expose the Navy to German air attack stung Sir Roger Keyes, the hero of the blockade of the German submarine base at Zeebrugge in 1918, into urging

4   B.H. Liddell Hart's *History of the Second World War*, Cassell, 1970, has been an invaluable work of reference.

Churchill to let him sail with his Royal Marines into Trondheim, in emulation of the feats of Wolfe and Saunders at Quebec, and of Hawke at Quiberon Bay. After trying in vain to open Churchill's 'overworked tired eyes' to his 'vision', he wrote again, bitterly disappointed, but still with the fire of bygone rugged sea captains, the last in the line from Drake to Fisher and Beatty.

7

'Your pusillanimous, self-satisfied, short-sighted Naval advisers'

Admiral Sir Roger (later Baron) Keyes (1872–1945) implores Churchill, First Lord of the Admiralty, to put his trust in him; he later became Director of Combined Operations at the age of sixty-eight.

29/4/40

I am not very quick with my tongue, and was not nimble enough to stem the flow of words you used to justify the shocking inaction of the Navy at Trondhjem, for which you and your pusillanimous, self-satisfied, short-sighted Naval advisers must bear the responsibility.

We have been three weeks at war on the Norway Coast, and many mistakes which were made in the conduct of the Gallipoli Campaign by the Admiralty and Government have been, or are about to be, repeated on the Norway Coast.

It is indeed a sorry tale. You were scathing, when I referred eleven days ago to the verdict which history would pass on Naval inaction, and said you were making war not history. Well you won't have to wait for history for the scathing denunciation you have merited. . . .

If the people responsible for the mess into which we have drifted cannot be induced to steel their hearts and make bolder decisions, they will be swept away. . . . There is still just time now to make a tremendous effort to turn the tide of retreat by capturing Trondhjem. Give me the small force I asked for and the Royal Navy and its Sea Soldiers will show the world that they can stand up to any German air attack. We will strike a blow which will help to decide the issue. For God's sake put your trust in me and don't waste any more time. We will have to do it in the end, and it will be far harder. . . .

At the same time, a force of 24,000 Allied soldiers, held up by snow and confusion, was very slowly closing in on the 4,000 Germans in the vital iron-ore port of Narvik. In view of the critical situation in France, and the threat of invasion of England, it was decided to take the town for face-saving but to sail home immediately afterwards. The newly appointed Army Commander under Admiral Lord Cork is fully conscious of the gravity of the situation, but seems most anxious not to sound pessimistic.

8

'It makes me sick with shame'

Lieutenant-General (later Field Marshal Sir) Claude Auchinleck (1884–1981) to General Dill, the new CIGS.

30 May 1940

. . . This is a queer show into which you put me! What with French, Norwegians, Poles and the Navy I find I have to keep a pretty wary eye on things and to cultivate a nimble tongue. I know you can't help it, but honestly Lord Cork and I are in a pretty impossible position at the moment. Nothing to France of course, but still just a wee bit difficult . . . The worst of it all is the need for lying to all and sundry in order to preserve secrecy. The situation vis-à-vis the Norwegians is particularly difficult and one feels a most despicable creature in pretending that we are going on fighting, when we are going to quit at once. . . .

It is not an easy war to wage but it is interesting enough! I hope I may be able to help you to make a new Army. It will have to be a very different one from our last. War has changed. We are in the same position as were Napoleon's adversaries when he started in on them with his new organization and tactics!! I feel we are much too slow and ponderous in every way. . . .

It is lamentable that in this wild undeveloped country where we, with all our wealth of experience, should be at our best, are outmanoeuvred and outfought every time. It makes me *sick* with shame. The French are all right, real soldiers.[5] As I said, our new armies will have to be very different from our old if we are going to recover our lost ascendancy in battle. . . .

[Across the top Auchinleck wrote: 'Before you read this, please be assured that I am *not* consumed with pessimism! I am very well and in good heart! So is everyone else.']

On 8 June, the aircraft-carrier *Glorious*, with an extra load of fighter planes and escorted by only two destroyers, was sailing 200 miles ahead of Lord Cork's convoy which was evacuating 24,500 Allied troops from Norway; she suddenly ran into the battle-cruisers *Scharnhorst* and *Gneisenau* against whose eleven inch guns she was defenceless. She was ablaze before her five unranged and unarmed Swordfish torpedo-bombers could load and take off, and sank after an hour, despite the smoke-screen and torpedo attacks from the brave destroyers. The *Ardent* went down too but the *Acasta* (Commander Glasfurd) bravely fought on alone and succeeded in inflicting such heavy damage on the *Scharnhorst* that she had to limp back to Trondheim under the protection of the *Gneisenau*. Thus the only lightly escorted convoy, unsupported by the Home Fleet, was saved;

---

5   *'Chasseurs Alpins'* under General Béthouart.

the *Acasta* finally sank too with the loss of its entire crew except one. The Germans made no attempt to rescue any survivors from the three ships, and nearly two thousand seamen, with twenty-five precious planes and their crews, perished in the sea.[6]

9

THE SOLE SURVIVOR OF THE *ACASTA*

Leading-Seaman C. Carter writes home.

[June 1940]

... On board our ship, what a deathly calm, hardly a word spoken, the ship was now steaming full speed away from the enemy and all our smoke floats had been set going. The Captain then had this message: 'You may think we are running away from the enemy, we are not, our chummy ship has sunk, the *Glorious* is sinking, the least we can do is to make a show, good luck to you all.' We then altered course into our own smoke-screen. I had the order to stand by to fire tubes 6 and 7, we then came out of the smoke-screen, altered course to starboard firing our torpedoes from port side. It was then I had my first glimpse of the enemy and we were very close. I fired my two torpedoes, the foremost tubes fired theirs, we were all watching results. I'll never forget that cheer that went up; on the port bow of one of the ships a yellow flash and a great column of smoke and water shot up. We knew we had hit, personally I could not see how we could have missed so close as we were. The enemy never fired a shot at us, I feel they must have been very surprised.

After we had fired our torpedoes we went back into our own smoke-screen, altered course again to starboard. 'Stand by to fire remaining torpedoes'; and this time as soon as we poked our nose out of the smoke-screen, the enemy let us have it. A shell hit the engine-room, killed my tubes' crew, I was blown to the after end of the tubes, I must have been knocked out for a while, because when I came to, my arm hurt me; the ship had stopped with a list to port. Believe it or not, I climbed back into the control seat, I see those two ships, I fired the remaining torpedoes, no one told me to, I guess I was raving mad. God alone knows why I fired them, but I did. The *Acasta*'s guns were firing the whole time, even firing with a list on the ship. The enemy then hit us several times, but one big explosion took place right aft, it seemed to lift the ship out of the water. At last the Captain gave orders to abandon ship. I will always remember the Surgeon Lt., his first ship, his first action. Before I jumped over the side, I saw him attending to the wounded, a hopeless task, and when I was in the water I saw the Captain leaning over the bridge, take a cigarette from a case and light it. We shouted to him to come on our raft, he waved 'Good-bye and good luck' – the end of a gallant man.

---

6   This disaster was due to a mentally unstable captain steaming off in a huff to deal with a court martial, without bothering to protect the *Glorious* by a Swordfish patrol, and the failure of the Admiralty to believe and pass on a warning from the code-breakers at Bletchley that the German battle-cruisers were lying in wait.

On the day of this tragic battle in the North Sea, Thomas Jones, Deputy Secretary of the Cabinet until 1931, who had twice visited Hitler with his friend Lloyd George in 1936 and was still close to Whitehall, assesses the profound change in outlook at home, brought about by the desperate situation.

10

'At last the country is awake and working'

Thomas Jones (1870–1955) to Dr Abraham Flexner of Princeton University.

Wittersham, Kent
June 8, 1940
. . . Everyone in England is abnormally sensitive to the beauty of this summer. Grasses look greener, scents are stronger, birds merrier in the trees because we feel all may be ruined in the next few weeks. From where I write I can hear the occasional booming of a gun in France. . . .

The coming of Winston to the top and the accession of Bevin and Morrison have wrought a profound change in the consciousness of the multitude. At last the country is awake and working. It began with Norway, and all that has followed since has quickened the pace of all in work, and the impatience of all not directly helping the national effort. Muddles and confusion there will always be and enormous leeway to make up, all the more after the gigantic losses of equipment which Winston openly admitted in his great speech. That is where we are so earnestly looking to you. . . .

Here on the home front the chief preparations are against P's and Q's, Parachutes and Quislings, and if we are given time – now so precious – we shall have some sort of protection devised. I hope you can hurry across lots of rifles and ammunition. . . .

Dunkirk

At Dunkirk I
Rolled in the shallows, and the living trod
Across me for a bridge
SIDNEY KEYES

When the German armour seemed to have the BEF in their grasp, Rundstedt, with Hitler's approval, suddenly halted ten miles from Dunkirk. What was the reason? Conservation of tanks for the conquest of France after the heavy losses inflicted on Rommel's 7th panzer division by a solitary depleted British tank brigade at Arras on 21 May? Goering's boast that the *Luftwaffe* would finish off the remnants of the BEF? Or, less likely, Hitler's hope to conclude a compromise peace with the British Empire he admired? Whatever the reason, helped by this short respite, the stubborn Franco-British rearguard actions by day and well-organized evacuation by night swelled the figure of 45,000 expected to be rescued by Operation Dynamo from the Dunkirk beaches, to an incredible 200,000 British and 140,000 French soldiers. They were picked up between 27 May and 4 June by destroyers with the aid of many hundreds of little private boats, bravely, if often inadequately, shielded by the RAF against Goering's dive-bombers. But the material losses were heavy: 228 ships, 177 planes, and all the 1,000 guns, 600 tanks, 850 anti-tank guns and vast stores which had to be left behind.

11

'Hell let loose'

A young Sussex corporal describes the anxious wait on the beach.

[June 1940]
. . . Dawn! Somehow, noboby knows why or how, we made our way towards Dunkirk. Each mile we met more men, trucks and guns, horses, everything in fact, on the narrow foul roads. At last far away in the distance we saw huge palls of black smoke reaching up to the heavens above. Hell let loose on earth! . . .

Subjected to the most incessant bombardment from several sides, and, of course, from overhead, we made our way through what remained of Dunkirk. The roads were covered with broken glass, telephone wires and tram cables here, there and everywhere; lorries, trucks, guns and motor-cycles lay about broken, smashed and never to be used again.

The beach at last. What a sight! Troops, troops everywhere, and out in the bay what remained of some boats . . . One hour, two hours, three, four, five, six hours, waiting there on the beach. At last we were moving? Yes! yes! towards the Mole. 'Make your way to the pier head along the Mole in batches of 50.' At last! Suddenly a high-pitched whine and a shell smashed into the Mole, right in a bunch of 50 men. It had started!

Then the order 'Forward the regiment!' Slow, slow, but each step bringing us nearer home, and also to that mangled mass there, left on the Mole. The fifties stopped. We were to wait there in the open until the next boat came up to the pier head. . . . We lay there, then once again towards the boat. At last we were on board and then they started to shell once again, but the shells fell the other side of the Mole, thank goodness!

12

'My only regret – one of our Rover Scouts was left behind'

Private J. Toomey, still dazed but indomitably cheerful, gives a graphic account of Dunkirk.

Darlington [n.d.]

Dear Folks,

Just a line to let you know that I am still knocking about. Would you like to hear all about the war straight from the horse's mouth? When the war started we moved so fast and often that I didn't have time to take any notice of names. . . . We drank a bottle of rum another of Cognac biscuit to get some sleep, the air raid siren was in the church tower opposite . . . . A day or two later we were in a chateau farmhouse affair when a dog fight developed about 1000 feet above and Messerschmitts, Hurricanes and Spitfires were having a hell of a good time. I don't know who won, I was being busy dodging planes bullets, and A.A. shrapnel. From that day onwards my tin hat stayed on my head even in bed sometimes. . . . Before we made the Dunkirk dash, the dive bombers came over and bombed us. Never look a dive bomber in the face, cos if you do you can bet your sweet life things are going to hum soon, but pray and pray hard and run, run like hell for the nearest ditches and dive into them. . . .

We had got separated from our crowd and were alone in the middle of the night in France or was it Belgium, anyway we were lost. As dawn came we found the main Dunkirk road and what a jam, after about ten hours of stopping and starting, driving into ditches and back into lorries we got near Dunkirk and here we had to dash thru' a barrage of shrapnel so we slammed the old bus into top and went flat-out down the road. When we were on the outskirts of Dunkirk we got out and looked up – there were about 70 bombers (German make, naturally, we hadn't seen one of our planes for three weeks!!!) knocking hell out of the blocks or what was left of them. From there to the beaches and they were black with troops waiting to go aboard only there were no boats. They gave us a raid that lasted from dawn to dusk, about 17 hours. The fellows laid down on open beaches with the bombs falling alongside us, lucky it was sand, it killed the effect of the bombs.

The following day dawn broke and we saw the most welcome sight of all: about a dozen destroyers off the beaches and more coming up – boats of all shapes and sizes, barges, skylarks, lifeboats and yachts. . . . We hadn't had water for a fortnight it was too risky to drink and all we could get was champagne and wines. Spirits only made us thirstier. However on the morning I had a drink of vin blanc and had to sit down I was drunk as a lord, the last time I had anything to eat was about three days off and on an empty stomach the wine had a devastating effect. That evening we went aboard after dash after dash up the jetty to dodge shrapnel. There were about 1800 of us on one small destroyer. When we were an hour's run off Dover and thought we were safe a bomber came down and slammed three bombs at us – missed us by 6 ft. We got to Dover at 2 am and climbed aboard a train, we were still scared to light cigarettes, a light on the beaches meant a hail of bombs, and we just drowsed, at Reading we got out and shambled to the road. It was about 8 am and people just going to work stopped and stared, we must have looked a mob, none of us shaved or wash for a week, our uniform was ripped and torn, with blood and oil stains. Two old dears took one look at us and burst into tears. I don't blame them, I frightened myself when I looked into a mirror. . . .

The times were rather tough and altho' I was scared stiff for three weeks it was something I wouldn't want to have missed. My only regret was that one of our Rover Scouts was left behind.

Still, *c'est la guerre*. Chin, chin. Love to all.

Jack

The civilian writer of the following letter sees it all in a haze of exaltation: another Corunna, on a much larger scale, and again glorified more than a victory! As for the soldiers, they were relieved to have escaped but had lost none of their assurance and good spirits.

13

'We held them; we held them'

A schoolteacher describes to a friend in America the trainloads of undaunted soldiers.

London, June 11, 1940

I got off last week-end and found there were no trains going to Reading as the B.E.F. were coming through every few minutes. I had a most roundabout journey and at Ascot had to wait for an hour, and on the platform was a whole trainload of the soldiers. They were unshaven and dirty, and their eyes looked as if they were at the very back of their heads, and many of them were stretched full length on the platform, in the hot sun, sound asleep. But the others! Their cheerfulness was beyond words and their faces were lit up and shining through the sunburn and dirt.

One, about half my size, gripped me by the arm and with his eyes blazing said, 'We held them; we held them; they were ten to one, but we held them.' It was no beaten army, it was a triumphant one, confident of the future and eager to get out and come to grips with the enemy again. They made you feel that it would be shameful to be downhearted or frightened and that the stuff that was England was there, as it must have been long before the Crusades. I passed trainloads of them, and at the stations they were hanging out of the windows, their tired faces cheerfully grinning, and behind them always men sound asleep. . . .

The novelist Alec Waugh evokes the momentous change in the character of war and the attitude to it. He recalls the 'complacent confidence' of the days of the 'phoney war' which seem to him so distant now, and his rude awakening to 'a new kind of warfare' in thirteen days of bombing terror in Flanders, worse than Ypres. He has become aware that 'total war is not waged along a fixed set line' and that there is 'no immunity in distance' any longer. Under threat of invasion, England is gripped by a new spirit of resolution.

14

IT IS TOTAL WAR NOW

Captain Alec Waugh (1898–1981) to his American publisher, John Farrar.

London, June [1940]

Is it really only seven weeks ago that I was writing to tell you how I had just joined the B.E.F., how I had finished a novel in my spare time during my last months of training at my depot; that I was describing how gay life had become in England in spite of the blackout and the budget, how crowded the London restaurants were, how Minsky's had nothing on the night club cabarets, how in the country town where my regiment was stationed, someone seemed to throw a party of some kind every other evening. That letter must have reached you just about the time that the Germans were pouring over the bridgeheads on the Meuse. It must have made strange reading.

Seven weeks ago. It seems incredible now that I could ever have written to you in such a strain. It seems incredible now that not only I but the whole country could have awaited for the long threatened spring offensive in a spirit of such completely complacent confidence. For we did. There was not the least sign of anxiety. . . .

I think now, most of us think now, that it would have been better if the war had really started in September. We were keyed up then for spectacular events. And when the curtain did not go up, unconsciously we relaxed. We did not know that we were relaxing, but we did. The B.E.F. was transported to France without the loss of a single man or gun. The income tax was raised. Blackout regulations were enforced. Production of war materials was increased. A strict censorship was imposed. There were evacuations not only of slum children but of whole office staffs. The training of the new armies was organized at a series of training centres throughout the country. We all believed ourselves to be working harder than we had ever worked before. As we were. The only trouble was that we were not working hard enough. Because there were no air raids, because there were no casualty lists, we relaxed to the sense of immunity bred in us by such phrases as 'Time is on our side'; 'We are waging a siege war'; 'Hitler has missed the bus'. We believed that we had only to endure with patience the trials of the blackout, the depredations of income tax, the dislocation of our private lives, for victory to fall into our laps.

It was in that spirit of complacent confidence that I was writing to you seven weeks ago. I believed, we all believed, that we were preparing for anything. And in a sense we were prepared. I wish you could have been with me on the Belgian frontier on the first morning of the Flanders battle. It was one of the most exciting days that I have ever known. That long stream of lorries, Bren gun carriers, howitzers, gun carriages, pouring forward to Belgium's rescue, was about the most inspiring sight that I have ever seen. The men looked so fit and lean and strong. And in every village the Belgians were waving welcome to them, were tossing branches of lilac on to the lorries. At last surely, it seemed, Hitler had met an adversary who was prepared for him.

I am not a military historian. I am not a student of strategy and tactics. I am not qualified to express an opinion on the sequence of tragic events that was within a month to drive that magnificent army, its equipment abandoned, upon the beaches before Dunkirk. Yet those thirteen days between the first air-raid warning over G.H.Q. and the docking at Dover of the steamer by which I was disembarked, were sufficient to convince me, as they convinced many thousand others, that we are confronted with a new kind of warfare, a warfare for which new weapons, new tactics must be forged. We had been prepared for one kind of war, but not for the kind of war we had been called upon to face.

There would be no point in my giving you actual details of those thirteen days. There have been so many descriptions of war's horrors; so many descriptions of frightened refugees. In the last war I was in three major battles – Passchendaele, Cambrai and the March offensive – and, in actual fact I saw during those thirteen days more actual bloodshed, more men killed before my eyes than I saw in those three battles, though I found the nerve strain of those incessant air raids greater than the artillery bombardments at Ypres, it is not by any accumulated recital of such details that the difference between this war and the last war can be conveyed. The different is not one of degree but of kind. This war is being waged on a different plane: where there is no immunity in distance, in miles, in the breadth of rivers; where there can be no safety until the thing you are fighting has been scotched at its very source.

Have I made myself clear? Perhaps I haven't. I'll take an illustration. I am writing this letter on the verandah of the Athenaeum: looking across Carlton Gardens toward the stuccoed façade of what was the German Embassy. On the left below the statue of the Iron Duke, workmen are busily constructing a series of air raid shelters. But apart from that brief burgeoning of yellow brick, there is nothing in the familiar scene to suggest any change of atmosphere; London in the bright June sunlight is its lovely, placid, immemorial self. Yet I know that London is no more safe to- day, however safe it seems, than that garden in Arras where I sat in a deck-chair under a cherry tree waiting for orders on the fifth day of the attack. There is no safety in distance, in rivers, in cement defences in this war of parachutes, of fifth columnists, of sweeping infiltrations, of air raid bombings where towns fifty miles from the firing line can become overnight a confused shambles of refugees and cut communications. A total war is not waged along a fixed set line. It is not waged only on one's front. It is waged behind one, and on the flanks, from above and from beneath. It is for that kind of war that we are preparing now.

You know that we are preparing for invasion, how we have destroyed every sign-post that might give assistance and direction to the enemy, how we have evacuated the South and East Coast towns, how we have mobilized the resources of the nation so completely that Bernard Shaw said we had done in two hours what Russia had only done in twenty-three years. We are too busy in our preparations to find time to apportion blame for the mistake of the last three years. There will be no equivalent for the munitions scandal of 1915. There will not be time for that. We have too much else to do. There is nothing that I can tell you of that you do not know already; nothing except the spirit in which this country is setting herself to those ten thousand tasks whose sum constitutes the one essential task. That I could tell you. But there is no need to describe that to you. The future will show you that. . . .

Churchill was hard pressed by the French to throw the whole of the remaining British fighter force into the Battle of France, but Air Chief

Marshal Sir Hugh Dowding gave a dire warning of the consequences of sacrificing it in a campaign which was lost anyway. Churchill explains to General Smuts why he must preserve the RAF for the imminent Battle of Britain to be able to carry on the war; 400 of the 650 Hurricanes and Spitfires were lost in France, and the shortage of trained pilots was even more serious as aircraft production got into its stride.

15

THE VITAL FIGHTER PLANES

Churchill to Smuts.

June 9, 1940

We are of course doing all we can both from the air and by sending divisions as fast as they can be equipped to France. It would be wrong to send the bulk of our fighters to this battle, and when it was lost, as is probable, be left with no means of carrying on the War. I think we have a harder, longer, and more helpful duty to perform. Advantages of resisting German air attack in this Island, where we can concentrate very powerful fighter strength, and hope to knock out four or five hostiles to one of ours, are far superior to fighting in France, where we are inevitably outnumbered and rarely exceed 2:1 ratio of destruction, and where our aircraft are often destroyed at exposed aerodromes. . . . Even if by using them up we held the enemy, Hitler could immediately throw his whole [air] strength against our undefended Island and destroy our means of future production by daylight attack. . . . I see only one sure way through now, to wit, that Hitler should attack this country, and in so doing break his air weapon. If this happens, he will be left to face the winter with Europe writhing under his heel. . . .

I am most grateful to you for cable. Please always give me your counsel, my old and valiant friend.

FIVE

Their 'Finest Hour': Alone Behind the 'Good Tank Ditch' (June 1940–June 1941)

Praise God now, for an English War . . .
When no allies are left, no help . . .
And only England stands
DOROTHY L. SAYERS (1893–1957), 'THE ENGLISH WAR'

General Weygand called the Channel 'a good tank ditch' and Churchill announced that Britain's 'finest hour' was about to begin. National pride and defiant determination were aroused by facing the enemy alone and a new grim confidence excluded any thought of defeat.

1

'It is our war now – every Britisher's war'

The wife of an RAF pilot killed in action two months later expresses the fearless vigour of a free people in adversity.

Sussex, June 25, 1940

What a sad day for the world.[1] For me, and for most of us here, I think, I feel tougher and somehow strengthened. No more complacency, no more uneasy doubts as to what the diplomats and foreign generals are cooking up, no more reading one day that such and such a town is of vital importance only to read the following day, when we have lost it, that it didn't matter much. The war is on our doorstep and it is our war now, and we are rather proud. We know our leaders, and we feel, most impor-

---

1   The fall of France.

tant of all, that they know how we feel. Adversity does strange things to free people, and like many others, I feel full of vigour and not the least bit frightened. It is about to be every Britisher's war, and that's how we want it. . . .

The Battle of Britain

I was ready for death,
Ready to give my all in one expansive gesture
For a cause that was worthy of death
TIMOTHY CORSELLIS, RAF (DIED 1941)

On 10 July an intensive *Luftwaffe* bombing attack was launched on the Channel ports to soften them up for Operation Sea Lion, the invasion of Britain planned for September. Rundstedt's twenty-five divisions were assembling hundreds of landing craft for an assault on the coast between Folkestone and Worthing, supported by parachutists. The German General Staff did not expect long resistance from the depleted British forces; they thought highly of the tough doggedness of the British soldier but not of the ability of the generals to cope with mobile warfare. Only fifteen infantry divisions on half strength in fixed defence positions and without the necessary equipment, and a single armoured division of only 160 light tanks with nothing but machine-guns, could be mustered for the defence of England. If the Germans had ever gained a firm foothold, there would have been no chance of driving them out again. Advice given to civilians on how to deal with German parachutists sounds rather quaint.

2

'I made 27 lbs of blackberry jam'
WAITING FOR INVASION

An English housewife tells her daughter in Canada how to tackle parachutists.

Sussex, July 8, 1940
Once more we are waiting and waiting for it to happen. No one can be lulled into a feeling of security as we were at the beginning of the war, for we are told all day and every day of the certainty of invasion and the things to do and not to do.
    There are a lot of soldiers billeted at Mrs G's, and she told me that they are all up at 3.30 and go far and wide watching for parachutists – it is supposed that they will land before dawn. I wonder if I have written to you since we heard the man talk on invasion. He had been through the whole thing in Finland – a war correspondent and the most brilliant speaker I have ever heard. We feel such things could not happen here in England. He says they will happen, that it is planned and cut and dried as only the Germans can plan; that the parachutists believed to be dropped in Sussex

will be men who have spent the last three summers on a walking tour here in these lanes and will know Sussex better than the local people.

His lecture told us how to observe intelligently and how to report what we did observe. He said if you are feeding the chickens or in your garden and should see a parachutist, don't run into the house and telephone; watch him; never take your eyes off him; see where he crawls into the hedge and watch until you can call to someone, or someone comes out. Then go to the telephone, call the police and report quickly parachutist seen in field No. 600 and drop the receiver as he wants all the lines to spread the report. You can see what good advice this was. He said if that parachutist is stopped in his first duty, the whole thing is delayed and possibly would fail. Surprise and quick action was what did it all in Norway and Holland, combined with treachery.

I made 27 lbs of blackberry jam yesterday.

George Orwell, back in England after being wounded in the Spanish Civil War, sees invasion as a means of getting rid of the appeasers.

3

AFRAID OF A PEACE OFFER

George Orwell writes to James Laughlin, his American publisher.

London, 16 July 1940

Things look rather black at the moment. We are all on our toes waiting for an invasion which quite possibly won't happen. Personally I am much more afraid of Hitler . . . making a peace offer. I actually rather hope the invasion will happen. The local morale is extremely good, and if we are invaded we shall at any rate get rid once and for all of the gang who had got us into this mess. . . .

But Goering believed Britain could be subdued by bombing alone, and Operation Sea Lion, with all its hazards, would therefore be unnecessary; he continued the assault on the coastal towns.

4

DIVE-BOMBERS LIKE A SWARM OF MIDGES

Private Geoff Jones describes an air battle over Margate to his parents.

East Kent, 9/8/40

Dear All,

Events have been moving very fast down here yesterday. By the hell, what a battle! The sky was absolutely full of planes of all descriptions. The scrap started at 24,000 feet and the first indication I had of anything amiss was something in the sky which looked like a flaming torch; it turned out to be a plane on fire, one of our own. I then started to scan the sky and it was not till I looked straight up above my head that I saw what was going on. My stomach turned over and I stood absolutely spellbound. They were just like a tremendous swarm of midges but when they came lower, by—what a din they made. The dive bombers came down and bombed Margate but there was not much damage. Official reports from Marston aerodrome this morning estimated the Jerry losses to be 60. We lost 16 planes, three pilots were picked up in the Channel.

The plane I saw in flames was right in the centre of Margate and he flew it into the sea and so saved a great disaster; he was, unfortunately, killed in doing so but no doubt he will get recognition.

The Jerries started at five yesterday morning and did not finish till last night. The sirens only went once as the scrap was off the coast. I happened to be lucky and was patrolling the beach on a bike all morning and saw everything there was to see. Five crashed in a bunch at one time; we could not make out the planes but could see the trails of smoke they left. They hit the sea near Dover.

You know what amazes me down here is, the civil population are not in the least afraid. I bet Kendal would get a queer shock if anything happened up there like that because 250 Jerries at once is no joke.

When British fighters shot down 236 German planes, for a loss of 96, the *Luftwaffe* attacked the aerodromes and radar stations on 12 August: it came close to success – losses were very heavy on both sides. When the German planes swooped down on the important forward aerodrome at Manston, most of the squadron based there were refuelling; they managed to take off just in time and shoot down five bombers and two fighters, but the bomb damage was so extensive that Manston had to be abandoned.

5

HOW MANSTON AERODROME WAS DEVASTATED

Private Jones writes home a fortnight later, less cheerful and more frightened.

24/8/40

Just a line to say that I am alright after a hellish do today. I have been on Manston Aerodrome all day and believe me I am just getting over it. I am the luckiest man on God's earth to be sitting writing this letter. . . . We went to see if the NAAFI was open for refreshments and found out much to our annoyance that it was not, but that fact saved my life. We got into our motor bike and sidecar and were riding very sedately down the road in the middle of the drome, I suddenly heard machine guns and cannons firing. Something like a golfball flew by my head and machine gun bullets were bouncing off the road in front of us. We got out like lightning. The first bomb then dropped. I saw the NAAFI (which I would have been in had it been open) absolutely demolished before my eyes.

I dived for the shelter and I had not got through the door before the swimming bath not twenty yards away was blown up and the blast helped me through by about five yards, had it not, I would have been cleaned up as a shell from one of the cannons went right through the concrete staples holding the door. When I managed to get out after they had gone the concrete staple was smashed to atoms and the doorway was blown across the road, the swimming bath was nowhere to be seen, the NAAFI was in ruins, not one brick on top of another, and the man behind me had a bullet in his leg which I would have got if *he* hadn't been there. I looked round at the devastation and thanked God. . . .

Manston was evacuated about an hour ago and only a skeleton staff left, the rest are nervous wrecks. A German prisoner told the authorities that his squadron has orders to blow Manston off the face of the earth. We were that nervous when we left the drome that we hit a wall, we were that much in a hurry we were doing about sixty down a country lane; we came through anyhow.

So long for now,

Goodnight,
Geoff

The attacks on the aerodromes had taken a dangerous toll of fighter planes, and – even more serious – of pilots, some of whom could fortunately be saved.

6

'Flames were blowing back in my face'

An RAF officer tells his mother how he was shot down; he was temporarily blinded and had shrapnel in his leg.

15th General Hospital, Hindhead, Surrey, September 4, 1940
Last Saturday at 8.30 a.m. we had started out for the South Coast on one of the brightest days that I have yet seen over here, looking for German bombers who were reported to be attacking. While doing this we had our faces to the sun and, although searching, we apparently failed to see some German planes above us.

The first thing I knew I had received a cannon shell through the lower left-hand side of my cockpit. I did a violent swing over the left to escape any further fire but some of my controls must have been shot away and I could not pull out of the spin into which I had got myself. The next moment flames were blowing back in my face and I endeavoured to undo my straps and get back the hood. I was a bit excited at first and failed to get my straps undone and almost gave up hope of getting out; however, I finally got the straps loosened and was able to bale out.

My parachute opened at about 16,000 feet and I floated safely to the ground but not without a feeling of fear that the German pilot would take a couple of shots at me on the way down, as they seem to be making a practice of in recent days.

Having landed, I took stock of myself and saw that my trousers had been practically blown to pieces and also part of my tunic, and that I had lost one of my flying boots, probably due to the explosion in the cockpit. I was not conscious of any pains at first. . . .

Had the nine clearly visible radar towers on the coast been knocked out first (only one was) and had the destruction of the aerodromes then been systematically pressed home, together with that of the fighter force, invasion might have become possible despite the naval barrier. But on 7 September, in revenge for small British night raids on Berlin and other German cities, Goering switched the *Luftwaffe* to massive day and night attacks on London by an average of 160 planes. Paradoxically, on the same day – the first one thousand bomber raid on the East End and the docks – church bells were rung in the belief that invasion was imminent.

A Hurricane pilot, one of the fighter force meeting the raiders, gives an account of the air combat with all the freshness of an exciting new experience.

7

ONE OF THE LEGENDARY 'FEW'

Flying Officer George Barclay (died 1942) to his parents.

North Weald, September 10th, 1940

My darling Mummie and Far,

. . . We have several times had some extremely exciting scraps with these vast Hun formations attacking London. Our fiercest hour was on the 7th, the day the Boche first attacked London Docks and the East End on a large scale.

We were sent up as a squadron to patrol over Maidstone – it was a grand day and from 15,000 ft. the view was so delightful that one was tempted to sit here and admire it instead of searching for the Hun. . . . Then over the wireless came a shout: 'Hullo, leader, Messerschmitt 109s behind us in the sun', and I'm sure twelve hearts suddenly beat double time! I looked extremely hard into the sun and cocked one wing up to cover it, so that I could look around without glare, but I couldn't see anything. We started to climb hard, turning to get a good look around – and there several miles away was a black line in the sky – 35 Hun bombers in close formation – and I gradually began to distinguish about 70–100 other little dots – Hun fighters.

The squadron turned to attack and I switched on the electric sight and turned the gun button from 'Safe' to 'Fire'. And then things began to happen – we went in at the bombers and as I broke away I saw two dropping back from the formation, streaming white smoke from one engine. But before one could take stock of the situation the Messerschmitts were on me. . . .

I turned quickly to see if there was anything on my tail and at the same moment two Me109s went past beneath my nose. I turned quickly, diving on one and gave him a burst – nothing happened – presumably missed him, but the noise of my eight guns gave me great confidence. I gave the second Me109 a burst and whoopee! A sudden burst of brilliant flame, a cloud of smoke, and a vast piece flew off it, and down he went. But no time to watch, there's something behind me shooting a grey line past me on the left (tracer bullets). I turned to the right and saw a Me109 go past with a vicious yellow nose and the large black crosses on the fuselage. At the same time I saw a Hurricane going vertically down pouring smoke (and later the pilot's parachute with another Hurricane circling it to protect him from the Huns). I dived to get away from the Me109s and levelled out at 6000ft.

I could still see the bombers 10,000ft above, so I climbed up keeping my distance until I was again on their level. They then made up my mind for me by turning straight towards me and I did a head-on attack on the leader. As I broke away my ammunition gave out, but I saw one of the leader's engines smoking. Now I couldn't see anything as oil was pouring out of the engine on to the windscreen and my engine gave signs of packing up altogether. I glided back over the Thames Estuary, noticing below a blazing oil tank with a thick cloud of black smoke up to 8,000ft, and a grey cloud of smoke over the Docks. I then realised I couldn't get back to the aerodrome and made a successful crash landing in a field about five miles away from here – quite OK and the Hurricane not much damaged. . . .

A few weeks later Barclay wrote:

We are having a grand time – I am realising an ambition, but it's a bit tough to see fellows wiped off one by one. . . . One gets used to people not coming back. Normally this warfare is thrilling, and a successful scrap puts one on the top of the world – but I won't deny it has its frightening moments, though having survived a frightening moment is also exhilarating![2]

The Blitz: London Can Take It

When our brother Fire was having his dog's day
Jumping the London streets . . .
LOUIS MACNEICE (1907–63),
'FIRE-WATCHER AT ST PAUL'S'

Could his limbs be found
Here would lie a common man . . .
ROY FULLER,
'EPITAPH ON A BOMBING VICTIM'

Every night of September from the 7th, London was bombed by about 200 planes, dropping a total of 10,000 high explosive, and countless incendiary

---

2 Barclay survived being shot down three times (once escaping from occupied France via Gibraltar) and became a famous flying ace; but he finally met his fate leading his squadron over El Alamein.

bombs which killed 5,730 people and destroyed 150,000 homes. This ordeal continued for nine months. But the effect of the Blitz was the opposite of what Goering had expected: civilian morale became only more grimly determined. Fifteen per cent of Londoners slept in the Underground every night, many of whom had been bombed out of their homes. A new feeling of togetherness in adversity eroded class barriers and created a spirit of self-sacrifice, but the greatest asset was the unquenchable humour. The following letters bear eloquent witness to the proud islanders' dogged defiance.

8

'The amazing grit of the people'

A civilian writes to a friend on the *Ladies Home Journal*.

Rudgwick, Sussex, and London [Autumn 1940]
Have you ever lain in bed, and listened angrily to a mosquito cruising around with malice intent? First you hope it will go away if you ignore it. Then you get so angry you determine to down the brute even if you do lose a shoe out of the window and break the mirror.

That is exactly what we are going through at the moment, only the mosquito, instead of gnawing a limb, drops heavy eggs around. The first bad raids caught me in my bath in Liverpool. I arose, put on my tin hat, and returned to my bath, a sweet sight, but one must wash. The place rocked, but next day one had to be told where the damage was, and go and look for it. On returning to London it was obvious Hitler's patience really was exhausted, and from 4 p.m. onwards every night we had it good and hearty. It does not make one in the least frightened, that's the funny part. It makes you damn angry! The trouble was as ever to get people off the streets, and the amazing grit of the people whose homes go is something that astonishes one most. 'High time it came down, anyway', was all one man said, as he vacated his tenement, or all that remained of it, with his worldly goods on a perambulator.

And who is to write the epic of the London taxi driver? In the worst raid, if you call 'Taxi', one arrives. The usual small rather cross-looking man with a moustache like an old nailbrush left too long in the soapdish. 'Where to?' is all he says. All night during the bad raids last week you heard them cruising around. If a whistling bomb dropped in the neighbourhood, they stopped for a moment. Then you heard again the comfortable familiar noise of their engines starting. That, and the distant whistle of a train that went on all through the raid, was one of the most comforting things I found. For three nights we didn't get much sleep, and on one of them I was on duty and had to drive through the inky streets myself. Maybe that is why I have sympathy for the taxi drivers.

All one night London was well lit up by the big fire, and it was quite unbelievable, with crashes and bangs going on all round, and the wireless going on gaily, just the same, and people walking around the streets saying 'Ooer, that was a big 'un.' Or sometimes just disgusted, 'The dirty . . .'

Yesterday, I came down to the Cottage, where I saw the most marvellous fight right overhead. A whole convoy of bombers came over and were attacked by Spitfires. I watched two bombers crashing down and in the field was a German pilot, dead before we got there. Just a boy, with the Iron Cross 1939 in his pocket, and a picture of a woman and a child. It makes one sick. . . .

It will be interesting to see what the outcome of all this is, and whether the machines or the men eventually win. All I know is, I don't envy Hitler if he ever should find himself landed in England. We are, by and large, a pretty dogged folk. I never realized it so poignantly as in Liverpool last week, where, with windows shattered and often the counter in splinters, shopkeepers carried on just the same. One man held out a loaf of bread squashed quite flat, and said facetiously, 'You can have this one cheap.'

9

'I wish I felt as unconcerned as I hope I look'
SLEEPING IN THE TUBE

A female civilian writes to a friend in America.

In the Tube, London, September 10, 1940
. . . If you could *see* the couple camped down next to us, draped in pink silk quilts and with their pillows placed on their faces; snores coming through . . . We stake our claims at about 6 p.m. and then settle down around 8 – and usually we go to bed at 6 a.m. I rather envy the air wardens and people who go out and do something; here we sit feeling convinced we are the next target. . . . There is a battle *royal* going on; all the tenement dwellers are sitting up and chewing chocolates! I wish I felt as unconcerned as I hope I look. . . . We have just had delicious cups of tea given us and are feeling a bit revived. It's a bit difficult writing on the floor by the light of a candle stuck in a bottle and *crash bang* as accompaniment to my thoughts. . . . We are all rolling up our sleeves for an invasion and we hope for this weekend, at last!

10

THE FEARLESS CHILDREN OF 1940:
IT'S HUMPTY DUMPTY TO LITTLE AUDREY

The same civilian writes a week later.

Audrey at the age of eight has a million times more spunk than I should have had at that age. During an air raid when we are in the shelter at night, before she goes to sleep, this is the sort of conversation we hear from her. 'Hark, Mummy, that's a Jerry.' 'It sounds like it.' Audrey – 'That's Cracking Ronnie – whoof.'

She has nicknames for all the different guns – you can more or less pick out the various types of guns by the cracks and bangs. 'Come on, give it to 'em,' she says. She imitates their sounds. Another is 'Humpty Dumpty' because she thinks it makes a noise like Humpty Dumpty falling off the wall. There's one sound she calls the 'Powder puff' because it sounds like little puffs. Sometimes they all seem to be going at once, and she gets quite excited calling encouragement to the A.A.

I remember at the age of fifteen I was simply squirmy with terror during the last war's raids, and I should have never thought it possible that there could be so much fearlessness amongst children. . . .

King George VI who had served at Jutland in 1916 was eager to share the danger with the people of London. He and the queen remained most of the time at Buckingham Palace during the Blitz and he practised shooting with tommy guns and carbines at the range with members of the royal family and equerries, to be ready for any invader. On Friday 13 September they had a narrow escape; fortunately the windows were open.

11

BLITZ ON BUCKINGHAM PALACE

The King to his Prime Minister.

We went to London [from Windsor] and found an air raid in progress. The Queen and I went upstairs to a small sitting-room overlooking the Quadrangle. All of a sudden we heard the zooming noise of a diving aircraft getting louder and louder, and then saw two bombs falling into the Quadrangle. We saw the flashes and heard the detonations as they burst about 80 yards away. The blast blew in the windows opposite to us and two great craters had appeared in the Quadrangle. From one of these craters water from a burst main was pouring out and flowing into the passage through the broken windows. The whole thing happened in a matter of seconds, and we were very quickly out into the passage. There were six bombs: two in the Forecourt, two in the Quadrangle, one wrecked the Chapel, and one in the garden.

12

SPY MANIA: A NAVAL CAPTAIN IS STRUCK BY THE MOB

Captain A.V.S. Yates recounts to an American friend, R.E. Gillmor, how he was arrested for photographing the house where a young boy had rescued a cat after an air raid.

4 October 1940

. . . I went down to a poor quarter of South East London, anxious to see conditions there for myself as the bombing had not seriously reached the West End. . . . A family of mother and four children ranging from 13 years to 15 days lost their house and practically all their possessions. This woman was absolutely splendid, never complaining about anything. The baby was quietly sleeping in the washing basket. . . . I asked how the cat had survived and was told that little Tommy, aged 13, had climbed up at great risk into the wreckage of the top floor of the house and pulled it out from underneath the plaster where it was trapped.

I told the mother that I would try and get a photograph of the building where Tommy had rescued the cat as it would be interesting to them in after life, and was in the act of taking photographs when an Air Raid Warden about 4 ft. high, accompanied by a youth he had pressganged, came up and asked me what sort of camera I was using. I thought this was a little inquisitive and I answered casually, 'it's a small Zeiss'. The Warden grabbed me by the arm and said 'come along with me', telling the youth to seize my other arm. Suddenly realizing I had been breaking the law by photographing without a permit, I completely unresisting went off with them towards the Police Station in order to explain that I was doing this for the former owner of the house.

Before I was half way there the rumour got around that the local Warden had captured a spy; people appeared in a flash from their shelters and before I knew where I was, I was in danger of my life – one soldier who had probably run like hell to Dunkirk dashed across the road and pinioned my arms as though I was trying to escape, regardless of the fact that I was already held by two men. By a lucky chance a police van suddenly came down the road. The Warden hailed the police (and I assure you so did I) and a squad of policemen hustled me into their van – not before I was struck in the face by an infuriated woman who had arrived too late to ascertain the facts and thought I had turned up by parachute. I learned a lesson with a crowd like that, that only the front row hears your explanation, the second row hears the word 'Spy', the third 'Jerry' and the fourth 'Parachute' and before you know where you are, no explanations are listened to.

We reached the Police Station and for the first time I was able to take off my mackintosh, revealing my uniform underneath. The soldier, thinking that he had perhaps been over-zealous, slunk silently away but no one else in that part of London recognised a Naval uniform and my identity card with photograph had not fully convinced the police. I refused to be locked in a cell until my identity card had been disproved and they compromised by locking me in a yard where there were about six cells, whilst they telephoned for detectives to question me.

After a short while the police also began to suspect that I was genuine and by degrees they made advances, first offering me a cigarette and then a cup of tea. Finally, the detectives arrived; one of them was a Plymouth man who believed my story at once but said he must prove I was the man I claimed to be. So we drove in the police car to the Admiralty.

Here my friends requested that I be taken back and locked up for the night which disconcerted the detective for the moment, until he realized that it was a joke. After being released I took them back to my flat for some beer and was only saved from running completely dry by the siren going off again, when they hurriedly left such an exposed position. The incident was instructive and at times alarming but it shows that care is at any rate taken before suspected spies are lightly dismissed.

13

'It's not the bombs that upset you, it's the lovableness of the people'
THE ARP WARDEN

The actor Stanley Lupino (1895–1942) describes to his wife in America the unbeatable cockney spirit.

London, October 13, 1940

The Battle of London is on. They are trying all the devilment that hell can supply them with, but it will not avail them one iota towards victory. There is hardly a district that is unfortified that they have not bombed. But they cannot beat the Cockney spirit. It is so wonderful, you would scarcely believe it. Homeless people sitting on their few belongings in the road, singing 'There'll always be an England,' 'Daisy, Daisy,' and hymns.

Us A.R.P. wardens have been at work from sunrise to sunrise. I have had two hours' sleep in one week (in bed). The intensified gun barrage we are putting up is so terrific all the birds in the trees are fallen dead in thousands. It is unceasing, the sky aflame with shells bursting like thousands of red-hot stars and shrapnel falling like rain. We do our rounds in complete darkness, and in dashes run, fall flat, wait, run, and so on. We have to put out incendiaries, and listen for the dull thud denoting time bombs dropped. This is the most hazardous job, and it means searching in darkness with only a tiny light for a hole. And it may go off at any time. It's a very windy job.

They don't laugh at wardens any more. They bless and look upon us as their greatest friends in need. Children run to us when they see the familiar black tin hat with the 'W' on it in white. Conductors won't take fares from us and shops hardly want to take payment when we walk in. We are policemen, nurses, firefighters, watchers for danger, aids in sickness, and give comfort and confidence to all and sundry.

During the night I visit the sleeping people in shelters. I never speak, only stand and inspect them, but they all say they feel my presence even in the darkness. And it gives them confidence. They know the familiar sound of my walk and the soft tread of my heavy gum boots. I never wake them, just stand in the dim light of a night light. If one wants to talk they whisper. One girl, a typist in the City, was awake in a shelter for 60 with 140 in it, huddled in heaps on the floor. She looked up and whispered, 'Hold my hand, sir, just for a minute.' I said, 'Of course'. After a while she pressed it to her face, and said, 'I feel better now. I haven't seen my man for three months and I am going to have a baby. I just wanted to feel a man's hand against my face.' This is only a few of the things that happen, choky, heart-hurting things that make you have to brace up and bite your lip. It's not the bombs, or the guns, that upset you, it's the lovableness of the people. Their hearts and souls laid bare – and when laid bare, so sweet to see. Neighbours who have never exchanged a word, huddled together for warmth and pity. I saw a pale-faced boy of eighteen with an old lady's head pillowed in his lap. He was stroking her hair. 'Your Mum?' I said. 'No, sir', he replied. 'I don't know her.' And then I trek back, dead streets, no human being to be seen, darkness, guns and thuds. . . .

One first aid worker, whose post was flooded with bad casualties, expressed her admiration for the elderly wardens who were always 'good-tempered and helpful' during raids at full blast, before quietly going off to their shops and offices in the morning, and added: 'The same applies to most girls at the Post; very few had seen blood en masse before, but they never turned a hair.' Other women drove ambulances in the midst of fires and explosions, or, unruffled by the night's bombing, just cleared up the rubble in their blasted offices and got down to work as usual.

14

'Anyone hurt here?' – 'All dead, go on'

An ambulance girl describes a night of duty in the blitzed dock area.

[September 1940]
We drove on quite alone through the street along each side of which were the low narrow slum houses. The streets were either away from the fire, and therefore pitch black, or else they opened right on to it, like rivers of light, with the silhouette of the houses cut out against them. Then we got into a jam of fire engines going over a narrow quay bridge into Victoria Docks. Everything was burning: every warehouse, every steamer, everything toppling and on fire. We went up one road in our attempt to get to Silvertown, and we could not get through – on account of the flames. We returned on our tracks and tried another way. Once more we came to a place where the road was jammed with traffic. A house feel right across the road some yards in front of us. We were pushed over a lot of debris by some of the firemen. When we got to the quayside, we called out to one man, 'Anyone hurt here?' He answered, 'All dead, go on.'

Then we picked up a man who was almost demented. He had lost his wife, and his grandmother and their house. We came to what seemed in the darkness a kind of village beyond a desert of flames. This was Silvertown. All the roofs of the houses here were blown off, and bombs were falling in rapid succession. We had to go on two wheels, skidding over some of the craters, until we came to a place like a Chinese war film. You know, just lots of ruins, and shell-holes, and an air of frightened people just daring to poke their heads out from under the ground. One man actually did rise out of a hole in the ground, and he asked us what we were looking for. We said that we were looking for a certain street in Silvertown. He answered, 'This is it. Every one is sheltering under those arches.' I took a stretcher and went with the man to this shelter, where there were forty people. I looked at them and said, 'Is anyone hurt?' But no one answered at all. They were shocked beyond words. Then some one said at last, 'Over there. A mother has just been dug up with a baby two days old.'

We filled the van with hurt and shell-shocked people. We found our way back as best as we could. When we got as far as Liverpool Street, the whole ambulance was lifted off the ground by a terrible explosion. We got back to the station at 2 a.m. But it all seemed much longer.

15

'Isn't this being a lovely week?'

'Molly' writes from Broadcasting House to Mrs Fawcett-Barry.

[May? 1941]

What a night! They say it was the heaviest yet and I can believe them, altho' of course first thing next morning always seems hopeless. . . . I went to bed about midnight and was wakened just before two by a terrific barrage. Then all our guns went quiet and our fighters went up and there seemed to be a terrific air-battle going on just over our heads. The wretched things were dive-bombing, which made it sound much worse. About 2.15 a plane zoomed down close to us. Then it roared up again and a few seconds later there was a sickening thud and the whole world seemed to shake, followed by several explosions. It was a Heinkel down on Campden Hill, Hammersmith suffered badly again and Oxford Street is closed from Marble Arch.

B.H. is all right, but all round it again caught it badly. Our building structure seems to have stood firm, but the inside is just blown out. We clambered up to our offices, over blown-down walls and doors, and floors littered with glass and rubble, and have spent the morning salvaging. I got busy with brooms and duster and actually our office doesn't look so bad. The telephone had been blown right out of the window, hanging down its cord and when I rescued it and put the receiver back on it rang – still working! . . . They are still digging for people under the pub just opposite our windows – it's rather sickening, but how those A.F.S.[3] men do work! It seems so heart-breaking, just as people were getting tidied up and rebuilt, to have the whole lot devastated again. But I suppose that's war – or this kind of war, anyway.

Isn't this being a lovely week? The sunshine does help up here. Now I am going to look for some lunch. Electricity seems to be off, but water supply and I hope gas is still functioning.

There can be no doubt that the English sense of humour and absence of self-pity made suffering more bearable, and the erosion of class barriers in face of death and adversity created a new human warmth. But the most amazing feature was the ability of people to adapt to the Blitz and be proud to be there.

---

3 Auxiliary Fire Service.

Blitz victims stand among the rubble, Marlow Road, Hackney, November 1940. (*London Borough of Hackney Archives Department*)

Special tactical recognition markings being applied to a 'Grizzly Bear' squadron Spitfire of the RCAF at Tangmere, 5 June 1944, the eve

16

'Hitler kept us waiting'

A civilian tells a friend in America how the 'old rigid society' is getting 'joggled up'.

London, October 1940

It may seem mad, but in spite of all the tragedy of this war, I wouldn't be out of England now for all the world, or even out of London. It is so worthwhile a fight, and the spirit in which people who have suffered most face up to it cannot be wasted in the ultimate purpose of world history. . . .

I think the defence that the Germans will never understand is our laughter. The way people take raids is so funny! We gave a lift to a working woman the other day on one of the very rare occasions when we have taken our car out. Rich and poor, high and low, high-brow or illiterate, we all have a common opening to conversation now. 'What was it like out your way last night?'

'Oh, I go to the shelter at the end of my road every night,' she said, 'and last night it was most annoying – the Germans were not punctual. I never give my children their hot drink till the guns begin, and there was I all ready, settled down with rugs and cushions and a thermos flask – and Hitler kept us waiting for ten minutes!'

We have all got used to our present fantastic life. By the way, there's a raid on at this moment – the barrage is shaking the house, and I am writing this dressed in my 'siren suit' and uniform greycoat, sitting at the kitchen table before going to sleep in the larder which being under the garden, makes a grand dug-out.

We're getting well joggled up this time and our old rigid society will be very different – and a good thing too! We are all learning how fine and interesting all the people we never used to meet are – that's the one part of war I think everyone enjoys. . . .

When 10 per cent of the invasion barges had been destroyed by the RAF and the *Luftwaffe* had failed to gain air superiority (they had lost 1,733 planes for 915 British fighter losses) and to demoralize the British people by the Blitz, Hitler cancelled Operation Sea Lion and turned his attention to the invasion of the Soviet Union. The Blitz continued until 16 May 1941, killing 45,000 civilians, half of them in London; then the bombers were sent to the Soviet border.

S I X

The Turning of the Tide (Summer 1941–3)

Forget for a moment the medals and the glory,
And clean shape of the bomb, designed to kill,
And the proud headline of the papers' story . . .
RUTHVEN TODD (1914–78)

The Bombing Offensive

This is a civilization in which a man, too squeamish to skin a rabbit,
can press the button that exposes the entrails of cities
R.N. CURREY

Churchill decreed that the German 'civilian population must be made to feel the weight of the war', and the strategic air offensive against German cities became the RAF's first priority, mainly for propaganda purposes: it improved morale at home and gave the lie to Goering's boast that British planes would never get through. But day raids proved to be suicidal and had to be abandoned, while a survey in 1941 demonstrated that night attacks were highly inaccurate, despite the pilots' wildly exaggerated claims to the contrary (only 10 per cent of the bombs fell within five miles of their target). The damage to the German war economy was so negligible that it did not make the still heavy British losses materially worthwhile; but it was then the only way of hitting Germany at all. In 1942, despite the recent contrary experience of the Blitz on England, Air Marshal ('Bomber') Sir Arthur Harris launched his Sterlings and Halifaxes, whose navigation and bombing devices had been improved, in a terror bombing campaign against German cities, in the obstinate belief it could win the war by itself.

1

BLITZING CITIES IS FUTILE

John Hughes tells his daughter Elizabeth in Sidney that the English are too 'unimaginative and stolid' to get scared but thinks bombing Germany equally useless.

3 April 1942

. . . Just imagine fighting the massed forces of the Luftwaffe, as we did for weeks, with searchlights and a few planes – no night fighters!!! The day and the night they first came over the Docks (Sept. 7, 1940) and set *17 miles of them* on fire and we could not retaliate! The sky a crimson blotch from the fires and the air humming with the noise of the Germans' engines. Half the East End on fire and then on December 29, 1940, half the City of London! Then the terrible raids in April on Wednesday and Saturday in one week.

Looking back on it all now it seems more like a prolonged chapter from Dante's Inferno than anything else. I honestly don't know how we stood it but we not only stood it but we became *indifferent* to it. That was because the English are unimaginative and stolid. Nothing in the air, on the earth and on the waters beneath scares them. They get annoyed but they never get scared. I honestly believe if hundred Nazi parachute troops came down to-night in Piccadilly Circus we would start queuing up to see how our Commandos would deal with them. The Londoner is great on queues. He queues for his bus for his breakfast lunch and dinner for the flicks and for the theatre.

As the average Londoner went through *92 successive days and many nights* of heavy raids and is walking about as perky as can be, you can conclude that Air Raids are not nearly such terrible things as people imagine. We are quite lonely, in fact, without them after ten months! All we get now night after night are beautiful searchlight effects over our Blitzed old city. . . . My own opinion for what it is worth is that prolonged Blitzes on strongly defended cities are downright bad business. You know my views on the bombing of civilians – it just gets you nowhere. Life in London has hardly been interrupted at all. Ditto in Berlin etc. It is futile.

The aim of attacking military and industrial targets, and weakening morale (particularly of industrial workers) now gave way to an attempt to take revenge for the Blitz: area by area in city by city was indiscriminately devastated and the population systematically exterminated. Berlin was obviously a prestige objective, but 21 of the 169 bombers raiding it in the night of 7 November 1941 were shot down.

2

THE TARGET IS BERLIN

Flight-Sergeant Richard Lord describes the raid and his crew's escape in their damaged plane.

. . . I looked over the heads of the men crowded round the board. Opposite Aircraft K.N.B. for Beer read, Sergeant Lord. Objective, Potsdamer or Anhalter Bahnhoff, Berlin. Berlin! I felt pleased that my chance to start exacting vengeance had arrived so soon. I had paid a visit to the Nazi Capital before (the ground defences gave me 179 shrapnel holes to remember them by). I know the Potsdamer Bahnhoff. It is on a level with the Anhalter Bahnhoff, and south of the famous *Tiergarten* and *Unter den Linden*. This was going to be a piece of cake!

The briefing officer told us individually what he wanted us to bomb, from what height and how we were to go in over the target. Maps were distributed and a large photographic map of Berlin was projected on a white screen. We were handed times of take-off, run in, bomb and return, a brief resume of weather conditions, and where to expect flak. We were to take off at 9 o'clock. Fair enough!

In the mess we smoked our pipes and cigarettes, played cards, but consumed no beer. We always swap yarns before taking off to batter the Hun. We tell each other stories of men and boys who have not returned and this seems to get our backs up; we give each other 'pep' talks! . . .

At 8 o'clock a lorry set us down K.N.B. for Beer. To-night was to be a big show. The new fellow, the Second Pilot, watched me working the cockpit drill. He said nothing, but, I guess, was thinking a lot. . . . I switched on the engines. Their mighty roar announced to the world at large that the lads were once more about to take disaster and havoc to the Nazis. I found my heart beating a little faster and I experienced a feeling of elation. With each steady throb of the engines my fears vanished. All thoughts of the task ahead drifted away. I found myself thinking of the darkening sky, the soft white clouds, of waves beating against sandy shores, a warm sun illuminating a Coral Island, of lazing beneath lofty palm trees.

We commenced our run. As we taxied towards take-off point, the silhouetted figures on the ground, the bold outline of the Control Tower, the black hulks of other aircraft, seemed removed from this November evening. We made for the blazing cans of oil. I steered the Whitley straight on the flare path. The control column stuttered in my hands as the aircraft lurched over the rough ground. Gradually I pulled back the stick, further, until at last the lurching halted. The 'plane grew steady, the stick stopped stuttering. We were airborne. In the light of the flares we could see another 'plane making that mile run. This 'plane was followed by another, and another. . . .

I began thinking of a game of tennis with – what was her name – ah! yes, with a girl named Irene. My thoughts wandered on. During the sea crossing I thought of many things, of the good times I had in the past, with Mavis and Pete. I remembered how, while we were still at school, his father used to cook buttered egg and insist on me eating it before I went home. I recalled the games of snooker in the local Y.M.C.A., when, just after Dunkirk, we watched maimed soldiers trying to play. It brought a lump in my throat – and I hoped and prayed I would never return to civilian life like those poor fellows. . . .

My thoughts were broken by Chuck, who shouted that we were approaching the Dutch Coast. There were unblacked out windows in 'V' formation and lamps signalled the famous Victory V in morse!

As we approached Berlin from the north we heard a German radio station. The bellowing voice of the Nazi announcer boomed through the inter com, yelling something about '*Blitzkriegen*'. Tysen stood it for a while, then he doused his light, opened his cabin window and released a large house-brick, shouting, 'I'll give you Blitzkriegen, you dirty Hun!' We keep these old house-bricks on board for stray searchlights. They do untold damage, gathering force as they speed down from 10, or 20,000 feet.

The cloud was thickening; we could see nothing but dark rolling masses of Mackerel sky. We were immediately over the suburbs of Berlin. It was deadly quiet. There were no searchlights, no flak and no enemy fighters. After having to battle through to the target so many times before it seemed uncanny. We were at almost 20,000 feet. I told the crew that I was going down and they gave me the 'thumbs up' sign. The Second Pilot looked green round the gills, but, as with all of us, the excitement of the adventure caught him in its grasp. He clenched his teeth and watched the instruments. At 10,000 feet there was still ten tenths' cloud. A gap in the billowing mass proved that the customary welcome was being prepared. Wavering Hun searchlights swept round to meet us. We could see nothing but glaring cones, Berlin was well blacked out. The searchlights gathered into a cone and fell accurately on us. For a moment I was blinded by the glare, and the I could faintly make out the course of the *Landwehrkanal*.

Chuck had apparently seen the Anhalter Bahnhoff. He shouted excitedly, 'Target located!' Luck seemed to be with us. The cloud broke and a clear path remained over Berlin. He took a landfall on a lake and putting setting on his bomb-sight as we made our first run in. I looked at my watch; we were a few seconds behind the scheduled time. 'Easy in a bit!' he ordered. We completed the run almost to time. Banking over Spandau we returned over the *Landwehrkanal*, stooging as Chuck took another landfall. We commenced our second run. There was still no flak, but the searchlights kept on us. Chuck said quietly, 'left-left, that's right – get her steady, Dick, steady – keep her that way – now hold it . . . bombs going . . .' I pulled on the control column, counteracted the bucking.

As the bombs went the Hun let loose. More searchlights were switched on us. I started violent evasive action, but they kept on us. Shells screamed up and exploded nearby. Again that nauseating stench of cordite, the deadly rattle as shrapnel fell on the roof of the 'plane, the stuttering of the control column as the shells burst close the machine. Tracers came out of the clouds like slow phosphorescent caterpillars. They fascinated me. I could see them leave the ground and trace their complete journey through the sky. Three shot through my port wing in less than a second, but they did no damage. The heavier flak became more accurate.

Climbing slightly, I managed to tuck the aircraft behind a cloud, but the orange searchlight which blinded me earlier on penetrated even this. Below us a great flash appeared. Our bombs had reached their target. Corrugated iron roofing, small girders, bricks and other pieces of debris were flung into the air. For a moment I could imagine bodies sailing upwards with the blast of the explosion. A large spiral of smoke wended its way through the cloud and the clouds seemed to be tinged with fire as they reflected the burning mass of the Anhalter Bahnhoff.

For a split second after the gigantic explosions there was a respite. The furious fire of the Hun was repeated, more deadly this time. I felt the 'plane go out of control as we received a direct hit from a shell. I could see tracers creeping towards the nose of the machine and realised that the nose was down, that we were crashing. I could do nothing. Another group of shells exploded. The force of them sent the Whitley spinning over on its back.

Somehow I managed to right the 'plane, but again we were hit and it sideslipped. The stick jumped forward, crushing both my hands against the instrument panel. The aircraft shuddered and bucketed about in the air to such an extent that I switched on the abandon aircraft light. I felt sorry for my second pilot. This was not exactly a 'piece of cake' for his first trip. . . .

Chuck spoke through the inter-com. 'You've knocked on the abandon aircraft light, Dick!' he said calmly. And we were spinning in towards the centre of Berlin at 2000 feet a minute. I barked back: 'Climb out!' and staggered towards the rear of the aircraft to get my parachute. Jock, the rear gunner, yelled, 'I'am staying!' The Second Pilot bit his lip and voiced the same sentiment. In a flash I made my way back to the controls. My hands were hurting me but the boys wanted to go down fighting, and I couldn't let them down. I switched off the abandon aircraft light and heard Tysen say, 'That's more like it.'

The Whitley was quivering, the wings were making terrible creaking noises and the engines were roaring at full throttle. The central column was jumping about like a wild horse and the instruments were flashing like an erratic adam's apple!

The Second Pilot proved himself to be a wizard fellow. He grabbed hold of the stick and helped me to pull on it. He saw that my hands were crushed and that they were of little use. For a few more seconds we fought for our lives, fought harder than any tiger or lion at bay. We righted the 'plane 600 feet above the Reichs Sportfield. The nose came up and the Whitley began to climb.

Reaching stalling speed, it stood still in mid-air, bucked, and we were crashing again. How we pulled our fists away from the stick and halted the spin I shall never know. I switched off the engines and cruised the 'plane. Flak was still being shied at us, but not so concentrated. Berlin was behind us. . . . The Whitley behaved magnificently. It bucked now and then, but we made good headway.

We climbed to 10,000 feet, but there was still ten tenths cloud. We had no way of telling where we were. I put the stick forward and we glided down to almost ground level. A few extra tall trees flashed by and Jock hissed through the inter-com that if I was going to stay at zero height he wanted to get out at the next station as he was running short of chocolate.

Pulling back the stick we climbed again. Through a gap in the grey fleecy mass we saw lights. 'What a target!' the second Pilot whistled. Chuck who had been making rapid calculations, said, 'Bomb that and we'd be responsible for another war!' We were off course, owing to the damaged rudder for which I had not been making allowances, and the lights below were the lights of Sweden. I altered course and climbed. It grew colder and colder. We used oxygen and plugged in our electric heating apparatus. Putting the Whitley on an even keel we stooged in the general direction of England.

We ran into a storm. Lightning flashed up and down the wings, blue veins, silvery, ghost-like waves jumped from one part of the machine to another. Jock reported that he could not touch his guns without receiving a shock, and said that he was frozen to his seat. It was 16° below zero; I put the nose down and we straightened at 14,000 feet. The cloud thinned out. Below we could see water – the North Sea. My petrol was low and one engine was behaving erratically. Water below and a faulty engine. I wondered if we could make the return journey. . . .

As the first rays of the morning sun shone up from the sea into our faces we cruised into the landing ground. 11 hours in the air.

The first thousand bomber raid devastated Cologne in May 1942 and in the total destruction of Hamburg in July 1943 a 800 degree 'firestorm' of incendiaries, together with repeated high explosive area bombing, killed nearly as many civilians as died in Britain during the whole war through German bombing (between 45,000 and 51,500). Even this massive air offensive of 1943–4, while reducing the cities of Germany to rubble, had little effect on morale, and war production continued rising rapidly; only in the last year of the war was dislocation, specially of oil production, caused. But the cost to the RAF was heavy: 57,000 airmen died in Bomber Command alone. Air crews had a survival chance of only 10:1 in each raid and were subject to LMF ('Lack of moral fibre') punishment, if they faltered. They were conditioned not to think of the horror they were causing, right up to the tragic and unnecessary devastation of Dresden and Würzburg when the war was all but won.[1]

After the disastrous Nuremberg raid of 30 March 1944, when out of 795 bombers 94 were lost and 71 damaged, Air Marshal Sir Arthur Harris had to switch reluctantly to selective raids on German industry. The first target was the vital ball-bearings plant at Schweinfurt. A Lancaster bomber navigator, fascinated by flying, but appalled by the slaughter of airmen, is torn between his anti-war feelings and the nightmare of a Nazi domination of Britain.

3

'Idealism is not enough'

Flight-Sergeant George Hull writes to Wren Joan Kirby, three weeks before being shot down.

26 February 1944

Well, they have not killed us yet, although in saner moments when I think back to these lively little affairs I wonder why. It made me burn with rage as we were going

---

1 Cp. R.J. Overy, *Air War 1939–45*, Europa, 1980, *passim*. Churchill was responsible for the protracted air offensive and never admitted it was wrong; but Harris was not honoured and the bomber pilots were not commemorated by a plaque in Westminster Abbey. (M. Walzer, *Just and Unjust Wars*, Allen Lane, 1978).

over to *Schweinfurt* to see the raid on London going on. I thought of your folks and mine underneath it all, and I would not have turned back if we had caught fire. . . . It rather added to my belief in the ultimate futility of all this slaughter but I never lose sight of the fact that if our feelings rule our judgement, we might suffer terrible consequences. Think of it, Nazis in Britain, desecrating our land, destroying these beautiful things that you and I hold dear, fouling our women in brothels, wholesale slaughter of people for arrogance's sake: perhaps your Dad shot for not obeying an order. . . . Can you see the Nazis sparing Britain, the country above all which held out against them, and turned the tables. Of course I hate the job, but Idealism is not enough.

In contrast, another airman quietly affirms his faith in the cause for which he is ready to die.

4

'Cheerio, Mother and Dad'

Flight-Sergeant Rowland Bennett writes a farewell letter to his parents before going on his last bombing raid over Germany.

[1943]

I am writing this on the eve of one of my operational trips. In the event of my not returning this will be forwarded on to you.

First of all, I do not want you to worry and fret, thinking you have brought me up to live a fine and decent life and I should go at the most precious time in life. You will understand my love for this country and for my work. It was my wish that I should take this job of flying, and I have never met a finer bunch of lads yet than there are on my squadron. You have given me the essentials of a good, decent life, and have done things for me which it is only possible for parents to do.

My only regret is that I won't be able to repay you and bring you the happiness I had planned when we were together after the war. I know you will find noble consolation in the thought that I died in a right and just cause, and that I went the way I wanted to go.

I want you to thank all my friends, who have shown every kindness to me. And so I will say 'Cheerio', Mother and Dad, and may you continue to live in good health and happiness and may God bless you both.

The Path of Victory in North Africa

We ploughed the sand with shell and burning bomb . . .
We hated sand
So loving warm, so thirsty for our blood . . .
T.W. RAMSEY, EIGHTH ARMY

In North Africa, General O'Connor's 7th Armoured Division, the 'Desert Rats', had chased vastly superior Italian forces across the Western Desert to Benghazi and El Agheila in February 1941, and were poised to advance on Tripoli to bring the war in North Africa to a victorious conclusion; Marshal Graziani's army had largely surrendered and the Italian Empire was crumbling. At that moment, Churchill, with fond memories of Gallipoli, revived the idea of a Balkan Front. General Wavell fully supported him[2] in what turned out to be a major strategic blunder: he stopped the advance of his desert army and ordered 58,500 troops into Greece where the Italian invaders were being driven back into Albania. Thereupon, three German panzer divisions with 10:1 air superiority descended on Greece on 6 April and, three weeks later, expelled the inadequate British force, taking 12,000 prisoners and all their tanks and equipment.

Well over half the British Army was evacuated to Crete by the Navy and the island was held by 50,000 British and Greek troops. On 20 May, in one of the most daring exploits of the war, 3,000 German parachutists cleared the way for an airlift of 20,000 troops in the first completely airborne invasion. After a week of heavy fighting the position of the defenders became hopeless, as 500 German bombers, unopposed by any fighters, were wreaking havoc at will. At the cost of three cruisers and six destroyers which were sunk with 2,000 sailors, and heavy damage to three battleships and the only aircraft-carrier, the Navy rescued 16,500 soldiers; but two thirds of the troops were either dead or prisoners. However, 4,000 of the German Parachute Division had been killed, and therefore Malta, Cyprus, and the Suez Canal were saved from a fate similar to Crete's.

5

'I could have sat down and cried my eyes out'
BLITZED OUT OF CRETE

Sergeant Edward Carracher writes to his aunt Alice from captivity.

25/6/1941

I've been through a very horrid experience since last February and believe me Aunt, I really don't think I could go through the same, and come out alive.

Last February we left Africa and went over to Greece. The Germans was pushing through on all Fronts, the Greeks had collapsed. We could not hold our front. Of course it was the German Air Force, they had already beaten our Force on the ground, and now they had no opposition. The most pitiful sight during our retreat

---

2   Wavell has stated that the gamble he deliberately took did not look as hopeless at the time
    as in hindsight, as he had no idea the Afrika Korps was on the way (*Army Quarterly*, 1950).

was when we came round the outskirts of Athens. The women and children giving us what little food they had, cool water and wine and these same people were machine gunned when the troops were.

Any old how we left Greece behind us and were bound for what later 'Lord Haw-Haw'[3] named the 'Island of doomed men', the isle of Crete. We had a few air raids on our way but our arrival on Crete was o.k. Jerry was over every day dropping his lot, but our six little Hurricanes would always give them a go, and come back and do the victory roll. . . . Jerry had left Suda Bay docks in ruins, the *York* was lying there crippled and so were so many other ships it was a graveyard for ships, our Hurricanes had left the sky we never saw them no more, we couldn't understand this.

Within the next few days the Blitz came. The sky was black with planes, and Gliders. We had to withdraw two miles the second day of the Blitz: he knock out our A A guns and his airborne troops were holding strong positions. His paratroop well they were our meat, I thought I was down old Daykins cellar killing off chickens, it was just like that anyway o.k. boy did they howl when they were getting theirs. I'll say they did. Yes they yelped like the swine they are.

This went on for six days, his airforce bombed and machine gunned everything before, we could not stand up to it any longer we had to retreat, he blew the dump to hell and anything around it. We held Jerry for the rest of the day, at 3 am next morning the news came through that we had to surrender, because the Navy would not be back and there would be no more evacuation. Gee I could have sat down and cried my eyes out; to think what I had been through, and it all had to end like this. We put up the white flag. . . .

Aunt Alice, I don't want to go through the experience again. Gee, but it feels good to be alive. Give my regards to uncle Bill I hope he is well, tell him to hope it wont be long before I shall be able to have a pint with him again. . . . Well roll-on till its over and we all get home again and settled down to a life of peace.

In the meantime, Rommel had landed in North Africa with a few mechanized battalions to launch a lightning attack backed by superior air support; to bluff his way through, he sported a large number of dummy tanks mounted on 'Volkswagen'. In twelve days his fifty (real) tanks, by ruse and mobility, drove the surprised British Army out of Cyrenaica right into Egypt, after most of their tanks had broken down and the three top commanders had been captured. The nadir of British fortunes had been reached.

In June the Germans attacked Soviet Russia, and Pearl Harbor followed in December: Britain no longer stood alone in suffering grievous setbacks but was sharing them with the most powerful Allies. In North Africa the position remained fluid, but owing to the claims of their Russian campaign the Germans could not match the build-up of the British forces. Churchill had high hopes of Lieutenant-General Auchinleck's imminent 'Crusader' offensive.

---

3   The Irishman William Joyce who broadcast German propaganda to Britain during the war, became, despite his shrewd comments, a figure of fun in Britain because of his accent and mannerism. He was executed in 1946.

6

'The eyes of all nations are upon you'

Churchill, writing to Auchinleck, foresees El Alamein.

15 November 1941

I have it in command from the King to express to all ranks of the Army and R.A.F. in the Western Desert, and to the Mediterranean Fleet, his Majesty's confidence that they will do their duty with exemplary devotion in the supremely important battle which lies before them. For the first time British and Empire troops will meet the Germans with an ample equipment in modern weapons of all kinds. The battle itself will affect the whole course of the War. Now is the time to strike the hardest blow yet struck for final victory, home, and freedom. The Desert Army may add a page to history which will rank with Blenheim and with Waterloo. The eyes of all nations are upon you. All our hearts are with you. May God uphold the right!

In December Rommel was at last forced to withdraw to Benghazi, with only thirty tanks left against two hundred British. The next letter evokes the atmosphere of a lull in the heavy fighting during Rommel's retreat from Cyrenaica, with the Eighth Army on his heels.

7

'This is the life for me'
BIVOUAC IN THE LIBYIAN DESERT

A young artillery officer writes home.

20th Dec. 1941

I'm writing at the Signaller's desk in the back of my truck, by torchlight, with the head-phones on, waiting for orders before we close down for the night. I can hear the voices of the rest of the vehicle's crew lying outside in the sand. They've put up their bivvy tents for the night, and we've just cooked our evening meal on a primus in the back here – and darned good it was too – a tin of sliced bacon, a tin of baked beans, some hard biscuit mashed in, and a mug of tea. This is the life for me; it has its discomforts and its small worries, but I'm well and very happy and on top of my form.

The cold nights have taken a bit of getting used to out here in the desert; we are carrying only sleeping-bag, pack with greatcoat, and small pack with eating and washing things. We get one quart of water a day for all purposes, and the going is thrashing the life out of our vehicles and guns. But somehow everyone has settled down amazingly quickly, and they're as happy a crowd as I could ever wish to serve with.

One subsection have been making our Christmas pudding – issue bread, dried figs, chocolate (for colouring), about 50% rum, army biscuit, condensed milk, sugar, and some private tinned fruit. They have been tossing it for the last hour. One bombardier graciously allowed them to cut off the leg of his bright-yellow pijamas for the purpose, so they're all set for their Christmas. . . .

Lieutenant D.G. Stallard, 73rd Anti-Tank Regiment, did even better. He wrote:

Hunting pig for Christmas dinner was our latest venture. When the Italian settlers left here the Arabs took their livestock, but apparently they do not like pigs, so there are numbers of them running about wild. We bagged three on Christmas Eve, so we all had pork for Christmas dinner.

In January 1942 a replenished Afrika Korps began to sweep back again 250 miles to the Gazala Line, and Churchill, in a black mood of frustration, vented his anger on Auchinleck over his postponement of the offensive to relieve hard-pressed Malta.

8

CHURCHILL'S MOODS

Lieutenant-General (later General Lord) Hastings Ismay (1887–1965), Military Secretary to the Cabinet, to Lieutenant-General Auchinleck.

3 April 1942
. . . You cannot judge the Prime Minister by ordinary standards. He is not in the least like anyone that you or I ever met. He is a mass of contradictions. He is either on the crest of the wave, or in the trough: either highly laudatory or bitterly condemnatory: either in an angelic temper, or a hell of a rage: when he isn't fast asleep he's a volcano. There are no half-measures in his make-up. He is a child of nature with moods as variable as an April day.[4]

At the end of May Rommel forestalled the British offensive and swept another three hundred miles across the desert in one week, right up to the Alamein line, with Alexandria – a mere sixty miles away – almost in his grasp. With 280 tanks against 850, he had inflicted a crushing defeat on General Ritchie at Gazala and Mersa Matruh, owing to his ability to change

---

4   General Sir David Fraser (*Alanbrooke*, Collins, 1982, p. 532) sums up Churchill's faults with which his CIGs had to cope: irrational, unfair, petty, foul-tempered, fond of unsound advice, lacking understanding of operational details and logistic constraints.

rapidly from fluid dispersion to intense concentration at the crucial point, in face of a general who frittered away his tank strength piecemeal in slow uncoordinated movements. No wonder Rommel found in British soldiers 'extraordinary bravery and toughness combined with a rigid inability to move quickly'. In desert warfare, which resembled naval operations on vast horizons of sand instead of sea, bold and lightning manoeuvre in the Nelson spirit was the way to success even against much larger forces; but the typical British regular army officer, sporting 'a certain affectation of easy-going non-professionalism', based on the background of a rural gentleman, found it difficult to adjust to this 'garage-mechanic's war' – he regarded technocracy as sordid.[5]

Even worse, after only one day's siege, Tobruk had fallen in June and 25,000 were taken prisoner: speed, daring and ingenious tactics had paralysed greatly superior British forces. Mussolini flew to Derna with his white charger, ready to ride into Cairo in a Roman triumph.

But the Afrika Korps, with only forty-four of its tanks intact, had at last overtaxed its capacity and was brought to a halt in the First Battle of Alamein which Auchinleck directed himself. His down-to-earth realism and rejection of hide-bound complacency made him stand out as a true professional. He was not dazzled by the Rommel myth and knew how to rouse the spirit of the Eighth Army after its recent reverses: 'The enemy is stretched to the limit and think we are a broken army. . . . He hopes to take Egypt by bluff. Show him where he gets off.' He wrote just before the battle: 'These damn British have been taught for too long to be good losers. I have never been a good loser, I am going to win.'[6]

In a slogging 'last ditch' battle of attrition, he called Rommel's bluff and fought him to a standstill which left both armies exhausted. But despite this crucial success, confidence had not been restored: rumours about an intended withdrawal to the Delta were rife. Churchill who, in any case, needed a scapegoat for the lack of successes in the war, rightly sensed that a change of commander would revive morale. He flew to Cairo to get a first-hand impression of the Alamein front and to dismiss Auchinleck, a week after he had halted Rommel's advance.

5 C. Barnett, *Desert Generals*, Pan, 1962, p. 99; *Britain and her Army*, Allen Lane, 1970, p. 441 f.
6 J. Connell, *Auchinleck*, Cassell, 1959, p. 627.

9

'A decisive victory can be won'

Churchill writes to his wife from Cairo.

9 August 1942

My darling,

I have been so busy at anxious work since I arrived here nearly a week ago that I have not found a moment to write. . . . It was absolutely necessary that I should come here. This splendid army, about double as strong as the enemy, is baffled and bewildered by its defeats.

Rommel is living entirely on transport, and food and fuel captured from us. He is living from hand to mouth; his army's life hangs on a thread, but meanwhile a kind of apathy and exhaustion of the mind rather than the body has stolen over these troops which only new strong hands, and above all the gleam of victory can dispel. I went to the front on Wednesday; saw the Alamein and Ruweisat positions and was everywhere greeted with rapture by the troops. . . .

In Montgomery, who should be here on Tuesday, we have a highly competent, daring and energetic soldier, well acquainted with desert warfare. If he is disagreeable to those about him he is also disagreeable to the enemy. I am confident that the new arrangement will work well. . . .

I intend to see every important unit in this army, both back and front and make them feel the vast consequences which depend upon them and the superb honour which may be theirs. The more I study the situation on the spot, the more sure I am that a decisive victory can be won if only the leadership is equal to the opportunity.

Here we live in Capuan luxury. The weather is delightful. . . . The wonderful air of the desert with its fierce sunshine and cool breeze invigorates me so much that I do not seem to need as much sleep as usual. . . .

I start at midnight Monday and have a bath at Teheran and should reach Moscow before dark on Tuesday. . . . I informed Gen. Auchinleck by letter yesterday of the decisions taken. He is coming to see me here in a few minutes. . . .

Not everyone agreed with Churchill's harsh decision; it drew some bitter comments on the interference of politics.

10

'WHITEHALL 'WANGLING, OGLING, JOCKEYING'

Major-General Sir Alexander Galloway (1895–1977) voices his frustration to Auchinleck.

War Office, 31 August 1942

. . . . I go home at night dead-tired with vexation because a third of every day is spent in fighting battles which are not against the Axis powers and I cannot see it is necessary. We have a hundred examples of the bad effects upon military conception of operations and upon their carrying out by political influence, wangling, ogling, jockeying and the like and yet every time that any military operation takes place it still suffers from the same thing, and as long as we go on as we do we shall continue so to suffer. It is a very great tragedy for it has cost the lives of thousands of men, prolonged the last two wars by at least two years and has lost us, and will continue to lose us, numbers of our best officers. It is pathetic to think that in peace time the Army struggles along stinged in every way so that even its thought is affected and this all due to political misconceptions and votecatching on an enormous scale, while when the war breaks out the Army has to stand the hardest knocks as a result, until, indeed, it is a wonder that it survives at all; and when everything does not go perfectly it is the subject of severe criticism from high-ups and even ridiculed by the man in the street. . . .

The newly appointed commanders, Alexander and Montgomery, adopted Auchinleck's defence plan: the turning-point had come in North Africa. On taking over, Monty proclaimed: 'We will stand and fight here. If we can't stay here alive, then let us stay here dead.' At Alam Halfa, early in September, he defeated Rommel's last desperate attempt to break through to the Delta, by drawing the German tanks to his anti-tank artillery screen and hull-down tanks with air support in a conventional defensive battle instead of the previous hazardous tank chases across the desert.

Monty's 'cautious, controlled, no-advance-without-security concept' of a slow methodical battle of attrition was based on First World War tactics: his material superiority was bound to prevail in the end. His order 'No more manoeuvre; fight a battle', supported by massive artillery and bombing, was more in keeping with British Army tradition and character than Auchinleck's mobile warfare which never matched Rommel's owing to the lack of concentration of force and coordination by badly chosen, ineffective commanders. Yet it was Auchinleck who had picked and fortified Alamein, flanked by the sea and the Qattara Depression; the chiefs of staff of both armies have testified that 'it was Auchinleck's personal assumption of command that restored the situation and paved the way for Monty's successful defence of Alam Halfa' (Major-General de Guingand), and 'if Auchinleck had not been the man he was – the best Allied general in North Africa during the war – Rommel would have finished the Eighth Army off' (Lieutenant-General Bayerlein).[7]

Monty has been called 'a past master in showmanship and publicity; audacious in his utterances and cautions in his actions' (Major-General Fuller), and a 'military Messiah', eccentric, arrogantly self-confident, precise and relentlessly energetic (Correlli Barnett). He was certainly the greatest field commander of the war, fighting the old 'encounter battle' with iron determination and professionally controlled coordination. Moreoever, he had the 'common touch' – a true soldiers' general, concerned for their welfare and instilling confidence, energy and affection by briefing them personally in clear terms. At the same time, he was ruthless in weeding out officers, disdainful of almost all generals, and ungenerous about Auchinleck ('should never be employed again in any capacity'). He boasted after Alam Halfa: 'Luckily I had time to tidy up the mess (and it was 'some' mess I can tell you) and to get my plans laid. I have won the first game, when it was his [Rommel's] service. Next time it will be my service, the score being one – love.'[8]

He wrote in the same vainglorious schoolboy style to the CIGS.

11

'Rommel has had to dance entirely to my tune'

General Sir Bernard Montgomery (later Field Marshal Viscount) to General Sir Alan Brooke, early in the Battle of Alamein.

1 November 1942

. . . I obtained complete surprise and broke into the enemy positions in the north; he was expecting the attack in the south and our deception measures worked well. A real hard and very bloody fight then began, and has gone on now for eight days. It has been a terrific party and a complete slogging match, made all the more difficult in that the whole area is just one enormous minefield. The artillery fire has been superb and such a concentrated use of artillery has not been seen before in North Africa. . . .

I have managed to keep the initiative throughout and so far Rommel has had to dance entirely to my tune. . . . I think he is now ripe for a real hard blow which may topple him off his perch. . . .

I am enjoying the battle, and have kept very fit and well. It is getting chilly now, especially at night, and I have taken to four blankets at nights.

My great task is to keep morale high and spirits up.

---

7 J. Strawson, *El Alamein*, Dent, 1981, *passim*.
8 Letter to Brigadier F.E.W. Simpson, 12 October 1942 (N. Hamilton, *Monty*, vol. I, H. Hamilton, 1981, p. 760).

The Second Alamein, which had started on 23 October, completed the reversal of the situation after a battle of attrition between 230,000 British troops with 1,440 tanks (and 1,000 in reserve) and 1,200 planes, against 27,000 exhausted Germans and 53,000 Italian veterans with 540 tanks and 350 planes between them; moreover, Rommel was on sick leave in Austria and his substitute Stumme died from a heart attack. When Rommel flew back straight from hospital, he found half of his tanks had been knocked out, and petrol and ammunition were running short; yet he held out for twelve days before starting his long retreat, with only 2,000 men of the Afrika Korps left with 30 tanks, facing 20:1 odds, and leaving behind 10,000 German prisoners with 450 tanks and 1,000 guns.

On 10 November Monty was triumphant:

The battle is over, in that Rommel's army has been smashed up and we are now in pursuit. What saved him from complete annihilation was the rain. . . . It has been a great party and I have enjoyed it. . . .[9]

He resented interference from Cairo HQ staff:

If I accepted all the advice I am NOW being given we might well have a disaster even now. There are in Cairo a complete lot of lunatics who sit in War Rooms completely out of touch with realities and who try & plan what I ought to do. . . . Alex is my great supporter; he never bothers me; never suggests what I ought to do. . . .[10]

Monty's view of battle was ruthlessly down to earth:

I am quite certain that the way to deal with the Germans is to face up to them in battle, and fight them; it is the only way to deal with them, because then you kill them. The trouble with our lads is that they are not killers by nature; they have got to be so inspired that they will want to kill and that is what I tried to do with this Army of mine. . . .[11]

He did not find it easy to rouse the killer instinct in his men.

9 Letter to General Brooke, in *Montgomery and the Eighth Army*, ed. S. Brooks, Bodley Head for Army Records Society, 1991, p. 83.
10 Letter to Brigadier Simpson, 19 November, 1942, in Hamilton, vol. I, p. 88.
11 Letter to General Brooke, 27 November 1942, ibid., p. 89 f.

12

EL ALAMEIN: ROMMEL IS ON THE RUN

Private Geoff Jones to his parents.

[Nov. 1942]

. . . We were to attack on the night of the 1st/2nd of November to make a bridgehead to put the armour through; this was to be the deciding factor for the Battle of Egypt. At one o'clock it opened with the usual heavy artillery barrage, and us advancing under it. We hadn't a great deal of trouble with his forward positions, prisoners were rolling in from every side. Another chap and myself rushed a machine gun post with bayonets, and two chaps surrendered without much ado. We had to slip by some Italian tanks dug in, but ran slap into one in the smoke and darkness, and I was very surprised when I found myself looking straight down the barrel of a tank gun. Someone fired through one of the slits and the bullet fanned my cheek; another five prisoners from that episode. We kept ploughing on until we ran into a string of German machine gunners; these were dealt with by the good old Mills 36's. We were then 500 yards beyond our objective and by a 'build up, scrape down' process we managed to get just below the ground before first light. The Tanks rumbled through us, over us, and around us, a terrific tank battle raged about our ears, the shelling for the next two days was a nightmare.

By November 4th we were all pretty 'Bomb Happy' and pig sick of it all. That night news came through that the Daba road was choc-a-block with enemy M.T., and a general movement Westwards was in progress; the armour was through. *The Boche was on the run*, our job was finished and glad we were. The battle of Alamein was over, and the advance had begun.

I thanked God that night the 5th Nov. Some of the boys had some captured Verey pistols and ammo, and they just about went mad. A 5th of Nov. in peacetime was put into the shade that night.

After that a brief rest, and on along the coast road with the blue Mediterranean like a mill pond. Who would have believed that there was a War?

13

'Several steps nearer home'

The young artillery officer writes again.

8th November 1942

. . . We had broken through on one small sector during the night, and at dawn the armour came up through the minefields, passed the infantry, and fanned out in the morning mist. As the mist lifted an hour later we found very much what was expected – a ring of 88 mm anti-tank guns on the high ground only 1500 yards away. Our armour was silhouetted against the mist, so you can imagine what sort of a time we had. . . . What was so distressing was that we gunners were there to knock out the anti-tank guns, but for at least two hours no one could spot a single gun-flash, owing to clever camouflage and that we were attacking up a slope. Still, although we were heavily shelled without stop, by the end of the day the Brigade was claiming quite a lot of tanks, anti-tank guns, etc.

Well, we had two more days of that, gradually getting on top so that when we made our final lunge forward we went straight through. The battle was of course quite the hottest I've ever been in, and one did feel that one was getting forward at last instead of the eternal retrograde movement. . . .

16th Nov.

We listened-in last night to the church bells ringing in England – a very great pleasure, as it was the closest we had felt to home for a long time. What an excellent show! I always felt Winston's propaganda was impeccable, and I'm sure of it now. The chaps of course are in great form, mainly because they feel for the time that they are several steps nearer home. . . .

29th Nov.

I suppose complete happiness is never attainable during a war of death, destruction and grief, but I seem to have got as near to it as possible. It's a real job, it's all-absorbing, it has a high standard of values at its core, it's constantly changing and is therefore invigorating and stimulating, and it's active and completely healthy. . . .

Three months later, after a 1,400 mile pursuit from Alamein, the Eighth Army entered Tripoli. Rommel could not persuade Hitler to withdraw his troops from North Africa to save them for the defence of Sicily and Italy; he gave up and flew home. Monty now turned the Mareth Line:

I enjoyed the battle more than any I have fought. Alamein was a slogging match. Mareth had scope for subtlety and resource, and for outwitting the opponent. The old value of initiative, and of making the enemy dance to your tune all the time, came out very clearly. . . . We very quickly delivered a smashing 'left hook' and knocked him out. . . .[12]

Now Monty attacked the last German defensive position on the Wadi Akarit, between the sea and the salt-marshes. A breach was made in the night of 5/6 April but not exploited to knock out the Axis forces; by the time Monty, in his systematic way, was ready to pursue, the enemy had once again escaped to the west.

12 Letter to General Brooke, 4 April 1943, ibid., p. 194.

14

'My troops are in TREMENDOUS form'

Montgomery reports to the Prime Minister in his characteristic terse style.

April 6, 1943

I delivered a heavy attack against enemy in Akarit position early this morning. I did two things not done by me before, in that I attacked centre of enemy position, and in the dark with no moon. Attack delivered by about three infantry divisions, supported by 450 guns, and enemy was surprised and overwhelmed and all objectives were captured. . . . The prisoners are estimated at 2000 after over six hours' fighting, and many more are flowing in. . . . My troops are in TREMENDOUS form and have fought splendidly. Will press on northwards when I have finished here.

15

'Rocks for a mattress and the stars for a blanket'

Private Jones gives a more detailed and human account of the battle to his parents.

. . . The enemy had a strongly fortified position along the line of the Wadi Akarit, and an order of the day from 'Monty' made it clear he wasn't going to stop there for long.

We moved over the start line at 3.30 on the morning of the 6th of April in pitch darkness. The barrage started as arranged, and hell broke loose for a while. Then it lifted and we stormed the hill at the point of the bayonet, and within 20 minutes Rumana was in our hands. It was such a surprise that the best part of the 126th Regt. of the Italian Spezia division were prisoners before they knew what had happened, together with a large number of Germans.

The Companies tried to consolidate on the top, but it was solid rock and an absolute impossibility to dig in, so they had to stop on the surface. The shells and mortars were coming down like hail; the shelling at Alamein was confetti compared to this, but they didn't shift us by trying to blast us off. The German crack division, the 90th light, launched the counter-attack and it looked as if they were going to succeed. It was a battle of machine guns, mortars and rifles at close range. Things were looking very bad when across the plain behind us came the Black Watch in open formation to give us a hand. The battle raged all day, our artillery laying terrific rolling barrages across the enemy gun lines. Six Junkers 88's came over to try to give us a hammering, but they reckoned without the Bofors guns. Not one of those six planes got back; they were all smashed to bits in mid-air by the finest piece of Ack-Ack shooting I've ever seen. I slept that night with three rocks for a mattress and the stars for a blanket.

Next morning at 5.30 the Intelligence Officer and myself went up the hill, and the birds were singing and everything was peaceful. As we stood at the highest feature of Rumana and looked around, the sight that met our eyes sickened us, hardened as we were to battle scenes. Dead Germans were lying everywhere, minus heads, minus limbs, some in four pieces. I've never seen so many dead Germans during my stay in Africa; they were only boys, most of them 17 and 18 which made it all the more terrible.

By this time our Armour was moving across the plain hard on the heels of the retreating enemy, and we watched for a while, and then made our way to where the boys were brewing up breakfast.

In the middle of the turmoil of battle there were some peaceful moments when a poet could admire the scenery.

16

'After that, who knows?'

Sidney Keyes writes to Renée-Jane Scott three days before he was killed.

26 April 1943

At the moment I am about 100 yards behind the front where I have just finished a course on demolitions, and should be going up to the front again to-night or to-morrow. I am writing in a tiny shut-in valley among the mountains with a clear stream in the bottom, and filled with cypresses and fig-trees. I can hear the Arabs shouting to their flocks, and playing crazily like crickets on their reed pipes. The whole scene is quite perfect, like something staged. . . .

I cannot think that this campaign can last much longer; but after that, who knows? The only way back seems to be through armed Europe. I am not in much of a hurry, but I will get back *some time* if it's humanly possible: and I've never yet failed to do anything I set myself to do.

Once the Wadi Akarit had been taken, it could not be long before the dwindling Axis forces would be trapped between the Eighth Army and the American Second Corps, advancing from the west. On 13 May, the remaining 250,000 Germans and Italians, who had run out of fuel and ammunition, surrendered. The war in North Africa was over.

17

'DERBY DAY' IN TUNISIA

General Sir Harold Alexander to the Prime Minister.

11 May 1943

. . . I expect all organised resistance to collapse within the next 48 hours, and final liq-uidation of whole Axis forces in the next two or three days. I calculate that prisoners up to date exceed 100,000, and they are still coming in. Yesterday I saw a horse-drawn gig laden with Germans driving themselves to the prisoners' cage. As they passed we could not help laughing, and they laughed too. The whole affair was more like Derby Day. The equipment of all sorts will take some time to count. No one has got away except a mere handful by air. We have recovered 2000 of our own prisoners. It is all very satisfying and augurs well for the future.

After the proud commander, a simple soldier shall have the last word to tell us what he considered the secret of the Eighth Army's victory.

18

'Like a happy family'
THE EIGHTH ARMY

Driver Alan Turnbull writes to his wife from Tunis.

The 15th Panzer Division surrendered to us after we had chased one another across Libya for two years. This Army is a grand mob to be in. There is such a spirit of helping one another in it. It does not matter which unit it is – 'tankies', gunners or infantry, they are all the same and just like a happy family, in which the officers enter into it like the rest. That, I think, is the secret of its success. We are proud to be members of it, and it was a fitting climax to the campaign out here that we should be the first to enter Tunis.

Sicily and Italy

> *Now in my dial of glass appears*
> *The soldier who is going to die.*
> *He smiles . . . I cry*
> *NOW . . .*
> *How easy it is to make a ghost*
> KEITH DOUGLAS, TANK OFFICER (DIED 1944)

In the first and largest sea-borne invasion of enemy-held Europe (Operation Husky), after bombing the airfields and dropping the Parachute Brigade of the First British Airborne Division, 150,000 men of Montgomery's Eighth Army and Patton's US Seventh Army landed from 600 ships and 2,100 small craft, commanded by Admiral Cunningham, on the coast of Sicily at 2.45 a.m. in the gale-swept night of 10 July 1943. Most of the 200,000 Italians offered only token resistance, but the 60,000 Germans made a tenacious stand on the slopes of Mount Etna.

19

'What fun we have in the middle of a war!'

Captain D.G. Stallard gives a glossy version of the landing with an eye on the censor.

July 25th

Yes, we have done it again I am proud to say, a perfect crossing, a wonderful landing and everything under control thanking the Navy and the R.A.F. The Sicilians are co-operating very well and all seem very pleased to see us – I do believe they look upon us as deliverers from Nazism! – Only yesterday when I was passing through a village, the populace turned out, gave the V sign and shouted 'Viva Churchill!' Now we haven't ordered that, in fact, we would rather they didn't because it becomes embarrassing when we have to treat them fairly but sternly.

It is awfully difficult trying to write a letter out here in the field – there are so many things I would like to talk about but would be censored. . . . Our contacts with home are the only thing which keeps us sane.

August 11

I am now in an orange grove. The oranges will not be ripe until Christmastime but the shade the trees afford is very pleasant. The irrigation system is very interesting – a large concrete tank with several sluices allow the water to take different aqueducts and each tree is watered daily. The concrete tanks are 9 ft. deep and make ideal bathing pools! What fun we have in the middle of a war!! I have been fortunate to be able to get around a bit on the island – having visited Syracuse and Augusta. Hope to climb Etna in a day or two, we shall put it down as 'training'!!

I hope more mail from you catches up with me before we push on to pastures new. I've always said I shall stay in the Grand Hotel Milan for Christmas! Here's hoping!!!

20

COMBINED OPERATIONS – A TERRIFYING EXPERIENCE

An infantry lieutenant to his father.

29th July 1943

. . . I've had amazingly little sleep for the past fortnight. My boots have just come off for the first time for five days and I've only had one wash and shave during that period BUT, and it is almost incredible, I've never been so fit in my life. No doubt about it if it wasn't for bombs and bullets war would be great fun! . . .

War and fighting is quite unlike what I had expected. A combined operation is the most unpleasant and terrifying experience devised by man once one gets into the assaulting craft. The only thing I can say in its favour is that it is a sure cure for sea-sickness! I've never been in as rough a sea in as small a boat and felt so little worried about the motion! But it was the only thing I wasn't worried about and therefore little comfort. However we landed intact, if not exactly 'according to plan' and my platoon proceeded to fight a little battle of its own with some surprisingly tenacious Italians. It was an amusing if trying day after we'd landed and one I shall enjoy to tell you of later – unless I'm so sickened of war when I get home I can't bear to talk of it. But I doubt it, as I find I have a mental robustness that overcomes the ghastliness of fighting. And frankly I can't imagine that I shall see anything much worse than I have seen in the last fortnight. . . . I was amazed how important trivialities become in even the most dangerous situations. I was much more fussed f.i. about my servant finding a handkerchief for me, than I was about three chaps who were making some very bad shots at me not more than 50 yards away! – Well, enough of war for the moment. I really must go to sleep now. . . .

21

'These are the ravages of war'

Army Nursing Sister Mary Luck describes how her hospital-ship *Dorsetshire* was bombed on 11 July despite being fully illuminated; she pities the wives of the blind and limbless soldiers.

We dropped anchor and could see the men landing and taking a zig-zag path up the rising ground from the shore; no patients were brought on board until about 5.30 p.m. That night we lay at anchor, with guns firing over us, and without our lights on.

On the second evening we were told we could undress for the night, as we were going out of the anchorage, and would have the ship's lights on again. About 5 a.m. I was awakened by a terrible noise and my tennis racket arriving on my head, and shrapnel flying across the cabin. I quickly donned my uniform overall and life jacket. I met the Chief Steward outside my cabin and between us we broke down the door on to the deck, as this was wedged, and I tripped down to my ward; I was met by the night orderly who said, 'He has gone, Sister, he died half an hour after you went off duty'. He referred to the man whose life we had been trying to save all day, and he thought this more important than the present happenings.

After our ship's engines were repaired, we sailed back to Alexandria with a full load of patients, then embarkation started again with patients to be taken home through the Straits of Gibraltar.

The men taken to Britain were the blind, the limbless, and the paralysed, people who would not be fit for war service again, yet they were so happy and excited to be going home. I often wondered how long they could keep up this front, when they had been separated from the mates they had shared experiences with, sent to specialised hospitals for their particular injuries, some to remain there for the rest of their lives, others to eventually go home and try to make a new life under difficult circumstances. Would the wives be able to cope with this changed situation? Not even able to recognise their own husband in some cases. These are the ravages of war.

On 17 August the Allied armies were finally able to join up at Messina, but they had failed to prevent 10,000 Germans and Italians being ferried across the straits to the mainland with all their guns, vehicles and stores. Meanwhile, Monty consoled himself with collecting birds; to the ADCs they were 'a bloody nuisance' and to Harold Nicolson another exercise in public relations, but they seemed to allay Monty's frustrations.

22

MONTY'S MENAGERIE

Montgomery writes to Phyllis Reynolds, foster-mother of his son David.

3 August 1943

All goes well here. I am extremely fit. . . . The present view form my caravan is quite wonderful. My HQ is right up on a mountain side and we look over a tangled mass of mountains, with Mount Etna towering above and dominating everything.

I have begun to collect birds, of which I have always been very fond. I now have some canaries, bought in Lentini, and in one cage I have a pair with a hen sitting on three eggs. She built her nest, laid the eggs, and began to sit, all in my caravan. We moved the HQ 30 miles yesterday, but she firmly sat on the eggs all the time.

I have also a peacock, given me by a grateful Sicilian; he is a very fine bird and struts about round my caravan and the mess. In the mess we have about twelve chickens and two turkeys; these are all very tame and walk about in the tent during meals and get fed by everyone. The turkeys now take food out of my hand. The hens lay very well; and we produced a family of three chicks, as we had a broody hen. So we are kept quite busy in our spare time.

A week later Monty reported: 'Today's bad news is that the hen canary has got fed up with sitting on her eggs and has deserted them.'

23

AMGOT: THE TASK OF RELIEF AND REBUILDING

An army doctor writes to his mother from Catania with a mixture of indignation and resignation.

Aug. 21, 1943

We bombed the aerodrome here to blazes and one end of the town is deserted and in ruins. The people are coming back but mainly the labouring classes who can do nothing else. There used to be 600 doctors in the town: with few exceptions all have fled. The Municipality seems to have had no control over *any* public utilities except the dust carts and they had all stopped working. There were trams. They now stand where they stopped when the current failed. Half the buildings are shuttered. There are no shops that have anything left to sell. The population was almost without food when our army arrived. Yet in our office the automatic telephones are working again (our Signals Corps), the Electricity and Water function again (our engineers) and N.A.A.F.I. talk of starting the Brewery again! The sun shines, the sea is blue, whilst the mountain [Etna] gives a beautiful setting to the place. Yet materially the town is as dead as if a tornado had swept through it and the people look hunted.

One sees masses of children, often quite happy looking, but thin and undernourished. Many are dirty and ragged. They all cry out to passing trucks for cigarettes and food. One little girl in a village made me laugh when she shouted 'Corrend beef'. She probably did not know what it meant but had picked up the words. Our emergency administration – Amgot – gives them rations of bread and olive oil and if necessary cash relief but all they can buy is fruit and vegetables. Meat is nearly non-existent and dairy produce so scarce we have had to send out dried milk for babies. . . .

I find my hatred for Germany grows every day, when I think of our future, progressing from one devastated town to another, one ruined and starving country to another – all to gratify their lust for 'blood and soil'. We can barely find enough to keep these people alive. Everywhere we go we shall meet the same famine and probably when winter comes typhus and epidemics. I hated the thought of this war that I knew was bound to come and the futility and slaughter all over again but, thank God, our vainglorious enemies made me feel that even another War was preferable to slavery of body and soul.

Now, just as we prayed in 1940, for strength to survive, I pray that we may have strength to rebuild when the War is over and that all the sacrifice and suffering of friend and enemy alike will not be so much 'Dead Sea fruit'. To have climbed up twice from the abyss for nothing is more than any sane soul could tolerate.

Yet I am fatalist enough to know that we must wait and watch as well as work. As the old priest said to me in France 'Courage mon fils, le bon Dieu aura toujours le dernier mot'.

On 3 September, Montgomery's Eighth Army crossed to the mainland where, after the fall of Mussolini, Marshal Badoglio had already negotiated the Italian surrender. The Germans were pouring reinforcements into Italy and their six partly incomplete armoured divisions threatened the Salerno beach-head of the Fifth US Army, including the British 10th Corps, by strong attacks which were overcome with the help of naval gunfire and air support. The Allied advance was very slow and made no further use of amphibious capacity – an omission which Churchill castigated as 'scandalous'. The opportunity for landing further north and taking Rome early had been missed through excessive caution: it took nine months of slogging up through the mountains, at the cost of 350,000 Allied casualties, to reach Rome. However, this exhausting frontal assault drained a large number of German troops away from Normandy and Russia, and contributed to later advances there.

On the Adriatic side of the Gustav Line, the important bridgehead over the Tigno was secured on 22 October; three days earlier, the welcome from the Italian population in one of the nearby towns had been, as everywhere, exuberant.

24

WINE AND KISSES FOR THE 'BONO INGLESI'

The infantry lieutenant writes home again.

19th October 1943

. . . We found the Boche in a bit of a pickle when we arrived on the scene and were able to get behind his forward troops. The enemy skinned out after two days of us and we had the amusing task of being the first troops to enter a town. One forgets all about war on these triumphal entries. Peace has come to the people and for the moment it seems to have come to you. Bread, eggs, hot figs, hastily fried up meat, vegetables, potatoes, marsala, vino, brandy and kisses are showered upon us. The old women are always in tears, the old men are drinking hard and shouting 'Viva' or 'Well done boys' according to their linguistic abilities. The children are frantic with joy; even the prettiest girls are allowed out in the streets: and for a while all is confusion. The Mayor, the chief of police, a few Italian officers immaculately dressed, are there to greet us. Scrolls are unrolled, flags are flying (the Colonel always pinches the best for his collection!). The 'sonofabitch' Tedeschi have gone and the 'bono Inglesi' have come. Information is always contradictory, but they all want to tell us what they know. There are spies in the village they say, or a few fascists, – 'Are they to shoot them straightway or lock them up' 'Lock 'em up' we say hastily, not wishing to get dragged into their local politics. The Germans have gone. That is what matters.

On the Anzio beach-head 50,000 Anglo-American troops were pinned down from January to April 1944 until they were saved by the advance from the south. The historic monastery of Monte Cassino, situated in a commanding hill position, was smashed to smithereens by 1,000 tons of bombs and nearly 200,000 shells, although there were no Germans there; but after this destruction, the German Parachute Division moved into the rubble, which was impassable for tanks, and repelled all attacks from the British 13th Corps, until General Anders' Poles stormed Monte Cassino in their fourth desperate attack, suffering 4,000 casualties. A stretcher-bearer gives a moving account of his battalion's hard-fought progress from the port of 'Hush- hush' through the mountains up to Monte Cassino.

25

THE SOLDIER MUST BE A 'HARD LIVE-FOR-THE-DAY FATALIST'

Private Walter Robson to his wife.

12.3.1944

Well, I'm not sure how much of it we can say, but we're in Italy. We landed at the beautiful port of 'Hush-hush' [Mondragone?], staggered off the ship tremendously laden with packs and two kit-bags. To land we had to scramble across the wreck of a bombed ship, its funnel broken and pointing out like an extra gun. There were Italian men begging for food and scrambling for any morsel thrown to them. The town was hollow and echoed like a city of the dead. Rubble intestines of lovely buildings were tumbled on to the pavement and shelling had obviously been pretty thick. . . . We went on and on, and climbed and climbed up in the snow. The moon was on the snow and it looked good but it was a sharp and disconcerting change from the Egyptian desert. . . .

27.3.

It is eerie in the mountains. The white rocks and stones can easily become skulls, specially when you come upon a lonely grave. 'Poor devil, he's well out of it.' But it's not them you think of, it's his people. Jerry ranged on more than an Italian slope when he got them. He ranged on an English home as well. He launched a shell and a letter. The shell brought peace to one, the letter misery to many, a wife, a child, a mother? Yesterday it was Jerry's grave. You thought the same thoughts. A home in Wilhelmshaven. You didn't gloat. Didn't even say that's one less. You don't hate Jerry. You just say why can't we all come to our senses and call the whole thing off.

31.3.

On my birthday I was up among the peaks, face to face with Jerry. You were drinking my health. It's good you didn't know where I was or you wouldn't have drunk a thing and my mother would have spent the night crying. How great a mercy indeed that we are insulated in that way – that we haven't got television sight. If we had, enjoyment and laughter would be forgotten, for there is so much tragedy simultaneous with the slightest laughter that the world would be sobered for ever. My mother, dear soul, says she feels guilty when enjoying the comfort of home and the thought of us occurs, as it nearly always does occur. We feel much the same way when being dished out with food within the hungry gaze of Italian folk. . . .

Mie was very glad when I became a stretcher bearer, 'So glad you'll be saving life, darling, instead of taking it', she said. And I, though I think I would soon dump a stretcher and snatch a rifle if we were attacked, would, I think, be haunted all my life if I knew I had killed anybody. I see the enemy too often as dupes rather than Fascists. I need to see a few atrocities, I suppose, and I'd be a hard and merciless killer. . . . Sorry about the gloom of this letter, ducky, the mood will pass. Good night.

20.7.

It is necessary to develop into hard live-for-the-day fatalists. The fighting soldier must be that. Then we may exult in the advances of the army as a whole, and not brood over the losses that go with victory. But it seems to me that he gets nearer to the animal then.

22.8.

I had a letter from Percy's wife, Hilda. 'I am being brave', she writes. 'No one ever broke their hearts with less fuss before. You wouldn't guess my world was in ruins when I discuss the good war news with people. You would never think that as far as I am concerned it can go on for ever and ever now.' – I promise to be very careful.

26

'We have taken Cassino' – 'when is this insanity going to stop?'

Private Robson to his wife.

22.5.

This letter is bound to be chaotic, which is not surprising, as I am chaotic. We all are at this moment. The papers are no doubt crowing about us and our achievements, but we aren't. We're bitter, for we've had a hell of a time, and are still pressing on. Everybody is out on their feet and one bundle of nerves. I can't tell you much yet and perhaps have already told you more than I should, but I can reassure you that the worst is over, and having come through the last nine days, will get through anything. . . . We've been Stuka'd, Mortared, Shelled, Machine-gunned, Sniped, and although we have taken Cassino, the monastery – none of us feel any elation. We've cracked the hardest nut of the campaign but the losses sadden and frighten us. Attacking with the tanks, bullets everywhere, front, behind, the flanks – phew! At such times you can be ice cool, all the same you don't think much of your chances. . . . We've attacked, attacked, attacked from the beginning with numbers dwindling all the time. We had a hideous 'Stukaing' one day during a tremendous counter-attack. We sat in holes and trembled. . . . And poor Gordon scrambled in head first, crying: 'I can't stand it. I can't stand it – my head, my head.' And he clutched his head and wept. I wiped his forehead, neck and ears with a wet handkerchief, and sang to him. Next day he conquered himself sufficiently to come out with me wandering around in no-man's-land searching for casualties among burning tanks and ditches full of German dead. When, when, when is this insanity going to stop? . . .

Postscript: Women in the War

Single women between the ages of nineteen and twenty-four were conscripted: they made a great contribution to the war effort in the services, civil defence and ordnance factories. The majority of the half a million servicewomen were volunteers, who very much enjoyed the experience of getting away from their humdrum lives and jobs at home.

27

'Isn't life grand'

A WAAF[13] girl writes to her parents.

[August 1943]

All I can say is, isn't life grand – On Tuesday at 15 minutes notice Molly and I left by train for —. We had drink and dinner in an officers!!!! mess and then toured the town which is all barricaded up, with a major driving; we just said 'smoke screen' and poodled through barriers, police and astounded civilians. We were left alone on a deserted football field from 11 p.m. to 1.30 a.m. doing our usual wind observations with torches. The sirens kept wailing but nothing was dropped. We were visited by a nice Second Lieutenant and the Major at midnight and they were perfectly sweet to us. At 1.30 we went to the mess again for some hot Ovaltine; then the Major said we were to be billetted with some A.T.S.;[14] he drove us to a large house, said good-night and told us to see the N.C.O. Well we went in, with a torch, had a jolly good wash in the sergeants' bath and as we'd not the courage to wake anyone and couldn't find an N.C.O. – it was by then 2.45 – so we found the sitting room and slept on a sofa, one each. At 6.30 we got up, went to breakfast – the A.T.S. took *no* notice of us – when the Major arrived we got into his car and away to the station!!! Extraordinary feeling just walking in, sleeping, having breakfast and walking out . . .

I really don't know why everything nice always happens to me – but I'm having a superb time. We did some road making as our 'site' is marshland and 6 feet deep dykes. I swung a pick-axe and shovelled up the remains – we all 'muck in' together here. To-day we started smoke work and did two trials. I had to cross 17 dykes and very few had planks across them. To-morrow we have to draw up the report! What fun!

Last night we escaped the beer session and cycled to a dance. We didn't know a soul, but had a grand evening; the hall was packed with gorgeous civvy girls and few men to go round. We think our Waaf uniform is original in these parts, so I expect that's why we got so many dances. To-morrow night we are to be taught skittles at the local!!!

The contribution made by hard-pressed housewives – many of them anxious mothers or wives of servicemen – who offered their spare-time services, without all the glamour and fun enjoyed by the girls in the Forces, will never be forgotten.

13 Women's Auxiliary Air Force.
14 Auxiliary Transport Service.

28

VOLUNTARY WORK

A country housewife writes to her soldier son, who had lately sailed for an unknown destination.

Nov. 19th, 1943

Darling John,

We are thinking so much of you darling and absolutely longing for a letter. Our thoughts and prayers are ever with you and I hope you can feel something of that, and are not lonely.

Life for the humble civilian is very drab; my friends are awfully good in rallying round now you have gone and are a great solace. . . . Your ancient Mother, aged 48, actually registered for National Service. I do several voluntary jobs – washing up at the school canteen, driving for the W.V.S.[15] etc. I often wish there were rather more interesting jobs here – I'd really like to work in a munitions factory where I should not have time to think. . . .

I felt my earlier work of cleaning up poor little slum evacuees more worthwhile, but the children are quite clean and respectable now. Some of them will find it difficult to go back to their squalid homes I am afraid, and in many cases their foster-parents will hate parting with them. I heard a touching story of a little girl who was so broken-hearted at being made to go back to her poor home where there were eight other children that finally her mother had to send her back again. But she only allowed her to stay long enough to get a new outfit of clothes!

Daddy is quite fit again after his flu, but he badly needs a holiday. He has not had more than a day or two since 1939, and his work is very exacting. His Home Guard work too keeps him out late many evenings, though as you know he really enjoys it. There seems to be a wonderful spirit amongst the men, and he says they would give a very good account of themselves if put to the test. He often looks very tired when he comes in, and of course 55 is rather old for such strenuous doings.

God bless you. Tons of love, Always and ever

Your loving Mummie

15 Women's Voluntary Service.

SEVEN

From Normandy to Victory (June 1944–May 1945)

He lies like used equipment thrown aside,
Of which our swift advance can take no heed,
Roses, triumphal cars – but this one died
GAVIN EWART

Your peace is bought with mine, and I am paid in full, and well,
If but the echo of your laughter reaches me in hell
DAVID GERAINT JONES, KILLED IN NORMANDY

At last the long-awaited moment had come when the Second Front was to open to liberate France. Churchill was determined to watch the D-Day dawn attack from the cruiser *Belfast* which was to bombard the German defences, make a short tour of the beaches after the landing and return in a destroyer. He brushed aside Eisenhower's protest but then the King asked him where he would spend D-Day and expressed the wish to join him; later, however, he had second thoughts.

1

CHURCHILL'S D-DAY FRUSTRATION

King George VI to his Prime Minister.

Buckingham Palace, May 31, 1944
My dear Winston,

I have been thinking a great deal of our conversation yesterday, and I have come to the conclusion that it would not be right for either you or I to be where we planned to be on D Day. I don't think I need emphasise what it would mean to me personally, and to the whole Allied cause, if at this juncture a chance bomb, torpedo, or even mine, should remove you from the scene; equally a change of Sovereign at this moment would be a serious matter for the country and Empire. We should both, I know, love to be there, but in all seriousness I would ask you to reconsider your plan. Your presence, I feel, would be an embarrassment to those responsible for fighting in the ship or ships in which we were, despite anything we might say to them.

So, as I said, I have very reluctantly come to the conclusion that the right thing to do is what normally falls to those at the top on such occasions, namely, to remain at home and wait. I hope very much that you will see it in this light too. The anxiety of these coming days would be very greatly increased for me if I thought that, in addition to everything else, there was a risk, however remote, of my losing your help and guidance.

> Believe me,
> Yours very sincerely,
> GEORGE R.I.

Churchill relates how the next day Admiral Ramsay tried to dissuade both, pointing out that they would see very little, while running considerable risks. The King agreed, but Churchill, who had to be forcibly restrained from watching air battles and raids from the Whitehall roof, insisted defiantly that it was his duty as Minister of Defence to go and that he would not need the king's permission to leave the country, because as long as he was in one of His Majesty's ships he was deemed to be in England. The King pleaded again with his impetuous prime minister.

2

George VI to Churchill.

June 2, 1944

My dear Winston,

I want to make one more appeal to you not to go to sea on D Day. Please consider my own position. I am a younger man than you, I am a sailor, and as King I am the head of all the Services. There is nothing I would like better than go to sea, but I have agreed to stay at home; is it fair that you should then do exactly what I should have liked to do myself? You said yesterday that it would be a fine thing for the King to lead his troops into battle, as in old days; if the King cannot do this, it does not seem to me right that his Prime Minister should take his place.

Then there is your own position. You will see very little, you will run a considerable risk, you will be inaccessible at a critical time, when vital decisions might have to be taken, and however unobtrusive you may be your mere presence on board is bound to be a very heavy additional responsibility to the Admiral and Captain. As I said in my previous letter, your being there would add immeasurably to my anxieties, and your going without consulting your colleagues in the Cabinet would put them in a very difficult position, which they would justifiably resent.

I ask you most earnestly to consider the whole question again, and not let your personal wishes, which I very well understand, lead you to depart from your own high standard of duty to the State.

Believe me,
Your very sincere friend,
GEORGE R.I.

In response, Churchill finally desisted, grudgingly, though with good grace. The incident illustrates what Churchill called the King's 'gracious intimacy' with him, without precedent since Queen Anne and Marlborough in the happier days of their relationship.

After tactical bombing of oil installations and communications in France (much more effective than the terror raids on German city centres), Operation Overlord got under way in the stormy night of 6 June 1944 on the fifty miles of beaches between the river Orne and the Cotentin peninsula. It was preceded by a softening up of the defences with 9,000 tons of bombs, and the capture of key bridges and destruction of gun emplacements by parachutists. An Allied army of 156,000 (swollen to two million in the next two months) landed from 4,000 assault craft under the cover of the battle fleet and over 10,000 planes. It was ultimately by far the greatest combined operation ever undertaken and yet surprise was complete: cleverly fostered feints had deceived the German generals (although not Hitler's intuition). They were expecting the main landing in the Pas de Calais and had kept their best troops there; relying on the unfavourable weather conditions, Rommel and other commanders were away and the reserves immobilized. The much-vaunted 'Atlantic Wall' was stormed.

3

OFF NORMANDY ON D-DAY

Sub-Lieutenant Sidney Montfort writes from the first destroyer to close the Normandy beaches.

12 June 1944
Now that strict censorship over the invasion has relaxed somewhat I'am able to tell you about my modest share in it. When the Admiral hoisted 'Good luck, drive on' we knew the time had come. 'Drive on' was the slogan of the Second Front operation. Everyone was happy that at last D Day had come. . . .

Still, as we watched the friendly shores of England fading away all had their own thoughts. . . . Well the long night passed and when dawn broke, cold and raw, with high seas running, we could see the coast of France. By this time we had overtaken the landing craft. We rapidly closed the beach then raced along the coast to our allotted position where we were to bombard a row of houses where the gun battery was believed to be hidden. As soon as we sighted our target we opened up and poured several hundred shells into these blinking houses, rapidly reducing them to ruins. But before we had fired many rounds Hell was poppin'. The other destroyers found their targets and blazed away, while the battle waggons whipped away 15" shells at targets further inland.

At the same time RAF planes cracked their bombs down on the shore defences, and the rocket-carrying sea-craft let off their death-dealing loads on the beaches, the most appalling and demoralising weapon surely ever devised! Shells from enemy guns landed on the beach and in the sea and occasionally German planes tried to bomb our troops, only to be chased away by the Spits.

By this time many buildings were ablaze and furious close-range cross fire was going on as our landing craft touched down and the Pongos[1] dashed up the shore to engage the enemy. I watched all this through my binoculars – a marvellous grand-stand view! I watched the battle raging all day as the troops struggled through booby traps and tried to catch the snipers. Gradually they established themselves, tanks and lorries came ashore and pushed inland.

Then in the evening came the most wonderful sight of all – the arrival of hundreds of gliders, packed with brave and gallant men. Boldly they went in to land through a curtain of flak and tracer. Then followed their stores and gear by multi-coloured parachutes. It was all vividly clear in the bright evening sky.

As darkness fell we left the French coast and headed for home. Then everything quietened and we pulled our dufflecoat hoods closer round our ears and settled down by the guns for the night. . . .

Allied superiority was overwhelming: 2,000 tanks against 100, 10,700 planes against 570. Only a quarter of the German army was in the west of which only thirty-six infantry and six panzer divisions were stationed on the coast, most of them in the Pas de Calais: Rommel's Army Group of nine infantry and a single panzer division was the only initial obstacle. But Montgomery could not be hurried in his methodical ways, even if the US generals felt frustrated. Instead of being taken according to plan on the first day when the way was clear, Caen fell only after six weeks' hard fighting in the biggest clash of tanks; the invasion armies were now able to fan out from the constricted beach-head area.

Churchill could not wait any longer and Monty commented condescend-ingly on his visit to Caen on 22 July: 'I don't like doing it as the place is very often shelled, but it will please the old chap and he likes to go to dangerous places. . . .'[2]

---

1 Soldiers of all ranks (Forces' slang).
2 Letter to Mrs Reynolds, in Hamilton, op. cit., vol. II, p. 750.

4

'I am in the pink'

An unknown soldier's letter, 'captured' unposted by a German near Caen, shows that First World War expressions were still in use.

July 12, 1944

Dear Ted and Brenda,

I am in the pink and have so far escaped a blighty one. I have no idea when I shall be home as I guess we will have to keep going after the retreating Germans. I suppose Paris will be our next objective, now Caen has fallen, and I hope it is. Not in ruins like the villages we have captured. There is no wine, women and song out here, as it is very seldom we see any civilians. After our last attack I don't want to go into another like it, as it was a real bloody battle. We had bread to-day for the first time since we came over here and I certainly did enjoy it; we only got one slice for breakfast, but really cannot expect too much yet. I hope to be able to see you very soon. . . .

5

LOVELY PLACES FLATTENED – IT MIGHT HAVE BEEN BURNESIDE

Private Geoff Jones to his mother.

[n.d.]

Dear Mam,

We are quite near a certain village here which has been reduced to ruins by shell fire, and the stink is enough to knock you over, absolutely revolting. The place might be Burneside, and it makes me recoil to think how near this was our lot in the first two years of this conflict. I pray to God this does not last long, lovely places being absolutely flattened. The world has truly gone mad. That was one good thing about the desert, you hurt no one who might be innocently involved.

There must have been thousands of head of splendid cattle destroyed across here since D Day. One can see them grazing in the fields of no-man's-land, those that have so far gone unscathed. We have had to shoot some which have been badly hit; it's the kindest way out. I have also seen the boys corner cattle which have gone unmilked for days, and fill a steel helmet with milk. There are brighter sides to everything, aren't there?

The fighting out here now is bitter, neither side seems to give any quarter. We have the Jerry outgunned, out-tanked, and are far superior in aircraft. The Royal Artillery never stop, it's just one continual hubbab night and day, which one has to get used to all over again. Where we are it's more or less like the last war, Jerry is only 300 yards away from me where I am writing this letter, the shortest no-man's-land I've ever been on. . . .

Last week we came by some pork, no questions, please, and commenced to fry it; but just as it was ready we had a direct hit on the cook house by a jerry shell, finished the pork, also two boxes of compo rations and our appetite into the bargain. I had a total black out and we had one man wounded, so we came off pretty well. The remains of the pork were later retrieved by some neutral who happened to be passing by, and devoured it with great relish, much to our annoyance.

Oh! one thing I really must tell you if the Censor will let me; – during one of my excavations of German gun positions I came across some marked maps, large scale artillery copies, giving the area from Carnforth to Carlisle on the West coast, and Leeds to Newcastle on the East. It gave me quite a turn I can tell you. But the beauty of it was that the backs of the maps had since been used for printing orders – the Boche dispelled from his mind any ideas he ever had of invading the British isles. Peculiar what one comes across, isn't it? It's quite feasible that he hoped to cut the British isles in half, probably from Arnside in the West and the Tyne in the East; please convey that to the Home Guard with my compliments.

I think Jerry is having quite a lot of trouble with his troops over here. There are so many of the Satellites [sic] with them, and they sometimes walk quite openly into our lines and surrender, and on interrogation give away stacks of information as to their dispositions, much to the delight of the gunners who slam 100 shells or so over, firing on information received from the prisoners.

Will have to close now as it is getting rather dark. Good night mam, God bless you. Fondest love as always

your ever loving son
Geoff

Paris was liberated on 25 August and the next day, Monty, now a Field Marshal, started his drive into Flanders to Antwerp and Brussels, which was liberated on 3 September.

6

NO SLEEP BUT 'TAILS UP & FULL OF BEANS'

Lieutenant Phil Crosfield to his parents.

5-9-44

The greatest pessimist must admit that things are full of hope. At times, I must admit that we almost wish the advance weren't so fast. Two actions in one day & then a long night march is no joke.

Typical of it was a few days ago. We were in action until about 5 p.m., then we did a long march of about 40 miles, arriving about midnight in a 'Hide' area where we fondly imagined we should spend what was left of the night. I told my chaps to put up their bivouacs & get some sleep & went off to get some food brewed up for them. When I got back we were told to be ready to go into action by daybreak. So I got reveille laid on for 2.30, and found myself with about half an hour in which to snatch some sleep. To crown everything, I had no tent and now it began to rain! So I put on my mac, crawled under a truck and got a precious half hour's sleep. Then up again, leading the guns in the dark, trying to map read, and reaching our new area at about 5 a.m., guns in action by 6 a.m. And now I hear we may move again, so no sleep for me. I have forgotten when I last took my clothes or boots off! Never mind, it's great to have him on the run. . . . I long & yearn to go to bed & sleep the clock round twice. On more than one occasion I have gone to sleep standing up in my truck. In spite of it all, I am very fit and we all have our tails up & are full of beans.

On 7 September Monty sensed that victory was within his reach:

The historical march of events continues, and we are now in Brussels and Antwerp. . . . We have reached a vital moment in the war and if we now take the right decision we could be in Berlin in three weeks and the German war would be over. . . . I fear very much we shall have a compromise, and so prolong the war.[3]

But the parachute drop on Arnhem on 17 September 1944 by the First Airborne Division which was to clear the way to the Rhine failed despite gallant resistance. A private in the 2nd S. Staffs Regiment who was killed in the action had written a farewell letter before, ready to die not so much for England or the liberation of Europe but for the little world centred around his Mom.

7

'I am no flag-waving patriot'

Private Ivor Rowbery to 'the best Mother in the world'.

Blighty (Some time ago)

Dear Mom,

Usually when I write a letter it is very much overdue, and I make every effort to get it away quickly. This letter, however, is different. It is a letter I hoped you would never receive, as it is just a verification of that terse, black-edged card which you received some time ago, and which has caused you so much grief. It is because of this grief that I wrote this letter, and by the time you have finished reading it I hope that it has done some good, and that I have not written it in vain.

Tomorrow we go into action. As yet we do not know exactly what our job will be, but no doubt it will be a dangerous one in which many lives will be lost – mine may be one of those lives.

Well, Mom, I am not afraid to die. I like this life, yes – for the past two years I have

---

3   Letter to Major-General Simpson, in Hamilton, op. cit., vol. III, p. 30.

planned and dreamed and mapped out a perfect future for myself. I would have liked that future to materialize but it is not what I will but what God wills, and if by sacrificing all this I leave the world slightly better than I found it I am perfectly willing to make that sacrifice. Don't get me wrong though, Mom, I am no flag-waving patriot, nor have I ever professed to be.

England's a great little country – the best there is – but I cannot honestly and sincerely say 'that it is worth fighting for'. Nor can I fancy myself in the role of a gallant crusader fighting for the liberation of Europe. It would be a nice thought but I would only be kidding myself. No, Mom, my little world is centred around you and includes Dad, everyone at home, and my friends at W'ton – that is worth fighting for – and if by doing so it strengthens your security and improves your lot in any way, then it is worth dying for too. If not then my sacrifice is all in vain. Have you benefited, Mom, or have you cried and worried yourself sick? I fear it is the latter. Don't you see, Mom, that it will do me no good, and that in addition you are undoing all the good work I have tried to do. Grief is hypocritical, useless and unfair, and does neither you nor me any good.

I want no flowers, no epitaph, no tears. All I want is for you to remember me and feel proud of me, then I shall rest in peace knowing that I have done a good job. Death is nothing final or lasting, it is just a stage in everyone's life. To some it comes early, to others late, but it must come to everyone sometime, and surely there is no better way of dying. . . .

My only regret is that I have not done as much for you as I would have liked to. I loved you, Mom, you were the best Mother in the world, and what I failed to do in life I am trying to make up for in death, so please don't let me down, Mom, don't worry or fret, but smile, be proud and satisfied. . . . . Remember that where I am I am quite O.K., and providing I know that you are not grieving over me I shall be perfectly happy. . . .

Good-bye, and thanks for everything,

Yr. unworthy son,

Ivor

Interlude: Doodle-bugs and Rockets on London

A week after the Normandy landing, pilotless jets each carrying one ton of explosive were launched from fifty-five ramps in the Pas de Calais against the London area; they were christened 'Vengeance weapon 1' (Vergeltungswaffe 1) by the Germans, and, with characteristic humorous derision, 'doodle-bugs' by the English. Their reassuring buzz and glow, and their alarming death-rattle and ominous silence before falling down and exploding, became part of London life: 9,000 were sent over in the next three months of which 2,340 got through the barrage of balloons, A-A guns and fighter planes; they killed 9,000 people and destroyed 23,000 houses.

The doodle-bugs were succeeded by the V-2 thirteen-ton rockets (forerunners of our intercontinental missiles), half a dozen of which were launched per day from Holland between September 1944 and March 1945; over 500 reached London, causing nearly 9,000 casualties.[4] Because their approach could not be heard, they were less nerve-racking but more frightening, and, being much bigger, they struck with a vengeance.

8

'Send exam form in as arranged'

Judy Murphy, a medical student, describes the effect of a V-2 rocket to her parents.

[n.d]

We were sitting at a lecture today at 4.10 pm when suddenly everything went black and the air was filled with glass and dust. The window behind Zoe and I sailed across the room and the frame fell on our shoulders. Then we were helped out and found we were all right. Some girls had bad cuts but I have only a bruise on my back.

The corner of the school where the V-2 fell is utterly destroyed. Many must be killed, especially at the Methodist HQ where there was a big office staff – completely gone. If the bomb had fallen just a fraction nearer there would have been about 200 medical students killed. Thank God we are safe.

P.S. Please send exam form in as arranged!

Monty planned to spend Christmas at Hindhead but could not because of the Ardennes offensive, Hitler's last desperate gamble to cut off the British Army in a second Dunkirk. He reported from the front on 12 December: 'All well here; dogs, canaries, goldfish, ADCs etc.' and again on Christmas Day: 'The Americans have taken a first Class bloody nose; I have taken over command of the 1st and 9th American armies and all troops in the north, part of the front, and I am busy sorting out the mess. . . . What a life!'[5]

The turning-point in the battle for the Rhineland came on 16–17 February in the Goch-Cleve area, the key to the Rhine approaches.

---

4 Cp. B. Collier, *Battle of V-Weapons*, Hodder & Stoughton, 1964. Hitler's Armament Minister, Speer called their blindly vindictive concentration on the relatively ineffective V-weapons their greatest mistake, at the expense of the development of jet fighters and ground-to-air rockets which he thought could have beaten the Allied air offensive in 1944. (A. Speer, *Inside the Third Reich*, Sphere Books, 1971, p. 493 f)
5 Letter to Mrs Reynolds, in Hamilton, op. cit., vol. III, pp. 181, 238.

9

'Truly thankful this was not our lot in 40–41'
IN GERMANY AT LAST

Lance-Corporal Geoff Jones to his mother.

20.2.45

I have just wallowed my way through what was once a peaceful German village, it is now flattened by our guns, bombers and infantry. Its 15th century church is roofless and holed like a sieve, but by some remarkable phenomenon the altar is still standing intact through it all. That always seems the case.

Here and there in the streets shattered furniture, and hanging out of one window a teddy-bear like a gaunt reminder that once a child has resided there, not even knowing what this war is all about. . . . I saw a Frau yesterday; she looked at me with eyes like a snake; they don't like this at all.

I'm writing this letter in a cellar amongst the ruination that I described before, about the only abode left to stay in. The hurricane lamp is shedding its pale light about me. I wish the people at home could see this in its stark reality; they would be truly thankful this was not our lot in the dark days of 40–41. . . .

The moonglow has just been switched on – a searchlight over the front to dazzle the Boche – and is making the broken walls stand out in clearer perspective. The guns are belching out, as they have been all day, in a drumfire barrage, seems to go on for ever without ceasing.

For the last 11 days I've slept on the ground, and have never had a dry blanket. I sleep fully clothed including leather jerkin and parachutist's jumping jacket; when I get in bed you should see the steam rise in clouds about me. . . .

Must draw to a close now, once again, once more, once less.

After a bombardment from over 3,000 guns and waves of bombers, the 21st Army Group launched on 23 March a night assault across the Rhine in the Rees sector, spearheaded by 150 Buffalo amphibious armoured personnel carriers, while the 6th Airborne Division was being dropped behind the German lines. The 1st Commando Brigade took Wesel, and when the stubborn defence of Rees by a German parachute battalion had at last been overcome, a twenty-mile bridgehead was established. A triumphant Monty, about to cross the Rhine, wrote to General Alan Brooke: 'My HQ are now in Germany. I have waited a long time for this moment and have travelled a long way before bringing it to pass. It is a great thrill. . . .'[6]

---

6 Hamilton, op. cit., vol. III, p. 418.

10

120 GERMAN PARATROOPERS SURRENDER
TO TWO LANCE-CORPORALS

Lance-Corporal Jones writes home from hospital.

4.4.45

After the great battle was over, the strip of land between the Maas and the Rhine, from Nijmegen down to Venlo, was one churned up desolate area of smashed homes, flattened houses and dashed hopes for the Boche.

The attack started at night 23rd, to the most ferocious artillery bombardment I've ever heard. The other two brigades of our division did the assault and us close at their heels in the early hours of the morning. Jerry fought stubbornly and pinned our Battalion to the road for nine hours before we took our first objective.

It was soon after 10 when the airborne started coming over. What a sight to behold! The Yanks came first, the aircraft flying in perfect formation at 600 feet; paratroopers, then gliders behind. All the guns stopped firing; there was silence except for the roar of the engines. Jerry must have been surprised; it took some time for them to get over believe me. The Sixth Airborne followed, being towed by the giant Stirling bombers. It took about 90 minutes, a sight well worth seeing. The bombing was terrific. I don't think Jerry has ever had before such a hammering. The cloudless sky was filled with planes from morning to night.

A squadron of tanks had to be brought up, it was my job to go back to bring them. I left about 5 a.m. and it's a good job I did, as Jerry counter-attacked 15 minutes after I left, and by the time I got back with the tanks, running the gauntlet of machine gun fire, I found Battalion H.Q. surrounded by the Boche. The situation was of extreme gravity. We got our artillery to lay down heavy fire, and our mortars and anti-tank guns added to the barrage. This helped to keep the enemy's head down till we got organised for a counter-attack. But we never did that counter-attack.

I was watching the terrific fire dropping a few hundred yards in front of me, when through the smoke came a German officer, an M.O., as it so turned out, and told my pal (who can speak German) that he thought his men would pack in if two of us would go with him. We never gave a thought to the possibility of it being a trap; all we thought about was getting the lads in Battalion H.Q. to safety. We took an automatic weapon each, and walked with the German officer into his lines.

Before we knew what had happened we were surrounded by paratroopers with their hands in the air, bawling 'Kamerad' at the top of their voices, some of them crying like babies. In all we took 120 prisoners between us. I'd never seen anything like this before. These fellows, the cream of the German army, are the most stubborn defensive fighters in the world; I was awestruck I can tell you. Our barrage had done its work. There were dead lying everywhere in grotesque attitudes.

Before I knew what was happening, our guns opened up in another ferocious salvo. The first few shells went over our heads, but one fell right amongst us, wounding me, and many Jerries were killed. The German doctor grabbed me and pulled me into a house, where he did me up, first stopping the bleeding. I thought what a funny situation to be in, wounded and being bandaged by a German.

I struggled to my feet eventually and staggered to the door, in time to see one of our companies marching by and take over. I gave them a yell to send back for an ambulance to cart the wounded away. Then I tried to get to the next house but I couldn't make it, as I was as sick as a pig and feeling very faint. Our vehicles eventually arrived, and I left the scene lying across the bonnet of a jeep. Believe me I thought that jeep had square wheels before, after a rough journey, I arrived at the 81st General, the same one as I was in, in Normandy, and coincidentally it was the same nurse that gave me the knock out drops. She put something in my arm, and I heard the organs playing as I sank into oblivion. It was a lovely feeling, after so much noise. . . .

The Second Army drove two hundred miles to the Elbe and liberated Holland on the way.

11

CHAMPAGNE WITH THE BURGOMEISTER

Major N. Geldard to his sister.

5 April 1945

On Easter Sunday we had orders to move up to a town in Holland and I had the pleasure of seeing what I had been longing to see – people celebrating their liberation. They did not actually cheer us in that town, but they were all out in the streets waving orange flags. It was an old moated town and three out of the five bridges were blown. There was a terrific traffic jam – with crowds of civilians looking on with awe.

We had a quiet but very sincere little party in the evening with the Burgomeister and leaders of the resistance – two bottles of champagne were produced – by the light of a hurricane lamp. A paratrooper from Arnhem who had been hidden for five months rolled up and two airmen hidden for five weeks. The Burgomeister, a forcible personage, had come out of hiding – went straight to the Town Hall and got on with his job and only asked for an hour off to go and see his wife. Stories of the underground people – the risks they had run and of those who had paid for it – of the people who had been tortured or undergone the third degree questioning – of good Germans and bad Germans and how none of them trust each other. An underground resistance man came in with wireless transmitting sets left with him by the Germans with instructions to send them reports of all our doings. . . .

On 30 April Hitler committed suicide in his Berlin bunker and on 4 May Montgomery accepted the unconditional surrender of the German forces in north-west Germany. After five years and eight months of war victory had been won in Europe, but the mood of the Army and of the people at home remained sober.

12

THE SMELL OF GERMANS

Lieutenant Chris Cross, 6th Airborne Division (Gliders) writes on the day of the Lüneburg Heath surrender, while coping with thousands of German troops and civilian refugees in 'unending streams of waggons', 'frightened out of their wits by the Russkis'.

4 May 1945

I suppose I should feel elated, but I feel tired and disgusted, and I can't get the smell of Germans out of my mouth and nose, no matter how much I clean my teeth. Disgust, contempt and a little pity mix ill. What now, I wonder?

13

REJOICING AND APPREHENSION ON VE DAY

Thomas Jones describes the atmosphere in London.

May 22, 1945

I was in London for VE Day. From the balcony of the Athenaeum I watched the rejoicing crowds and saw Winston passing through them waving his hat and making the sign of victory. A more orderly or happy crowd never thronged a public thoroughfare, certainly I saw no excess anywhere. The mood of the people is too serious for extravagant demonstration; all the camp revelations were fresh in everybody's mind and we are still anxious about the way the Three Powers will work together in Europe. Last Sunday's papers were almost as depressing as on any Sunday in the war.

The soldiers had many extraordinary tales to report when censorship was lifted: one story may illustrate their never failing cheerfulness and humour, and their acceptance of what fate had in store for them.

14

HOW THE SARISBURY GREEN WOMEN'S INSTITUTE'S NOTICEBOARD WENT TO WAR

Bombardier E.D. Bickers writes to the Ladies from Germany.

27.5.45

You will doubtless be extremely surprised to hear from me, a complete stranger. Methinks you will be even more surprised when you learn about what I am writing.

Have you ever missed a notice-board from your Institute? Probably not. It is the sort of thing that wouldn't be missed in a hundred years. But that it is missing is a very definite fact, because I have it here in Germany. I will explain.

Early last June we were in bivouac at Sarisbury Green, awaiting our turn to sally forth and participate in the jolly old free-for-all that had just begun on the beaches of Normandy. It so happened one morning that we required a flat surface to do duty as a card table (we were playing poker), so I said, 'Right-ho, chaps, leave it to me', and promptly heaved along and swiped your jolly old notice-board. With every intention, of course, of returning it before we beetled off. Unfortunately, we were suddenly told, without any fore-warning what-so-ever, to grab our guns and get to the wag-gons, as we were OFF. Well, in the general shambles that ensued, the jolly old board got slung into the back of a truck and came over with us.

Chapter Two. Whilst we were exchanging hot words with the fearful Boche round the battered city of Caen, an exceedingly nasty missile that whistled 'Deutschland über Alles' as it came through the air, fell where I'd been standing a split second before and blew my Map Board to wherever it is that true and trusty map-boards go when they leave this muddled world of ours. A map-board being to me as necessary as is a powder-puff to the modern girl, I came upon your notice affair. So I converted it forthwith. And it has seen service ever since.

It was with us when we smashed through Caen and bottled the Hun in the Falaise Gap, when we crossed the Seine and chased him the length of Belgium and into Holland, when we fought down to the Maas and along the river throughout the win-ter; it was there at the crossing of the Rhine and the Elbe and was nearly at the Baltic when friend Fritz threw in the towel. Now it is doing duty with the army of occupa-tion in the area of the Kiel Canal. One day I hope it will make the journey back to Sarisbury Green, there to rest in the peace and quiet, surrounded with the halo of all honour and glory for having been the first Women's Institute Notice-Board to go through a major campaign.

You may doubt the sanity of one who troubles to write up on such a subject, but the fact is that your jolly old board has become a sort of mascot with little me. If it becomes necessary for me to totter along to add my humble weight to the argument that is proceeding round and about Japan, then your jolly old board will totter that-a-ways also. . . .

E I G H T

The War with Japan (December 1941–September 1945)

You who fell beside us, pioneers
Shorn of the future – you who chose to be
The hopeless van of the victorious years . . .
BRIGADIER BERNARD FERGUSON,
RETURN TO BURMA

The war with Japan, like that with Germany, started disastrously and for similar reasons: initially forces, equipment and training were insufficient to cope with Japanese superior fighting capacity and tactics.

Singapore: 'the worst disaster in British history'

A general's duty to win, as soldier's duty to fight
FIELD-MARSHAL VISCOUNT SLIM

At the same time as they attacked Pearl Harbor, the Japanese landed in the north of the Malay peninsula. Admiral Sir Tom Phillips sailed from Singapore with the newly arrived battleship *Prince of Wales* and the battle-cruiser *Repulse*, in an attempt to cut the Japanese invasion supply line in the Gulf of Siam. To succeed he needed fighter cover and surprise; but the fighters did not arrive till it was too late and enemy submarines had spotted the ships. Eighty-five Japanese naval planes flew 400 miles from Saigon and sank both vessels with torpedoes and bombs, for a loss of only three planes, despite the 175 anti-aircraft guns of the *Prince of Wales*: nothing like it had been done before and it stunned Britain more than any other disaster.

1

TALKING TO THE BISCUIT BOX

An unidentified survivor of the sinking of HMS *Prince of Wales* on 10
December 1941 writes home.

Singapore, 17 Dec.
. . . We were hit by at least four yellow belly torpedoes. We also got hit by a bomb in
another attack and that killed a good many men. I was standing in what was known
as the Admiral's Bridge and certainly had a marvellous view for nearly two hours.

We saw the first torpedo coming towards us and felt it hit a nasty jar but very little
noise in the midst of all our own anti-aircraft. This gave us a list to port. I remember
the Fleet Gunnery Officer and I having quite an argument as to how many degrees of
list we actually had. . . .

A good deal later on, when the second main torpedo attack was made on us, after
Repulse had disappeared I saw about four tracks of torpedoes coming towards us and
remember telling the Flag Lieutenant to watch a particular one that was coming
straight towards us. Sure enough one of them hit us under the forecastle and the one
we were watching hit about four or five seconds later dead under where we were
standing, throwing up a huge spray of water right in front of us, at the same time the
sky seemed full of these yellow bellies and another torpedo hit us on the other side.
There were of course several misses but the Japs had done their work.

About half an hour later, nine bombers came along at a fair height in a perfect formation of line abreast they did not seem to mind all the A.A. Barrage which we put
up against them. They came along like a solid steel rod straight for us and dropped
their bombs. We fell flat on the deck and while lying there waited for the bombs to
explode. I remembered having read in some A.R.P. pamphlet that one should put a
pencil in the mouth which I did. The one bomb that hit us was a big one possibly
1000 lb, and it burst about 200 ft. from us and made a hell of a noise.

Although I don't think that the bomb made very much difference to the ship, it
appeared at the time to have put the finishing touch to us, the engines had stopped
and there we were quite useless waiting for the next attack which thank God never
came! It was not necessary. . . .

We were all still watching proceedings from our bridge when the order came to
abandon ship. To get down in comfort on to the upper deck would have meant going
down no fewer than six ladders. By the time I was half way down the first ladder
however, the ship was beginning to list really badly and my only real anxiety was not
to hurt myself before getting in the water and thereby spoil my swimming. After getting down the first ladder I was in what is called the 'flag deck' which by that time
was about 12 ft. instead of about 50 ft. above the water on one side and quite unget-
table on the other side. I decided to jump on the low side. Before doing so, I jerked
my binoculars, cap and shoes off; this could not possibly have taken more than two
seconds but when I looked at the water again the 12 ft. drop had gone and I just
stepped in, as one would go into a swimming bath by the shallow end. I swam like
hell. I did not get very far away however when I was closely pursued by the ship's
mast which hit me very slightly on the head and pushed me down under water for

what seemed an eternity. However, I disentangled myself from the rigging and shot up like a piece of cork, as a result of my life belt being blown up. I just had time to get my breath (a very quick one) when a nest of guns from the other side of the ship came tumbling down and took me down in the depths again, this time I thought I was done for. But Providence was on my side, I bobbed up again, looked round to see if anything else was coming up to hit me and saw the old ship upside down and bottom up. My next thought was the danger of being sucked down again when the ship finally disappeared and so I started swimming like hell again toward the most beautiful biscuit tin that I have ever seen floating about. I think I reached that tin not a minute too soon! It kept me afloat beautifully and gave me time to recover my breath. It was such a beautiful biscuit box, darling, I remember being very silly and talking to it, 'You and I are going to be great friends for a long time'.

After a time, I started to swim again with my biscuit box until I eventually reached a carley float with about six men in it. A carley float is one of those oblong life saving contraptions which hang about ships. Three men hauled me on board and I was saved. . . . There were still a large number of men in the water and as most of us were too weak to swim and rescue people, the only thing I could do was to talk to some of these men by encouragement and gentle persuasion make them swim or drift slowly to the float. I also got together another couple of laden floats and so ended up with a little party of about twenty.

I found a cask of water and had it passed round and we all felt better. In the meantime, two of the ship's motor boats had floated off the ship as she went over and these together with a boat from a destroyer went round and picked up all the stray people in the water who had not been lucky enough to find a carley float. They were all taken on board the same destroyer who had been alongside the ship. But she was getting very full and just could not hold any more men. She eventually went off at full speed but not before another couple of destroyers had hove in sight. We were eventually taken off about 3.15, the ship having sunk at 1.20 p.m.

I was in a shocking mess after my long immersion in a mixture of seawater and oil fuel but my watch was still working perfectly! We messed about for a couple of hours picking people up and eventually pushed off home at full speed and got there at midnight with about 700 men on board. What a party. I was able to get a sort of wash and discarded my filthy clothes and settled in the wardroom which was packed full of men who had been hurt and about thirty officers. The hospitality was good, very good in difficult circumstances and I must admit that I had an incredible quantity of whisky which made absolutely no difference to one's head. One might have been drinking water; but it was very soothing.

The discipline and the calmness of all the lads in the P. of W. was simply magnificent and knocked all the usual Daily Mirror stories into a cocked hat.

Frightened? Yes of course I was frightened and yet I had keyed myself up for unpleasant events anyway, after that first torpedo and so one did not sort of worry much. . . . And that my darling is the whole rather lamentable story! I think it was a miracle that a good many of us got away with it and I thank God for it.

Eleven Buffalo fighters appeared on the scene just in time to see the survivors being picked up by the escorting destroyers; more than two thirds of the crews were saved but the admiral went down.

2

'Something above human nature'

A Buffalo pilot describes to Vice-Admiral Sir Geoffrey Layton how ship-wrecked survivors of the *Prince of Wales* waved to him like Brighton holiday-makers.

[10 December 1941]
. . . It was obvious that the three destroyers were going to take hours to pick up those hundreds of men clinging to bits of wreckage and swimming round in the filthy, oily water. Above all this the threat of another bombing and machine gun attack was imminent. Every one of those men must have realized that. Yet as I flew round every man waved and put up his thumb as I flew over them. . . . Many men in dire danger waving, cheering and joking, as if they were holiday makers at Brighton waving at a low-flying aircraft. It shook me, for here was something above human nature. . . .

Three Japanese élite divisions, including the mechanized Imperial Guards, descended six hundred miles through the Malayan jungle in less than two months, shattering all British attempts to halt their advance towards Singapore. They were aided by their armour and 4:1 air superiority, but rigid British textbook drill was, in any case, quite unsuited to cope with their imaginative infiltration tactics. Like Rommel, General Yamashita was a thoroughly up-to-date professional in his use of speed, daring, and cunning, and his fanatical troops were even more ruthless and hardy than the Afrika Korps.

'We had been caught napping, everyone of us: civilians in self-indulgent blind contentment with present prosperity; soldiers in conceited complacency; government in abstractions,' wrote an inhabitant of Singapore.[1] Years of inertia, neglect and wishful thinking bore their bitter fruit: the fixed cannon of Singapore were facing the sea, their trajectory useless against an enemy coming from the north, and General Percival had taken no defence measures for fear of alarming the soldiers and civilians. Despite the air raids, life in the city went on 'as usual' right to the last moment: cocktails, bridge, cricket – while the Governor called rhetorically for 'total war – shoulder to shoulder'.

1 *Blackwood's Magazine*, vol. 251, May 1942, p. 372.

3

'Will they have the cheek to attack?'

A correspondent in Singapore wonders and thinks they will be all right if they don't get rattled.

17 January 1942

Singapore is the greatest surprise: very peace-timey, though full of refugees. The district round Cirano's all gone; the Alhambra too – one somehow didn't expect it here. But Singapore goes on much the same, and doesn't seem to understand the Japanese are almost on our doorstep. Troops are pouring back. Surely we should have stood longer in Johore!

We don't hear much about reinforcements. Some Hurricanes have arrived, but not nearly enough. We want three times more of them. We must be inflicting quite ten times the casualties on them, and yet they keep coming on. New troops all the time, while ours are wearying. Leeches in the Ulu, torrential rains, the mosquitoes . . . and not knowing where they are. But how they manage the jungle fighting – that jungle that was to be our sure shield! Will they have the cheek to attack the island itself, I wonder; or just bang at us from Johore?

25 Jan.

'Raffles' go on just the same: dancing every night, only you have to get your drinks now; the 'boys' have all run away. . . . The British are wonderful people for carrying on and not worrying. But we seem quite incapable of any war ideas or ruthless feelings.

1st Feb.

We are under gunfire now from the mainland; one finds how much worse bombardment is than bombing. . . . It is getting *bad*. Singapore is utterly unprepared for a show like this. There is the devil of a time going on in the harbour: dive-bombing the shipping; fires in the town, at the naval base. Immense numbers of troops and transport tearing here and there night and day. We should be allright for a long time if we don't get rattled. . . .

At midnight on 8 February four thousand Japanese crossed the Johore Straits in two hundred launches, expecting to be met by a barrage of burning oil and petrol poured onto the sea, but not even a searchlight was turned on them. There were sporadic brave attempts to hold off the invaders, but the defence was too static and dispersed. The city, whose population had been doubled by the influx of refugees to one million was soon burning under a hail of bombs and shells; after the destruction of the airfields, the few remaining British planes flew to Sumatra. The garrison of nearly ninety thousand troops, almost two thirds Asian, lost heart and began to desert, and the water supply was running out; no one knew that the Japanese were short of ammunition.

On 15 February Singapore surrendered with a garrison larger than the Japanese army in the whole of the Malay peninsula, in what Churchill later called 'the worst disaster and largest capitulation in British history'. The following exchange of cables during the fatal last five days of the drama show the different attitudes of the three principal leaders: Churchill's romantic insistence on a fight to the death for the sake of British honour, Wavell's loyal transmission of this ruthless order – though modified by escape clauses – and Percival's concern for the lives of the troops and civilians in his charge in a hopeless situation.

4

FIGHT 'TO THE BITTER END'!

Churchill to General Wavell, Supreme Allied Commander.

10 February 1942

... There must at this stage be no thought of saving the troops or sparing the population. The battle must be fought to the bitter end at all costs. ... Commanders and senior officers should die with their troops. The honour of the British Empire and of the British Army is at stake. I rely on you to show no mercy to weakness in any form. ... The whole reputation of our country and our race is involved. ...

General Sir Archibald (later Field-Marshal Earl) Wavell (1883–1950) to General Percival.

13 Feb

You must all fight it out to the end. But when everything humanly possible has been done some bold and determined personnel may be able to escape by small craft to Sumatra. ...

Lieutenant-General A.E. Percival to General Wavell.

13 Feb

Enemy now within 5,000 yards of sea-front, which brings whole of Singapore town within field artillery range. We are also in danger of being driven off water and food supplies. Troops already committed are too exhausted either to withstand strong attack or to launch counter-attack. ... In these conditions it is unlikely that resistance can last more than a day or two. My subordinate commanders are unanimously of the opinion that the gain of time will not compensate for extensive damage and heavy casualties which will occur in Singapore town. ... There must come a stage when in the interests of the troops and civil population further bloodshed will serve no useful purpose. Your instructions are being carried out, but in above circumstances would you consider giving me wider discretionary powers?

Wavell to Percival.

14 Feb

You must continue to inflict maximum damage on enemy for as long as possible by house-to-house fighting. Your action of tying down enemy and inflicting casualties may have vital influence in other theatres. Fully appreciate your situation, but continued action essential.

Percival to Wavell.

14 Feb

As a result of extensive damage to mains our water supply now limited to maximum 48 or possibly only 24 hours. If enemy captures pumping station which he is now attacking this will be further reduced. This has now become governing factor as prospect coping with million civilians without water has produced entirely new situation. Am watching developments and fighting on but may find it necessary to take immediate action.

Wavell to Percival.

15 Feb

So long as you are in position to inflict losses and damage to enemy and your troops are physically capable of doing so you must fight on. Time gained and damage to enemy are of vital importance at this crisis. When you are fully satisfied that this is no longer possible I give you discretion to cease resistance. . . .

Percival to Wavell.

15 Feb

Owing to losses from enemy action water petrol food and ammunition practically finished. Unable therefore to continue the fight any longer. . . .

In face of an onslaught for which they had not prepared, Churchill's categorical order was as powerless as Hitler's at Stalingrad, and all that could be done was to demolish guns, docks and bombs. Churchill diagnosed correctly that British prestige in Asia would never recover and that the Empire would come to an end.

Forty of the forty-four ships, crammed with refugees, which were trying to get away from Singapore were sunk by bombs and shells, but some soldiers escaped in rowing boats.

HMS *Prince of Wales* at Singapore. *(Royal Naval Museum, Portsmouth)*

5

Escape: 'I really believe there was someone on our side'

A soldier, one of the few who reached Indonesia, describes his month-long odyssey to his mother.

13th March 1942

Well I am safe. You must have been worrying a great deal, as I have not written for so long. Reason well, I can leave that to your imagination. Yes, Singapore was no place for a peaceful man, right up to the finish of this great tragedy, bombs and shells flew round. Believe me when I say that I am ashamed to have taken part in this disastrous campaign. Still, I know now what war is really like.

After many a long day of shelling and bombing, the whole terrific noise suddenly stopped, and we all knew that the worst had come. We were told that an Armistice had been signed. Four of us decided that we would have a shot at getting out, and look for a boat. Naturally there were a great many more with the same idea, and after a search of three hours, we found a small sampan or rowing-boat. We had to rescue it from the burning docks, and as we had only two hours until dawn, the chances were pretty thin. We rowed like hell – dawn was just breaking when we sighted a small island not far off, as we could see the many fires of Singapore very clearly. Before we knew what was happening, the boat was dashed against the very rocky coast of the island, almost capsized, and all our stores, water-bottles and equipment were washed away! After quite a long struggle we managed to beach the sampan, and as we were utterly worn out, we crawled into the undergrowth and promptly fell sound asleep.

The sun was well overhead when I awoke and much to our relief some Chinese appeared with a lovely mug of cold water and plenty of biscuits. Was I thankful to see that water! The Chinese were absolutely grand. When we landed they had seen us and had rescued our boat which had drifted out to sea, mended a small hole, built a sail and replaced the three oars we had lost. They made us coffee and gave us tinned sardines and told us which island to make for.

We set off again with renewed confidence just when dusk was falling. We had about three miles of open sea to cross and the wind was blowing up strongly. The tide took us along at a tremendous pace and when dawn broke we managed to paddle into a native village. We had decided only to travel at night as there was a danger of Jap planes – all day long we heard the drone. This village was very kind to us. The small Malay boys climbed trees and threw down coco-nuts. Others brought coffee and some curried rice they had cooked for us. It was jolly good and we had some lovely fruit to finish off the meal.

After a good rest two Malays said they would take us to an island from which they knew large boats were taking people away. For protection they put a small covering which we hid under when we heard a plane. After many a weary hour we arrived at this island and after two days a Chinese junk took us off. The next four or five days were pretty dreadful. We existed on rice and water with a few tins of 'bully'. By walking, motor-boat, motor-bus, train and steamer, in three weeks we eventually arrived here. The amount of stories I can tell you of these three weeks when I get back will keep you going just as long. When I look back I really believe there was someone on our side, the amount of luck we had. It all seems just a dream.

The Burma Campaign

When you go home
Tell them of us and say
For your to-morrow
We gave our to-day
(ON THE MEMORIAL AT KOHIMA)

When 130,000 men had been taken prisoner in Malaya the Japanese occupation of Burma became inevitable: after a five-month defence, the British forces retreated a thousand miles across the Chindwin into India. The re-conquest of Burma was going to be one of the most arduous tasks in the whole war.

Wavell's Arakan campaign of 1942–3 was forestalled by the Japanese and met disaster in the trackless forest jungle, but in February 1944 the Fourteenth Army under William Slim – perhaps the most brilliant general of the war in its most difficult campaign – was ready to take the offensive in the coastal Arakan and break the myth of Japanese invincibility.

6

'I ought to say "Ha, ha, among the Trumpets"'

The poet Alun Lewis (1915–44) writes the last letter to his parents, filled with premonition, before starting out on the Burma offensive in which he was killed.

[India] Feb. 8, 1944

Dear Mother and Daddy,

. . . It's very peaceful this evening: the sun and the shadows in the angle of the hills: and the snows and the odd voices carrying from soldiers chatting. I don't know why I'm so preoccupied these days. I seem to live with hooded eyes. I ought to say, 'Ha, ha, among the Trumpets', and dash off and swim, but somehow I don't contrive . . . Bless you, for your New Year's greetings. I feel the protection of your wishes for our strength and safety: and I'll carry them with me wherever the months take me. And you two, look after yourselves, won't you? . . . I miss you all very much: much more I can ever say or feel: and it's because you've enriched us with so much love and happiness and guidance all the years we were together. The world makes a boy tough: he becomes less generous, more supicious and cautious, but the boy you made is still as he always was deep inside the shell of the infantry officer: and no matter what happens to the infantry officer, my love and my essential self will never be diminished, so purely was it made.

Excuse this, if it hurts you. I only say it because it should be said sometime. I'm saying it to myself more than to you. And now I'd better do some work and get some supper before we go out on a night exercise: poor dabs!

So long now, all my love,

Ever,
Alun

7

'The fundamental unchanging things . . . sing out in my heart'

Alun Lewis's last letter to his wife.

[n.d.]

. . . If by some magic we were together I'd tell you quietly all that I cannot tell you in a letter. The only things they permit me to say are the fundamental unchanging things that don't help the Japs or interest the fifth columnists: things of no conse-quence to the fighting world, the world of telegrams and troop trains and supply columns. But they sing out in my heart like a branch of cherries and seven singing dwarfs, louder than all the trumpets, and it's the only true meaning in the sunshine and the scene. . . .

As I write now, Indian troops are shouting and squabbling about their dixies full of dahl and chapatis[2] and curry and the air is trailed and lined with the smell of their food. Hobnailed boots clattering back and fore, and men asking questions, and birds flying over in the wide blue sky. Last night I felt the moving active qual-ity in the star-grown sky and the dark night and the silent watchful land – and there seemed to be a marvellous depth and freedom as well as danger and secrecy in it all. . . .

I must run now. Sorry I have to go. And God be in our heads and in our eyes and in our understanding. Buy me a typewriter when someone has one to sell, and I'll buy you a beautiful beautiful emerald or maybe a sapphire or maybe something neither of us knows.

The Japanese 28th Army pre-empted the advance of General Christison's 15th Corps towards Akyab by secretly infiltrating one division to capture Taung Bazaar and General Messervy's 7th Indian Division HQ by surprise. They cut the crucial Ngakyedauk Pass through the Mayu Range and

2   Thick lentil sauce and grilled wheat pancake.

encircled the isolated 'Administrative Box', a vital maintenance centre on the road the Engineers had constructed for tanks and artillery. The Japanese planned to destroy the 15th Corps and invade Bengal in the 'March on Delhi' they had proclaimed. For three weeks, an incessant hail of shells and mortar bombs poured down from the surrounding jungle-covered hills on the besieged in their exposed position; but Geoffrey Evans' 9th Brigade held out with unflagging courage despite severe casualties. Sustained by air supply, after the Spitfires had shot the Zero fighters out of the sky in the biggest air battle in Burma, they beat off the Japanese assault until they were relieved by the breakthrough of the 26th Division from the north. The remnants of the Japanese division, decimated by their stubborn 'do or die' attacks and running out of food and ammunition, were driven into the jungle where few of them survived. It was the first Japanese defeat and the turning-point in the Burma campaign.

8

'Hold out and you will make history!'

Captain Anthony Brett-James, Signals Officer 9th Brigade, 5th Indian Division, later a military historian, gives his parents a vivid description of what it felt like in the midst of the nightmare of this desperate battle.

[Ngakyedauk Admin Box] 19 February '44

That I have been unable to write for so long will have caused you anxiety, and it is still not possible to post letters to the outside world.

This business began on the 6th and next morning disturbing news filtered in that the enemy had been seen in strength high up on our left flank. The Brigadier instructed me to open a signal office one mile back in great haste. It started life at the head of a narrow gulley, overgrown with bushes and tall grass; bamboos and a tarpaulin made a roof and an old tent served as the fourth wall for blackout.

The first two nights we remained ceaselessly awake, vigilant upon every sound, calculating the proximity of every outburst of firing. Sergeant Yates and I watched down the gulley, our rifles loaded, a bren gun and revolvers at hand; we kept two grenades to hurl, and incendiary bombs for burning secret documents in case of dire need. . . .

We set off along the wooded track towards the end of the Pass. So slippery was the mud that we had to cling to branches. Carriers were stuck, mules were trying desperately to clump their way up. . . . I returned to the hub of battle. Everywhere was depression, gloom, uncertainty, confusion, mud and wet, slithering feet and useless vehicles. Everybody seemed to be waiting for something to happen. No one knew what had happened. In the tent one wireless set was working, around which an anxious group of officers had assembled, as though the set were our sole salvation. The

General sat rather forlornly, pale under his bush hat.[3] I heard him remark: 'These things usually turn out all right in the end', and he laughed nervously. The Japanese were only two or three miles away.

Outside the tent which was now the command post for the constituted 'Box', our Brigadier stormed and stalked, galvanising energy concerning manning of defences; he seemed able to cleave a path through the rain and gloom and uncertainty. A wireless message came in from Lord Louis Mountbatten to say 'Hold out and you will make history!'

All our supplies are dropped from the air; every day the Dakotas come, sometimes twice daily, to circle low above the Box, while bales and tins are pushed through the side hatch, and drift to ground beneath a host of white parachutes; in gayer mood, these are red, green, blue, yellow, orange, a vivid picture, coloured like some regatta on a day in summer. Our fighter planes roar at tree-top level to drop messages wrapped in streamers. Three times the enemy have dive-bombed us, the wings of their machines blobbed in red, but this does not compare with a Desert Stuka raid! . . .

On the night of the 8th some 50 Jifs[4] and Japanese slipped through the dense jungle and entered the Main Dressing Station hospital. Here they murdered every doctor they could find, and several score of the British patients; two doctors owed their escape to the perfect black-out of their dug-out in which they were performing an operation at the time. The enemy were finally driven out the following afternoon with the aid of tanks. The remaining doctors worked like heroes, for the casualties from wounds, malaria and dysentery increased rapidly, and not one man could be evacuated. . . .

Life has become monotonous and stagnant in the nothingness-to-do, nowhere to go; we count the minutes to the next cup of tea, and in sleep we find fitful escape, plunged into dreams of machine-gun fire, only to wake to reality. . . .

23 Feb.

This has been my most eventful war-time existence and yet utterly static. We have withstood a siege for a fortnight. Parties of Japs infiltrated on every side, gaining positions on the hills that overlook us, were blasted off again by the tanks and held back until a company of West Yorks could hasten from the other end of the Box to counter-attack. The tanks' concentrated fire-power is an awful sight: a wooded hillside seems to erupt and crumble in belching smoke and yellow dust, tree trunks topple, branches snap, green foliage falls in shreds and, when all has quietened, bare sanded patches scar the slope. The huge medium guns were turned upon the ridge at 300 yards, mortars and mountain guns ranged, and this weight of ammunition was unleashed against the advancing Japanese infantry. Fearsome to witness, this onslaught succeeded in holding back the enemy. I must admit to a hollow feeling in my stomach that noon, when doubts assailed me as to our power to last out the day, let alone the harassing darkness.

Ammunition dumps have exploded for hours on end over our heads, small arms crackling like some bamboo forest in flames, shells whining above the hills. In the dark the glow and the noise are as unnerving as the enemy's attacks. We have been mortared and shelled: one shell passed visibly two feet above the signal office roof

---

3 Frank Messervy who fought more battles in the war than any general, had lost his red gener al's hat when his HQ was overrun early that morning; it was later recovered from a Japanese.
4 Indian Nationalists.

with an eerie hiss, to land in the gulley just below. Pieces of shrapnel hum through the air, hot to the touch and jagged, and everyone ducks, or leaps into a slit trench or hugs the earth.

Throughout the hours of darkness we hear the rattle of machine-guns, shouts in the dark, the explosion of grenades and mortar shells, pops and crackles from all directions, the brassy hammering of the Brownings, tanks rumbling along the dusty tracks, red tracer scurrying overhead, the whine of bullets and the upward weave of verey lights. The glow of ammunition still exploding is broken by the sudden flare and strident hum as the fire touches off yet another shell. Then is all the earth cast into weird light and shadow, and men lower their heads lest they become silhouetted. Vehicles gleam, white orange smoke is spewed into the blue darkness. Orion and Sirius look down upon us as we wait, tense, uncertain of what moves beyond. . . .

The strange, controversial genius of Orde Wingate, a cousin of T.E. Lawrence, combining utmost audacity and harshness with Old Testament mysticism and melancholic sympathy,[5] had fired Churchill's romantic imagination: he agreed to the creation of the Special Force of Chindits (named after the half-lion, half-griffin beasts guarding Burmese temples, symbolizing the concept of mobile air-supplied columns behind enemy lines) by this non-Jewish Zionist who was dreaming of leading the Israeli army he had helped to found into Palestine. The first Long Range Penetration brigade had been tried out early in 1943, and now six brigades of ten thousand men with eleven air squadrons were ready to spearhead the 1944 offensive in central Burma by establishing bases from which to disrupt Japanese communications.

9

'War is a necessary evil – as is a surgical operation'

Major-General Orde Wingate (1903–44) writes to his wife Lorna, who was expecting a child, before the start of the second Chindit expedition.

21 January 1944

Beloved,

I have had three letters from you. It relieved me of some anxiety. I continue to enjoy excellent health. I have just completed a tour with Godfather [Mountbatten]. He is a

---

5 Captain N. Durant characterized Wingate after his death: 'His eyes and his voice were sharp as steel with both of which he seemed to stab anyone to whom he was talking. He was a man in whose presence anyone from Lt.Gen. to Pte. felt uncomfortable and aware of his faults and shortcomings. He spared no one in his criticisms and never used soft words to the victims, he had absolute mental and moral courage allied with a complete lack of pity.' (Imperial War Museum, Box 80/49/1)

splendid person. Apart from him and a few others my reception generally in British Army circles is that of Pasteur at the hands of the French medicos! What a mercy it was that the Prime Minister recovered and is again on the war path. . . .

I spend much of my time in the air. My old dislike of flying is quite gone. . . . War is I suppose a necessary evil – as is a surgical operation. The drugging by one human being by another, the hideous mutilation by the knife, are in themselves an evil but become good through the motive. Can one fight in war with good motives? If not one ought not to fight. I believe one can. On the contrary. It is a police operation which has in view the welfare of the criminal as well as of the community protected. . . .

God bless you, my dear love, in 1944, and give you a safe delivery. I am happy to be married to you. May we have many years together. I love you very much.

Orde

Sixty-two gliders dropped nine thousand men in the 'Broadway' area on 13 March but the overland attack on Indaw by Bernard Fergusson's brigade was repulsed. On 24 March Wingate's B.25 bomber crashed into the mountain jungle at night after he had started a letter to Lorna: '. . . I am suffering from too great placidity these days. I wish I . . . .' Major-General Lentaigne, who succeeded him as LRP commander, captured Mogaung on 6 June after desperate fighting, despite the great hardship caused by malaria and the monsoon.

10

THE COMFORTING CHATTER OF THE WRISTWATCH IN THE LONELINESS OF THE JUNGLE

Leo de Filippis describes the jungle exploits of the Chindits.

[June ? 44]

. . . You may be interested in some of my adventures with the Chindits in the labyrinthian horror that is *Burma*. . . . We had reached our first objective: an important stretch of railway, and our job was to blow up the bridge that spanned a fairly wide and deep gorge. I was momentarily blinded by a brilliant orange flash that was followed a second later by a thunderous roar as the bridge disintegrated in a welter of flame and smoke. The whole railway cutting was choked with thick dark-brown dust that changed the sun-drenched afternoon into murky twilight. . . .

With the successful conclusion of its first mission, the column prepared to make a quick fade-out. Suddenly and without warning a furious drumming of machine-gun fire burst from a point on the opposite side of the line, a stinging, high-pitched note very much like the wacking of a whip. The Japs had their fire concentrated on that part of the line we were crossing, and had turned it into a bullet-swept No-man's-land. We dispersed into the undergrowth. . . .

The machine-guns had stopped firing, and sinister silence hung over the jungle-clad hills, a tense nerve-stretching stillness that could almost be felt. 'This is it', was my thought as I lay behind my big pack which I was using as firing cover; the moment had arrived when the long and arduous months of training were about to be tested. We were to get across as best as we could. . . . It was impossible to move silently; the trees and vegetation are so interlaced that we had to back our way through with machettes. It was hard going, continually stumbling over hidden roots and getting entangled with creepers. . . .

At length, panting and streaming with sweat, we reached the small plateau on the hill-top. We were soon all set to cover the others in their dash across the line. The Japs again opened up with their machine-guns, but this time their position was spotted and in the next moment the deeper roll of the platoon's four Bren guns was added to the din. Under the sustained and accurate fire from our Brens the Japs abandoned their position and dispersed into the jungle. Meanwhile, the platoon below had taken the opportunity given by the effective covering fire above to complete the crossing *en masse*, and were now in the comparative safety of the jungle. . .

By now the darkness had set in – the black-ness so intense that everything was blotted out. To have moved even a short distance in any direction would have been the utmost folly: it was all too easy, even in daytime, to get lost in the jungle. Night in the jungle is a weird experience; a strain on the strongest nerves. As I lay on my blanket it seemed to me that I was alone in the world – but I had one friend with me in the black void: the cheery, luminous face of my wrist-watch. I held it close to my ear for a while, listening to its incessant chatter and I was somewhat comforted by the busy little voice that was a symbol and a reminder of my own world. . . . It was 9.30. That meant that in England it was three o'clock in the afternoon, and the day was Saturday. I began thinking of the fantastic difference between myself and people back home, where they were either finishing lunch or having tea, or perhaps in cinemas or crowding the High Street; while here was I, wrapped in my blanket and lying among the decayed vegetation of a Burmese jungle, with every possibility in the near future of some Japs handing me a in-way ticket to Paradise – or elsewhere! . . .

In the morning no song of birds here; only the prospect of another day of back-breaking toil over mountains and the foulness and stench of jungle and swamp. . . . To lighten the burden of equipment, with most of the others I had thrown away my waterproof cape when the monsoon broke on us suddenly in the wilds of a range of mountains, the crossing of which had been estimated to take at least five days. . . . The bright sunlight was quickly changing to a reddish haze and in less than half an hour the sky was now a leaden grey. We had not gone far when a brilliant flash of lightning split the gloom, followed almost immediately by a deafening clap of thunder; then came the rain – a solid curtain of water. In a few seconds I was drenched, and half drowned in the torrential downpour. . . .

All I possessed now was what I stood in – a shirt and a pair of slacks! The column was reduced to utter chaos. It was impossible to continue upwards without continually slipping full length in the muddy water and starting to slide downwards. The order to bivouac was passed down the column. We were able to rig up a shelter of sorts by tying the corners of our groundsheets to the trees.

It was in these conditions that the column made a forced march of 18 miles to occupy a pass on the mountains that lined the Mogaung Valley, the only escape route for the Japs retreating before the advance of General Stillwell's forces. We got there a few hours ahead of the enemy, and for three weeks were hard pressed by the Japs, who attacked continuously, using every trick in their efforts to break through. For three weeks we endured the strain of sleepless nights, living on half rations, and drinking the rain-water caught in our ground-sheets, since the one stream nearby was fouled with the bodies of the slain, our own as well as the enemy's. . . . The remnants of the enemy were forced to the hazards of crossing mountains and going through swamps that had become tenfold more deadly through the rains, and when we left the pass after blowing up the road in several places, the air was heavy with the stench of death.

With the final clearing of the Japs from Mogaung our task was ended. The last lap of our 600 mile march was along the main road littered with the debris of war. . . . Then our plane took off on its way to India, and we were high in the air and looked through the circular window on to the forbidding aspect of the wild mountains and jungle below, it was somehow hard to realise that for five months we had lived and moved in that nightmarish tangle that hid in its dim recesses the last resting-places of so many of our lads.

On 14 August 1945, eight days after the explosion of the first atom bomb at Hiroshima, Emperor Hirohito announced the Japanese surrender: it meant liberation for the British prisoners who had survived cruel hardship.

11

'The iron entering into the soul'

Major-General Degge Sitwell (1896–1973), GOC Java, who had been in Japanese prison camps in Taiwan and Manchuria since his capitulation in May 1942, tells his wife what he has been through.

Hoten POW Camp, Mukden, 19 August 1945

My darling girl,

Thank God these little brutes have collapsed at last, and are now whining for mercy, like the bullies and braggarts they are. 17 August 1945 a wonderful day, I shall keep it as an anniversary for the rest of my life. . . . First of all, bar the fact that I am very weak and thin through three and a half years starvation, I am absolutely well, physically, and none the worse for the purgatory we have been through. I now understand what they mean in the Bible about 'the iron entering into the soul', having been kept in manacles for a month at one time. . . .

After the capitulation, they tried to make us do a 'death march' like the Americans had at Bataan; seeing what it would mean, Maltby[6] and I flatly refused to give orders to march. Rather to my surprise, we got our way, and the men were transported by train, but I then had to pay. I was stood up against a wall faced with a firing party and kept in handcuffs for three weeks of which ten days were behind my back; it was absolute agony; in addition, I was beaten up a good deal. They gave me up after a month as a bad job.

---

6   Major-General Maltby was GOC Hong Kong in 1941.

The Japanese attitude throughout has been to degrade us in every possible way, and to set our own men against us: to drive the officers mad with starvation, whilst giving the men more than they could eat, under threats of imprisonment if they gave the officers any, hoping to make officers try to steal the men's food. . . .

What I really look forward to, on getting back: Eating proper meals with knives and forks at a table, instead of hogwash out of a pig bucket as we have had for three and a half years! English food, particularly a steak and a Welsh rarebit . . .

All my love darling to you and all our dear ones, and thank God for peace once more, I can hardly believe it even now.

Ever your loving

Degge

P.S. I am lucky but I am afraid about half of my poor soldiers were dead at Japanese hands whilst POW.

NINE

The Certainties of Self-Sacrifice: Unquestioning Faith and Instinct without Reason

Here not the flags . . .
Nor the names cut in brass.
Not the drum
SIDNEY KEYES

If you can go
Knowing that there is no reward, no certain use
In all your sacrifice, then honour is reprieved.
To fight without hope is to fight with grace
HERBERT READ, 'TO A CONSCRIPT OF 1940'

The Second World War had come as a profound disappointment when gradually all idealistic hopes of permanent peace through international cooperation had proved illusory.

> We who have put our faith
> in the goodness of man and now see man's image debased
> lower than the wolf or the hog –
> Where can we turn for consolation?

asked Herbert Read in his 'Dunkirk Ode'. Shrinking from the futility of war and burying one's head before its horrors made its reality all the more rude an awakening. But as disillusionment had set in well before the war, there was none of the initial enthusiasm and subsequent painful disenchantment which had marked the First World War: there was only sober and cheerful acceptance of the sacrifice which had become necessary to defend the country, not against a rival imperialism as in 1914, but against an evil tyranny which would make life not worth living. The greater the Nazi threat became, the more steeled became resistance to it. In the atmosphere of the dire threat to survival in 1940, war was welcomed in absolute faith as offering the chance of justifying life by the measure of its sacrifice.

1

'This war is a very good thing'

Flying Officer V.A.W. Rosewarne wrote a farewell letter to his mother before being shot down, which was found when his body was washed ashore; he expresses his gratitude to her, to England and to God.

[June 1940]

Dearest Mother,

Though I feel no premonition at all, events are moving rapidly, and I have instructed that this letter be forwarded to you should I fail to return. . . . Though it will be difficult for you, you will disappoint me if you do not at least try to accept the facts dispassionately, for I shall have done my duty to the utmost of my ability. No man can do more, and no one calling himself a man could do less.

I have always admired your amazing courage in the face of continual setbacks; in the way you have given me as good an education and background as anyone in the country; and always kept up appearances without ever losing faith in the future. My death would not mean that your struggle has been in vain. Far from it. It means that your sacrifice is as great as mine. Those who serve England must expect nothing from her; we debase ourselves if we regard our country as merely a place in which to eat and sleep.

History resounds with illustrious names who have given all, yet their sacrifice has resulted in the British Empire, where there is a measure of peace, justice, and freedom for all, and where a higher standard of civilization has evolved, and is still evolving, than anywhere else. But this is not only concerning our own land. To-day we are faced with the greatest organized challenge to Christianity and civilization that the world has ever seen, and I count myself lucky and honoured to be the right age and fully trained to throw my full weight into the scale. For this I have to thank you. Yet there is more work for you to do. The home front will still have to stand united for years after the war is won. For all that can be said against it, I still maintain that this war is a very good thing; every individual is having the chance to give and dare all for his principle like the martyrs of old. However long the time may be, one thing can never be altered – I shall have lived and died an Englishman. Nothing else matters one jot nor can anything ever change it.

You must not grieve for me, for if you really believe in religion and all that it entails that would be hypocrisy. I have no fear of death; only a queer elation. . . . I would have it no other way. The universe is so vast and ageless that the life of one man can only be justified by the measure of his sacrifice. We are sent to this world to acquire a personality and a character to take with us that can never be taken from us. Those who just eat and sleep, prosper and procreate, are not better than animals if all their lives they are at peace.

I firmly and absolutely believe that evil things are sent into the world to try us; they are sent deliberately by our Creator to test our metal because He knows what is good for us. The Bible is full of cases where the easy way out has been discarded for moral principles.

I count myself fortunate in that I have seen the whole country and known men of every calling. But with the final test of war I consider my character fully developed. Thus at my early age my earthly mission is already fulfilled and I am prepared to die with just one regret, and one only – that I could not devote myself to making your declining years more happy by being with you; but you will live in peace and freedom and I shall have directly contributed to that, so here again my life will not have been in vain.

Your loving Son

The attitude of many women in the Forces was similar: sacrifice was accepted without hesitation.

2

A WAAF GIRL SHIELDS A PILOT FROM A BLAST

Corporal Joan Pearson, a medical orderly on an aerodrome, was the first woman to win the George Cross when she saved a pilot from his blazing plane despite the explosion of two 120 lb bombs – a fine example of absolute devotion to duty.

May 1940

I had just dozed off in a fitful sleep – it was difficult to sleep long or soundly because machines were always being 'revved' up or patrols going out. Being in the medical we were always on the alert and on the spot even if off duty.

It was about 01.00 hrs. Awakening I heard a machine approach, one engine cut out, then a rending crash, silence and engines roaring up. I believe my trousers and fisherman's jersey were on by then, it was dark, can't remember whether I put on gum boots or shoes, but was running out in the wet grass and across the cement road towards the guard house. A few flames were moving in the air and there must have been the noise of the crash.

A twinkling light showed at S.H.Q. – that meant the ambulance – must warn the guard to undo the gates and be ready. The guard grunted as I ran by him, he knew me, I shouted to him the ambulance was behind.

I kept running hard and came to a RAF police. He tried to prevent me from climbing the fence – men were shouting for doctor, ambulance. I yelled 'Coming'. There was a blazing fire started. The nettle stung me in the ditch on the other side. A figure panted up and I saw another silhouetted against the light. A man was dragging a harnessed figure – I told him to get the fence down for the ambulance. I tried to drag the pilot further away from the blaze, but he was groaning and so decided to render first aid immediately in case of further damage. I took his parachute harness off and found his neck was causing great pain. He told me to keep clear as he had a full load of bombs aboard. The petrol tanks blew out and so I lay down and tried to shield the light from his face as he was suffering from shock. A huge bomb went off but I was holding his head to prevent further dislocation. The bomb took all the oxygen. As there was another bomb to go I ran to the fence to help the M.O. over with the stretcher. We got aboard the ambulance and got into camp. The other bomb went off worse than the first. The Sick Quarters was all ready and we finished our work about 3.00 hours. Sick parade was as usual 08.30 hours.

In Churchill's words, the Battle of the Atlantic was the dominating factor of the war, on the outcome of which everything ultimately depended – in the same way as in the First World War when Britain was nearly defeated before convoys were introduced. To counter the Asdic detection device and deadly depth-charge the Germans switched to wolfpack surface attacks at night: at the peak, 1–20 March 1943, 107 ships were lost, two thirds in convoys, but air escort carriers and long-range planes turned the tide in May.[1] The stories of self-sacrificing rescue are countless: one example is Squadron-Leader H.R.K. Wells, who was on his way home for leave from the Western Desert when his ship was torpedoed.

3

A MORTALLY WOUNDED AIRMAN SAVES A NURSE FROM DROWNING

Doris Hawkins, who was returning from Jerusalem hospital on the same boat as Squadron-Leader Wells describes to his parents how he swam for both of them.

[1943]

When we were torpedoed I was taking home my friend's infant daughter, and when I arrived on deck I found that our lifeboat had been blown away. There was no one to direct us, and in the pitch dark, with the ship listing heavily, I could not move about carrying a 15-months-old baby. Squ.Ldr.Wells came upon us, and had it not been for his help little Sally and I would have gone down with the ship. He took Sally from me and we went from boat station to boat station, and finally, got us into a boat. It capsized and little Sally was drowned.

After some time of swimming I heard Squ.Ldr.Wells calling from a raft and he swam towards me. At that moment there was a terrific explosion from the ship, and

1   D. Macintyre, *Battle of the Atlantic*, Batsford, 1961, *passim*. In the whole war, 2,828 merchant vessels and 175 warships were sunk by 1,173 German submarines for the loss of 789 of them; but the 5,000 tanks and 7,000 planes which got through in Arctic convoys to Murmansk probably tipped the scales on the Russian Front.

the blast caught us as we swam. He curled up, but got me on to the raft, although I am sure he had internal haemorrhage.

The next day the U-boat surfaced and began pulling people on board by a lifeline. Squ.Ldr.Wells then tied a tow-rope round his body and struck out, towing two rafts and nine people. When within 100 yards of the submarine it went off in another direction. He was terribly exhausted and bitterly disappointed. We were just beginning to dread a second night when the submarine turned and came straight towards us, threw a lifeline, and took us all on board.

Unfortunately, Allied 'planes spotted the submarine and commenced to bomb it. The captain decided that he must submerge, and as he could not do so with all of us on board he was forced to put us into the water. We found ourselves once again swimming for life. Once more Squ.Ldr.Wells helped me. I am a poor swimmer and he a magnificent one, but he was now a very sick man. He gave every ounce of his strength to get me to the boat. We were swimming for 50 minutes, and most of the time I was towed by him while he swam for both of us and he would not abandon me. He was taken into one boat and I into another, and he died a few days later. . . .

What is there that I can say? I do wish that I could do more than just write a letter, and I feel it must be some comfort to you to know how selfless, gallant, and chivalrous he was, and I shall always be proud to have known him.

Beside the many thousands sacrificing their lives in unquestioning faith, there were those acting in the same way but without the supporting certainties of traditional beliefs. Richard Hillary was one of the first fighter pilots shot down in the Battle of Britain: severely burnt, he baled out over the North Sea from his blazing Spitfire and was eventually picked up unconscious by a Margate lifeboat after failing to drown himself, to put an end to his agony. Blind for a time, he insisted on returning to operational flying after two years of plastic surgery operations. In the famous book he wrote during convalescence with utterly unsentimental detachment, he saw Death as 'The Last Enemy' to be vanquished by overcoming the evil of the Self. In the event of his own death he asked his commanding officer to inform his girlfriend ('who can take it') four hours before his mother, so that she could break it to her gently.

4

INSTINCT BEFORE REASON IN THIS 'COMIC WAR'

Richard Hillary (1919–43) writes to his mother after returning to active service; he was killed seven weeks later.

19 November 1942

Mother Darling,

I just want to say thank you for always having faith, for not questioning my decision, for never betraying that you feel unhappy and, above all, for your unfailing sense of humour. We do not often speak together about it and for this and many other things I am so deeply grateful. I know what you think of my going back and if I were outside looking on I would agree with you. Yet I am glad the decision has been left to me. One can go on arguing the thing out rationally *ad nauseam*. I can write I am more useful on the ground, I only want to go back so that people may say 'well done!' and to get a medal. I am frightened of going back, I only want to make a name, etc.

Finally one must listen to one's instinct, and the time will come when I shall know that my instinct was right and my reason wrong. You must try not to worry about me and to have the same faith I have that I shall be all right, for I know it. . . . It may be that a thousand things will happen. I do not know. But that it will be all right, I do know. I should not be at peace with myself if I did not go back. There are very few things to which one can cling in this comic war, to see straight and know where one is heading is perhaps the most important of all. God bless you always.

Richard

Quoting in his book Verlaine's lines:

Quoique sans patrie et sans roi . . .
J'ai voulu mourir à la guerre,

Hillary expressed the belief of the 'lost generation' of young intellectuals that they were sacrificing their lives in war, not for king and country, but as an attitude of defiance of death in their comradeship. Michael Howard, a young army officer who was to become a distinguished war historian, belongs to the same élite who, by the constant proximity of death, were stimulated to ardent discussion. The search for answers was agonizing, as traditional faith was no longer acceptable to them: 'Having been born into the age in which all previous ages had been successfully "debunked", we can have no heroes on which to base our lives,' wrote another lieutenant.[2] Howard found in Hillary's book, 'a desperate ignorance, and absurd faith in spite of it, a deep trust in the value of friendship and a great joy in living', which he shared: 'We don't know; we don't even feel; we accept. . . . We have faith, but no real Faith.' And he asks: 'What *is* this faith, which seems to have no object?'[3]

2 E.M.G. Belfield, in *Horizon*, vol. VII, no. 42, June 1943, p. 432.
3 Quoted from the letter which follows in its unabridged version.

5

'Our standards of battle are banners without marks'

Lieutenant Michael Howard, later Regius Professor of History at Oxford University, to the writer Arthur Koestler.

[1943]

This letter is occasioned by your article on Richard Hillary in *HORIZON*, to try to amplify some of your remarks. It would be presumptuous to claim anything of Hillary's qualities, or of his insight and sincerity; all I can say of myself is that I am of his generation; that I am about to go into action with an army wherein not many young officers do survive, and that these similarities give me a little shadow of understanding of what must have been Hillary's state of mind when he was waiting to die. . . .

I have talked so much with friends in the same position, who face a probable death, trying to probe and analyse their attitude in order to understand my own, and always it comes back to the same dead end: we don't know; we don't even feel; we accept, and we know we must accept this extraordinary role which we must play, with an absence of bitterness which is inexplicable. There is no disillusionment, because there have been no illusions. We have faith, but no real Faith. . . . I would suggest that there are two great components of our attitude towards our future. First, an ignorance of what we are fighting for which no amount of propaganda or religion will enlighten. As you say, it is a different war to the newspaper 'Men Who Know No Fear' stunt. We are not fighting for England in the charming Rupert Brooke sense or the stirring Newbolt sense. We are not fighting for democracy – many are temperamentally anti-democratic. Our standards of battle are banners without marks. But against that ignorance we have an obscure and (for us) quite inexplicable faith that to fight and to die is right, and perhaps the best thing we can do for this wretched world. Don't understand me to say that we believe war to be right as such: as you know, we detest and loathe it. Yet, for some reason, we are prepared to fight for something we don't know, which we can never express. But what *is* this faith, which seems to have no object; can we never know?

This is the background on which we fight; the foreground is occupied with friendship and good fellowship, as though because of a common faith, we are drawn so close to our friends that they embody all we believe in – a shield of affection which can hold out the horrors of the night outside. We depend almost desperately upon one another. The loss of a friend is a tearing of your soul, and if friends are lost we replace them by a stopgap of acquaintances, parties, drinks, anything to give security. Sometimes, whatever happens, you find yourself alone: and then there comes a wild regret for all the beauty and splendour of life, a passionate longing for a golden and exaggerated past. Even then our odd negative faith keeps out bitterness. We are still ready to die. Perhaps the shadow of death does heighten our senses, makes us see beauty more fully and makes us live every moment as deeply as we can. There is such a lot to be crowded in. Please God if I survive that I don't lose this intensity of life. . . .

After the anguished intellectual quest for certainties about the condition of man at war, let us conclude by going back to our stretcher-bearer in Italy. He is concerned with the effects of prolonged fear which turned so many soldiers into psycho-neurotic cases: 'battle fatigue', as it was called euphemistically, accounted for 15 per cent of casualties and reduced strong, courageous men to 'whimpering wrecks, crying like children'. The soldier's only antidote against ever-present fear was a combination of good-humoured stoicism, cynical fatalism and obscene jokes, shared, like his suffering, with the fraternity of comrades who were his only real world. Self-respect and affection for his comrades gave the soldier the courage to over-come the fear of death and face self-sacrifice.[4] The 'steady carrying out of your job' was the only way.

6

'The hurdle of time'
THE STRETCHER-BEARER'S DREAM

Private Robson writes to his wife from Italy.

25.6.44

... I'm glad you liked the letter I sent you. I have sent you so many lately that I think I would be ashamed to read whining, self-pitying things of no possible cheer to you. They haven't been brave, firm, cheerily swashbuckling. Though recognizing the part we are playing, they show no desire to play it further. They have been personally defeatist, have they been cowardly?

We all know fear, and I think the best antidote to it is the steady carrying out of your job. It is strange, but it is not so much the fear of death with me, as a fear of never seeing you again, of never embarking on our wonderful plans. It is that that frightens me. But now it is more serious. I am, we all are, in the S.B.s, more nervy. The nerves get worn. Way out of the line, we react slightly to gunfire and our own planes passing over provoke a nervousness we never felt before. It's only small, but it's there, and it may increase. Really I suppose we all need a period of convalescence, even perhaps with treatment. In the line again we'll be all right, but for how long? We won't manage for so long without sleep, we won't be able to stand the same amount of fatigue. If we try it, I'm afraid the nerves will win, and we'll go back psycho-neurotic cases. . . .

I've seen men duck at the buzzing of a bee, and a whole platoon go to ground when a chap innocently gargled his throat. And consider the case of the sentry who fell and accidentally shot himself – before we got him to the R.A.P. he was murmuring in delirium: 'The Dodecanese, we've lost all those islands now. Where were the

4 J. Ellis, *The Sharp End of War*, David & Charles, 1980, *passim*.

aircraft. Poor lads, they didn't stand a chance.' And so on. And though we were taking him in with a wounded leg he was complaining about his chest, that he couldn't breathe – because he was wounded there in the Dodecanese. Now the stuff on that man's mind! And how much are we going to be affected in the same way, and will it change us much?

I don't want to frighten you, darling. We treat it with humour, this nervousness. Maybe it is this humour that will save us. The war cannot last much longer, that is a comfort. . . .

I want the cottage on the edge of the village about which you wrote in your lovely last letter, I want the walks home under the elms when the leaves are whispering lullabies to the young rooks, and on across the stream where the water lillies are, and where, if we are very still we may catch the blue of the kingfisher. . . .

How high and how wide is the hurdle of time we both long to jump?

But 'Robbie' never jumped the 'hurdle of time' – he sacrificed his life, wearing out his lungs in saving the wounded so that they could live and return home in peace.

Envoy

I shall come back,
And see again the clover and the rose
Blooming anew, and bending to each summer wind that blows,
And, being back, shall find again,
When war is over,
The gates of heaven are but the cliffs of Dover
CORPORAL KEITH WATSON, RAF

Conclusion:
English Attitudes to War 1914–45

The two world wars, fought under entirely new conditions and brought about by the development of the tools of war, induced a considerable departure from some of the English attitudes prevalent in previous centuries. Boastful nationalism and hero worship had gone; indiscipline, hatred of foreigners and feelings of vengeance occurred only rarely; the influence of religion had declined, and women were increasingly to share the burdens and dangers of war and contribute to the war effort on a large scale. The whole nation was gradually plunged into war. Perhaps the most poignant experiences were those of the Tommy in the trenches of 1914–18 and the desert rat of the Eighth Army or the Chindit in the Burma jungle, of the soldier landing at Gallipoli or in Normandy, of the air ace of the First World War or the bomber crew of the Second, or of the sailor at Jutland or in the *Prince of Wales*. Mutual loyalty between servicemen grew strongly:

> The soldier became increasingly bound up with his tiny fraternity of comrades who shared his suffering and they alone came to represent the real world. In the last analysis, the soldier fought for them alone, because they were his friends and because he defined himself only in the light of their respect and needs.[1]

In this concluding analysis we can follow the evolution of English attitudes to war between the two conflicts, characterized by a certain erosion of the barrier between servicemen and civilians, and between men and women.

Joyful bellicosity. Winston Churchill confessed in 1914 that the outbreak of war held for him 'a hideous fascination' (p. 4), a midshipman found the battle of Heligoland Bight 'jolly exciting' although admitting that he was at times 'in a beastly funk' (p. 6), and Captain Julian Grenfell enthused about 'the joy of battle' in France and adored the 'great game' of war which for him was 'all *the* best fun' (p. 13). In 1917 Captain Greenwell enjoyed the 'gay life'

---

1 J. Ellis, The Sharp End, Windrow & Green, 1990, p. 315.

(p. 73), and the war artist Paul Nash was enraptured by 'these wonderful trenches at night; at dawn; at sundown!' (p. 76); Duff Cooper gloried in 'a feeling of wild and savage joy' at the sight of an artillery barrage (p. 36); a lieutenant in the tank corps found an attack as exhilarating as a big school match (p. 84), and the war poet Wilfred Owen sang the praises of the exultation of going over the top (p. 102).

Enthusiasm tended to be more muted in the Second World War, but a Battle of Britain pilot rejoiced in the thrill of aerial combat (pp. 136–7), and an artillery officer bivouacking in the Libyan desert confessed 'This is the life for me' (p. 155), while Montgomery wrote from El Alamein: 'It has been a great party and I have enjoyed it. . . . Rommel has had to dance entirely to my tune' and was going to be 'toppled off his perch' (pp. 160–1).

Patriotism. In the same way as on the eve of the Somme offensive in 1916, a lieutenant was ready to die doing his duty 'to my God, my Country, and my King' (pp. 60–1), a flying officer recounted in a farewell letter to his mother in 1940 the sacrifice of those who had given all for the higher civilization of the British Empire: 'I shall have lived and died an Englishman' (p. 208), and the wife of an RAF pilot affirmed: 'It is to be every Britisher's war, and that's how we want it!' (p. 132); Dorothy Sayers too praised God for an English war, standing alone without allies (p. 131).

Courage and endurance. In 1915 Captain Grenfell, dying of a cracked skull, was able to joke about 'Julian of the 'Ard 'Ead', (p. 14); Lieutenant King-Hall described how he continued to take notes at Jutland while standing in flames (p. 55); a captain narrated how in the siege of Kut (1916) they held out against the Turks for five months on a diet of mule and grass (p. 68); and a private related how they did the same at Passchendaele wading up to their waists in mud, sprayed with machine-gun fire and suffocated by mustard gas (pp. 81–2). However, Harold Macmillan of the Grenadier Guards took a more qualified view of courage when he wrote in 1916: 'Bravery is not really vanity, but a kind of concealed pride, because everybody is watching you' (p. 23).

In 1940 the sole survivor of the destroyer *Acasta* related how they kept on inflicting damage on the *Scharnhorst* until they sank (p. 123), and a pilot flying low over the shipwrecked survivors of the *Prince of Wales* saw them cheering and joking (p. 193). A nurse torpedoed on the way home from the western desert in 1943 told how a mortally wounded airman saved her from drowning (pp. 210–11); a WAAF corporal, the first to win the George Cross, dragged a pilot who had crashlanded clear of his blazing plane despite the explosion of two 120 lb bombs (pp. 209–10); and the plucky girls driving ambulances in the Blitz on London should also not be forgotten (p. 143).

Facing death. Lieutenant Harold Alexander told quite impassionately how, on the retreat to Mons in 1914, he found himself in a death trap without cover, 'preparing to die on top of the mound' (p. 12), and a lieutenant affirmed in his farewell letter to his parents on the eve of the Somme offensive in 1916 that he was ready to die 'in the cause of civilization' in 'the most important moment' of his life (p. 60). In another farewell letter, from Arnhem in 1944, a private proclaimed that there was 'no better way of dying' and that death was 'nothing final and lasting . . . just a stage in everyone's life' (pp. 182–3).

The ready admission of fear of death was a new feature of the twentieth-century wars. Harold Macmillan, lying wounded in a trench on the Somme recounted that he felt 'no need to show off any more, no need to pretend. I was frightened,' (p. 23). Likewise, the captain of the destroyer *Achilles* facing the *Graf Spee* on the River Plate in 1939 confessed he felt 'awfully frightened' every time the enemy guns went off (pp. 117–18), a private admitted having been scared stiff at Dunkirk (pp. 126–7), and a lieutenant recounted the terrifying experience of the combined operations landing on the coast of Sicily in 1943 (pp. 167–8).

Cynicism and humour. Bitter irony, mitigated by anti-heroic humour, constituted a defence mechanism against the horrors of trench warfare. Raymond Asquith's sparkling wit oscillated between impassive lucidity and lighthearted banter, a posture of irreverent cynicism and upper-class contempt for sentiment (pp. 26–7), reminiscent of Battle of Britain Richard Hillary's attitude twenty-five years later, though without the hilarity and facetiousness of an earlier age; Hillary saw in instinct the only thing to cling to in this 'comic' war (pp. 211–12). More down to earth, Robert Graves was a source of anecdotes of macabre humour about 'cushies' and return tickets to 'Blitey' (p. 33), a lieutenant saw shelling in the trenches in terms of an exchange of turnips and sausages (p. 29), and a colonel at Gallipoli appreciated 'Johnny Turk's humorous banter' (p. 41). A Londoner living through the Blitz complained that Hitler had kept him waiting for the usually punctual air raid and thought laughter a defence the Germans would never understand (p. 145), and a survivor of the *Prince of Wales* sunk by Japanese planes in the Gulf of Siam related how he talked to a biscuit box to which he was clinging (pp. 191–2).

Loyalty, comradeship and regimental pride. A music scholar, serving as a private in 1916, extolled the companionship of soldiers behaving coolly and kindly to each other without swank: 'English virtues at their best and least demonstrative' amid the desolation and obscenity of war (p. 31). In 1918 Wilfred Owen too found comfort in the comradeship of the 'smoky cellar' dug in the trenches to provide shelter from the shells crashing outside and called it 'a good life' (pp. 102–3), and a colonel regretted in 1919 the good fellowship and lack of humbug in the trenches, looking back to it 'with something like affection' (p. 99). Likewise, in 1943, a driver wrote from Tunis that the Eighth Army was 'a grand mob to be in . . . just like a happy family in which the officers enter into it like the rest' (p. 166), and Lieutenant Michael Howard spoke of friends with a common faith drawing together in the regiment: 'They embody all we believe in – a shield of affection which can hold out the horrors of the night outside. We depend almost desperately upon one another,' (p. 213).

Invasion scare, spy mania, and the attitude towards total war hitting the home country. The age-old English apprehension of aggression from the continent revived in 1914. Admiral Fisher related with a pinch of irony the latest rumour of an imminent German invasion of Scotland with a feint at Norwich, while F.S. Oliver reported the alarm that 250,000 Germans were poised to disembark in Essex and Suffolk to strike at London (pp. 10–11). In 1940 the threat became much more real. A housewife described how they were told to behave if German parachutists were to arrive (pp. 132–3), and a naval captain related how he was struck by the mob when he was arrested while taking a photograph of a bombed house in the East End of London: spy mania, fed by reports from Holland, was widespread (pp. 140–1). A civilian expressed his admiration for the 'amazing grit of the people' pursuing their business as usual in the midst of the Blitz on London and paid a special tribute to the coolness of the taxi drivers; another was impressed by the fearlessness of the children of the bombed-out sheltering in the tube stations; and an ARP warden, the actor Stanley Lupino, praised the unbeatable cockney spirit and confessed himself to be upset not by the bombs but by 'the lovableness of the people' (pp. 138–42).

Complacency, unpreparedness, incompetence and blunders. A long tradition, highlighted for the first time in the Crimean War, continued. A colonel in the Dardanelles was critical of the authorities for underestimating the task of occupying them in 1915, adding: 'It is not for us to reason why, we must go on and see it through' (pp. 42–3). In 1940 Captain Alec Waugh severely criticized the widespread wishful thinking during the 'phoney war' that 'Hitler missed the bus', only to face a rude awakening when a new kind of warfare caused casualties worse than at Passchendaele (pp. 128–9). At Singapore in 1941 the neglect of defence measures (fixed cannon facing the wrong way!) led to a humiliating capitulation to a far smaller Japanese force which spelt the end of British reputation in Asia: a civilian accused the military of 'conceited complacency' and 'self-indulgent blind contentment' (p. 193).

Servicemen's recriminations against civilians, politicians and generals. Admiral Fisher derided the 'criminal folly' of sending BEF 'play soldiers' to France in 1914 (p. 5) and dubbed Churchill who was responsible for the then imminent 'very great national disaster' in the Dardanelles as 'a bigger danger than the Germans' (p. 44). In 1916 soldiers and officers resented that civilians 'grow fat on big money' while 'the poor Tommy [was] shivering in the trenches' (pp. 71–2). Some generals like Robertson were equally disdainful of politicians who 'have no idea how war must be conducted' and thought French generals 'a peculiar lot' (pp. 88–9). The panic caused by air raids on London between 1915 and 1917 which seemed insignificant to the soldiers in the trenches angered them (p. 83), while a small band of officer-poets scorned their generals who from the safety of French châteaux sent them into murderous offensives which seemed to them devoid of purpose (p. 89). Finally, Captain Herbert Read deplored the clamour for revenge among the civilian population after the armistice in 1918 (pp. 97–8).

In the Second World War criticism of that kind was more muted, although Admiral Sir Roger Keyes raged against Churchill's 'pusillanimous, self-satisfied, short-sighted Naval advisers' in 1940 (p. 121), and Major-General Galloway voiced in 1942 his frustration with Whitehall 'wangling, ogling, jockeying' (p. 159).

Brutalization. Captain Sorley was appalled by the insidious progress of brutalization in 1915 against an enemy he held in high respect (pp. 21–2), in 1916 Lieutenant Engall was revolted by the use of flame projectors, adopting the Germans' 'foul and hellish methods' and remarked that 'your meek and gentle old Jack' had become bloodthirsty and gloried in it, while another lieutenant was horrified about feeling 'the primitive passion for slaughter let loose' in him, and a captain feared 'we shall become all that we hate' (pp. 63–6). Attitudes in the Second World War were much more impassive and clinical: Montgomery complained that he did not find it easy to rouse the killer instinct in his men who 'are not killers by nature' (p. 161), but a flight-sergeant felt pleased he could exact vengeance on the Berliners for the bombing of English cities (p. 148).

Compassion for the enemy and fraternization. This was a feature of the First World War when a certain comradeship in suffering reached across some of the lines at Christmas 1914 before brutalization had set in: for example, a captain described how fraternizing soldiers were singing, drinking and hare-hunting in no man's land. Fellow feelings extended more readily to German prisoners than to the French allies through disbelief in the alleged incurable barbarism of the Germans, quite in contrast with the Hun-baiting hysteria at home (pp. 17–19). Similarly a midshipman thought it beastly to have 'the duty to send the poor chaps to the bottom' when they had stopped firing in Heligoland Bight, and another sailor took pleasure in saving 'such plucky foemen' at the Falkland Islands (pp. 8–9). In the Second World War the ideological gulf was too deep to generate warm feelings for the Nazi enemy.

Religion and farewell. A letter from a lieutenant on the eve of the Somme offensive in 1916 placed his soul and body in God's keeping: 'I am going into battle with His name on my lips . . . trusting implicitly in Him', and a captain wondered 'how sad He must be sometimes, when even a little heart like one's own nearly bursts with pity' (pp. 60–3). In 1944 Alun Lewis in his last letter to his wife from Burma wished that 'God be in our heads and in our eyes and in our understanding' (p. 199), and a flying-officer expressed his gratitude to his mother and to England in a farewell letter in the belief that evil was sent 'by our Creator to test our metal' (pp. 208–9).

Disillusionment, alienation, nostalgia, and solitude. These sentiments grew largely out of the impact of the unchanging nightmarish conditions of the First World War trenches on sensitive souls. For Sergeant-Major Keeling the 'delightful picnic' soon turned into hell (p. 24), for Captain Greenwell such warfare 'reduces men to shivering beasts, nothing fine or sporting' (p. 58), and Raymond Asquith saw in war only senselessness without 'a single redeeming feature' upon which he looked with 'invincible pride and stiff indifference to the brutal muddle of the universe', death being 'the only solution of the problem of life' to set anxieties at rest (p. 26). Captain Campbell felt alienated in the dead trench land without a sign of humanity with thousands of men 'like rabbits concealed', perceiving in their eyes frightened with piteous wonder the question 'What the blankety, blankety hell *is* this?' Despairing of an early end of the war he sought comfort in the redeeming vision of a civilian ploughing between the lines in 1930 (pp. 36–7).

Major Alan Brooke getting a bird's eye view of the Somme offensive felt like looking at a cinema film dream (pp. 57–8); for Lieutenant Gillespie 'the nightingale's song was the only real thing' in the infinitely sweet and sad moonlit night (p. 28); Captain Nevill was charmed by the antics of 'Freddie the mouse' nibbling his hair 'as one would drink coffee and liqueurs'; and Duff Cooper was enraptured by the sight of a beautiful hand sticking out of the earth (pp. 34–6). The war artist Paul Nash pictured Nature's victory over monstrous devastation (pp. 76–7), while Harold Macmillan escaped from the desolation of shattered trees with no humans for miles to nostalgic dreams of the 'glamour of red coats and the martial tunes of flag and drum', the splendid charges, the glittering lances, the flashing swords (p. 23).

The mobile warfare of the Second World War did not allow time to indulge in such visions and sentiments – everything had become more technical and down to earth; only in extreme circumstances like the Burma jungle an officer could feel himself 'alone in the world', comforted solely by the chatter of his wrist watch (pp. 203–5).

Obscenity of war and anti-war feeling. Criticizing writers on war for ignoring the '*individual* horror' of being 'smashed suddenly into red beastliness', Captain Wilson described war as an obscenity (pp. 62–3), and Private Gurney asked why 'high triumph be signified by a body shattered, black, stinking . . . an offence to the hardest' (p. 31). There were macabre sights: Ivo Grenfell saw a toad sitting on the chest of a skeleton in a Loos graveyard, mice playing on the bones (p. 35), and Raymond Asquith described cats nesting in corpses while rats were getting them under in a war of attrition like all wars (p. 26). Wilfred Owen 'suffered seventh hell' at the sight of men drowning in the mud of waterfilled craters in the 'Slough of Despond . . . pockmarked like a body of the foulest disease – its odour the breath of cancer' (pp. 100–1). T.E. Lawrence felt his nerves going after the 'potting' of a train on the Hejaz Railway, at the spectacle of Turks lying around in bits but still alive (p. 69), and Bertrand Russell confessed to hating even the pacifists who kept saying human nature was essentially good despite daily proofs to the contrary and exclaimed: 'I hate the planet and the human race – I am ashamed to belong to such a species' (p. 74). In the Second World War, however, he changed his mind and recognized its necessity like most people: the obscenity of war was then more efficiently disguised – yet Private Robson could cry out: 'When, when, when is this insanity going to stop?' (p. 173).

Acceptance and self-sacrifice. Readiness to see the war through to the bitter end unquestioningly has been exemplified for the First World War by Harold Alexander and Colonel Hardman. Battle of Britain pilot Richard Hillary echoed Raymond Asquith's defiance of death, characteristic of the 'lost generation of intellectuals', most aptly defined by Michael Howard: 'We don't know; we don't even feel; we accept . . . we have faith, but no real Faith,' who goes on to ask himself: 'What is this faith, which seems to have no object?' Without being able to explain why, although detesting war, he felt it 'right' to fight and die (p. 213). For Private Robson and thousands of others there was no such soul searching: they were just 'hard live-for-the-day fatalists' (pp. 172–3).

Sources of the Letters

PART ONE: THE FIRST WORLD WAR

1. From Offensive to Deadlock (1914–15)

1 Churchill, Randolph, *Winston Churchill*, Heinemann, 1969, vol. II, 710 f.
2 King-Hall, L., *Sea Saga*, V. Gollancz, 1935, p. 375.
3 *Correspondence of Admiral Lord Fisher*, A.J. Marder (ed.), J. Cape, 1959, vol. III, p. 55.
4 Walker, C.F., *Young Gentlemen*, Longmans, 1938, p. 203.
5 Ibid, p. 221.
6 *Cornhill Magazine*, XXXVIII (1915), p. 541.
7 *Letters of Rupert Brooke*, G. Keynes (ed.), Faber & Faber, 1968, p. 632.
8 *Fisher Correspondence*, p. 89 f.
9 Oliver, F.S., *Anvil of War*, S. Gwynn (ed.), Macmillan, 1936, p. 53.
10 Nicolson, N., *Alex*, Weidenfeld and Nicolson, 1973, p. 30.
11 Housman, L., *War Letters of Fallen Englishmen*, V. Gollancz, 1930, p. 118.
12 Mackenzie, J., *The Children of the Souls*, Chatto & Windus, 1986, 183 ff.
13 Greenwell, G.H., *Infant in Arms*, introd. J. Terraine, Allen Lane, 1972, p. 12 ff.
14 Baynes, J.C.M., *Morale*, Cassell, 1967, p. 69.
15 Housman, op. cit., p. 143.
16 Ibid, p. 293.
17 Ibid, p. 144.
18 *Letters of Charles Sorley*, Cambridge University Press, 1919, p. 305 f.
19 Macmillan, H., *Winds of Change*, Macmillan, 1966, p. 82 f.
20 Keeling, F.H., *Letters*, Allen & Unwin, 1918, pp. 225, 229 f.
21 Ibid, p. 233 f.
22 Asquith, R., *Life and Letters*, J. Joliffe (ed.), Collins, 1980, *passim*.
23 Gillespie, A.D., *Letters from Flanders*, Smith Elder, 1916, p. 132.
24 Ibid, p. 195.
25 *J. Masefield's Letters from the Front*, P. Vansittart (ed.), Constable, 1984.
26 Laffin, J., *Letters from the Front*, J.M. Dent, 1973, p. 65 f.
27 Gurney, I., *War Letters*, R.K.R. Thornton (ed.), Carcanet New Press, 1982, pp. 89 f, 170 f.
28 Graves, R., *Goodbye to All That*, Cassell, 1929, p. 94 f.
29 *Selected Letters of Robert Graves*, Paul O'Prey (ed.), Hutchinson, 1982, p. 42 ff.
30 Harris, R.E., *Billie, The Nevill Letters*, MacRae, 1991, p. 57.
31 Mackenzie, op. cit., p. 207 f.
32 *The Letters of Duff and Diana Cooper*, A. Cooper (ed.), Hamish Hamilton, 1983, pp. 94 f, 104 f.
33 Campbell, I., *Letters*, privately printed, 1917, p. 60 f.
34 Ibid., p. 71.
35 Wester Wemyss, Baroness, *Life and Letters of Lord Wester Wemyss*, Eyre & Spottiswoode, 1935, p. 220.
36 Rhodes-James, R., *Gallipoli*, Batsford, 1965, p. 118.
37 Imperial War Museum.
38 Mackenzie, op. cit., p. 196 f.
39 Darlington, H., *Letters from Helles*, Longmans, 1936, p. 34 f.
40 Imperial War Museum, 76/27/1.
41 *Fisher Correspondence*, p. 237 f.

2. Trench Stalemate and War of Attrition (1916)

1 MS.
2 MS.
3 Briscoe, W.A., and Stannard, H.R., *Captain Ball V.C.*, Oxford University Press, 1921, p. 162.
4 Ibid., p. 156.
5 Ibid., p. 201.
6 Ibid., p. 263.
7 *Fisher Correspondence*, p. 334.
8 Bennett, G., *Naval Battles*, Batsford, 1968, p. 167.
9 Wheeler Bennett, J.W., *King George VI*, Macmillan, 1958, p. 95 ff.
10 King-Hall, op. cit., p. 467.
11 Bennett, G., *The Battle of Jutland*, Batsford, 1964, p. 89 f.
12 Fraser, D., *Alanbrooke*, Collins, 1982, p. 73 f.
13 Greenwell, op. cit., p. 126 ff.
14 Ibid., p. 144.
15 Letters of K.E. Luard, R.R.C., in *Unknown Warriors*, Chatto & Windus, 1930, p. 83.
16 Housman, op. cit., p. 106.
17 Ibid., p. 168.
18 Ibid., p. 298.
19 Engall, J.S., *Subaltern's Letters*, Griffiths, 1917, p. 96 f.
20 Ibid., p. 106 f.
21 Housman, op. cit., p. 120.
22 Ibid., p. 82 f.
23 MS.
24 National Army Museum, 6709–16.
25 Stewart, D., *T.E. Lawrence*, Hamish Hamilton, 1977, p. 178 f.
26 Ibid., p. 178 f.

3. From Failure to Victory (1917–18)

1 *Fisher Correspondence*, p. 351 ff.
2 Feilding, R., *War Letters*, Medici Society, 1919, p. 133.
3 Greenwell, op. cit., pp. 159, 198 f, 251.
4 Russell, Bertrand, *Autobiography*, Allen & Unwin, 1968, vol. II, p. 77.
5 Charteris, J., *At GHQ*, Cassell, 1931, p. 242.
6 Nash, P., (ed.), *M. Eates*, Lund Humphries, 1948, p. 15 f.
7 Scott, A.J.L., *History of the 60 Squadron, R.A.F.*, Heinemann, 1920, p. 50.
8 Ibid., p. 92.
9 Ibid., p. 95.
10 Ibid., p. 101.
11 Feilding, op. cit., p. 188.
12 Moynihan, M., *Greater Love*, W.H. Allen, 1980, pp. 83, 86 f.
13 Imperial War Museum, Wilkinson, No. 55.
14 *Luard Letters*, p. 197.
15 Housman, op. cit., p. 159.
16 Read, H., *The Contrary Experience*, Faber & Faber, 1963, p. 99 ff.
17 Oliver, op. cit., p. 204 ff.
18 *Private Papers of Douglas Haig*, R.N.W. Blake (ed.), Eyre & Spottiswoode, 1952, p. 122 f.
19 Ibid., p. 217.
20 Maurice, F., *Life of General Lord Rawlinson*, Cassell, 1928, p. 204 f.
21 Owen, F., *Tempestuous Journey*, Hutchinson, 1954, p. 449 f.
22 Housman, op. cit., p. 182 f.
23 Greenwell, op. cit., p. 225 f.
24 Charteris, op. cit., p. 318.
25 Maurice, op. cit., p. 231.
26 Read, op. cit., p. 145.
27 Imperial War Museum, Wilkinson, No. 96.
28 Feilding, op. cit., p. 373.
29 Owen, W., *Collected Letters*, H. Owen and J. Bell (ed.), Oxford University Press, 1967, p. 427 ff.

30 Ibid., p. 457 ff.
31 Ibid., p. 590.
32 Ibid., p. 590 f.

PART TWO: THE SECOND WORLD WAR

Prelude: The Spanish Civil War (1936–9)

1 *Penguin Book of Spanish Verse*, V. Cunningham (ed.), J. Cape, 1980, p. 117 ff.

4. From the 'Phoney War' to Dunkirk (September 1939–June 1940)

2 *War Letters from Britain*, D. Forbes-Robertson and R.W. Strauss (ed.), Jarrolds, 1941, p. 6.
3 Ibid., p. 10 (reprinted from *Time*).
4 Johnston, G.H., *Battle of the Seaways*, V. Gollancz, 1942, p. 121.
5 Imperial War Museum, 71/19/9–10.
6 *War Letters*, op. cit., p. 52.
7 *Keyes Papers*, III, P.G. Halpern (ed.), Allen & Unwin, 1972–81, p. 36 ff.
8 Connell, J., *Auchinleck*, Cassell, 1959, p. 139 ff.
9 Churchill, W., *Second World War*, Cassell, 1948–54, vol. I, p. 517.
10 Jones, T., *Diary with Letters*, Oxford University Press, 1954, p. 459 f.
11 Beckles, G., *Dunkirk*, Hutchinson, 1940, pp. 129, 136.
12 Imperial War Museum, Misc. 361, Box 16.
13 *War Letters*, op. cit., p. 32.
14 Ibid., p. 26 ff.
15 Churchill, op. cit., vol. II, p. 129 f.

5. Their 'Finest Hour': Alone Behind the 'Good Tank Ditch' (June 1940–June 1941)

1 *War Letters*, op. cit., p. 75.
2 Ibid., p. 47.
3 *Collected Essays, Journalism and Letters of George Orwell*, Secker & Warburg, 1968, vol. II, p. 33.
4 MS.
5 MS.
6 *War Letters*, op. cit., p. 79.
7 Barclay, G., *Fighter Pilot*, H. Winn (ed.), W. Kimber, 1976, p. 52 ff.
8 *War Letters*, op. cit., p. 62.
9 Ibid., p. 81.
10 Ibid., p. 89.
11 Churchill, op. cit., vol. II, p. 334.
12 Imperial War Museum, Box P 178, No. 14.
13 *War Letters*, p. 127.
14 Spender, Stephen, *Citizens in War*, Harrap, 1945, p. 43 f.
15 Imperial War Museum, Misc. 29, Item 516 T.
16 *War Letters*, p. 115.

6. The Turning of the Tide (Summer 1941–3)

1 Imperial War Museum, 75/9/1.
2 Lord, D.R., *Germany Quivers*, P. Rance (ed.), A.V.H. Productions, Woking, 1942, p. 29 ff.
3 Imperial War Museum, Box 89/12/1.
4 *Daily Mail*, 23 October 1943.
5 Imperial War Museum, 3513 P 100 T.
6 Churchill, op. cit., vol. II, p. 493.
7 *Blackwood's Magazine*, April 1942, p. 271.
8 Connell, op. cit., p. 472 f.
9 Gilbert, M., *Road to Victory. Winston Churchill 1941–45*, Heinemann, 1986, p. 167 ff.

10   Connell, op. cit., p. 721.
11   Hamilton, N., *Monty*, vol. I, Hamish Hamilton, 1981, p. 835.
12   MS.
13   *Blackwood's Magazine*, May 1943, p. 344.
14   Churchill, op. cit., vol. IV, p. 688 f.
15   MS.
16   Keyes, S., *Minos of Crete*, M. Meyer (ed.), Routledge, 1948, p. 183 f.
17   Churchill, op. cit., vol. IV, p. 695.
18   *Westmorland Gazette*, 19 June 1943.
19   MS.
20   MS.
21   Pack, S.W.C., *Operation 'Husky'*, David & Charles, 1977, p. 129 ff.
22   Hamilton, N., *Monty*, vol. II, 1983, p. 349 f.
23   MS.
24   MS.
25   Robson, W.S., *Letters from a Soldier*, Faber & Faber, 1960, pp. 73, 83 ff, 119, 130.
26   Ibid., p. 96 ff.
27   MS.
28   MS.

7. From Normandy to Victory (June 1944–May 1945)

1   Churchill, op. cit., vol. V, p. 549.
2   Ibid., II, p. 335.
3   Imperial War Museum, p. 270.
4   McKee, A., *Caen*, Souvenir Press, 1964, p. 263.
5   MS.
6   MS.
7   Imperial War Museum, Misc. 83, Item 1256.
8   Ibid., 'P' 370 T.
9   MS.
10 MS.
11 MS.
12 Imperial War Museum, Box 91/8/1.
13 MS.
14 MS.

8. The War with Japan (December 1941–September 1945)

1   Imperial War Museum, Misc. 153, Item 2374.
2   Kirby, S., *War against Japan*, H.M.S.O., 1957, vol. I, p. 198.
3   *Blackwood's Magazine*, May 1942.
4   Churchill, op. cit., vol. IV, p. 91 f.
5   *The Watsonian*, Summer 1942, p. 90.
6   Lewis, Alun, *In the Green Tree*, Allen & Unwin, 1948, p. 61 f.
7   Ibid., p. 65 f.
8   MS.
9   Sykes, C., *Wingate*, Collins, 1959, p. 503 f.
10 *Blackwood's Magazine*, October 1945, p. 259 ff.
11 Imperial War Museum.

9. The Certainties of Self-sacrifice: Unquestioning Faith and Instinct without Reason

1   *The Times*, 18 June 1940.
2   Goldsmith, M., *Women at War*, L. Drummond, 1943, p. 76 ff.
3   *Daily Mail*, 9 March 1943.
4   Dickson, L., *Hillary*, Macmillan, 1950, p. 171 f.
5   *Horizon*, VII, No. 42, June 1943, p. 430.
6   Robson, op. cit., p. 114 ff.

Index of Letter Writers

C640